Battles and Borders

Perspectives on Cultural Transmission and Literature in Minor Language Areas

Studies on Cultural Transfer and Transmission

Volume 7

Series ISSN

1879-7350

Series editor

Petra Broomans

Faculty of Arts

University of Groningen

P.O. Box 716

NL-9700 AS Groningen

p.broomans@rug.nl

www.petrabroomans.net

Series publisher

Barkhuis

Kooiweg 38

NL-9761 GL Eelde

info@barkhuis.nl

www.barkhuis.nl

Battles and Borders

Perspectives on Cultural Transmission and Literature in Minor Language Areas

Edited by **Petra Broomans** (chief editor),
Goffe Jensma, Ester Jiresch,
Janke Klok and Roald van Elswijk

Barkhuis
Groningen
2015

Cover design and typesetting: ColtsfootMedia, Nynke Tiekstra, Rotterdam
Book design: Barkhuis & Nynke Tiekstra
Index and bibliography: Karina Smits

ISBN 9789491431791

For information about the series see 'About the Studies on Cultural Transfer and Transmission series', at the back of this volume

This publication was supported by a grant from the Groningen Research Institute for the Study of Culture (ICOG), Groningen Research School for the Study of the Humanities (OGWG), The Nordic Council, Stichting Groninger Universiteitsfonds (GUF), Stichting Scandinavisch Vertaal- en Informatiebureau Nederland, Embassy of Sweden – The Hague, Norwegian Embassy – The Hague, Hauge-Tveitt jubileet 2008, Mentanargrunnur Landsins – Tórshavn, The Department of Frisian Language and Culture (Groningen), The Department of Scandinavian Linguistics and Literature (Groningen)

Table of Contents

Preface

The essays in *Battles and Borders. Perspectives on Cultural Transmission and Literature in Minor Language Areas,* the seventh volume in the series Studies on Cultural Transfer and Transmission (CTaT), reveal how literature, literary history and cultural transfer function in conflict zones, as well as in both peripheral and central regions, against the background of shifting national borders during the last two centuries. Special attention is paid to minority and migrant groups in Northwest Europe. This book was produced as part of the research project 'Peripheral Autonomy? Longitudinal analysis of cultural transfer in the literary fields of small language communities', which started in 2006 and concluded with the publication of *Rethinking Cultural Transfer and Transmission. Reflections and New Perspectives* in 2012. The book concentrates on one of the central topics of the project: that of cultural transfer issues within minority cultures. It can be seen as a possible survival strategy, a way to remain visible against dominant languages and/or within state borders. It also indicates another new topic for further study: the importance of cultural transfer for migrant groups. In the SOCTAT-internet forum (www.soctat.org), which can be considered to be the follow-up of the 'Peripheral Autonomy?' project, a group has been created called 'Migrant and minority cultures and literatures', where scholars can share information, articles and opinions related to this topic. New directions require definitions and concepts to be rethought. The present volume aims to kick-start a reconsideration of the concepts of 'minority' and 'migrant' cultures and literatures.

We thank our contributors for their collaboration and for many valuable discussions. We would also like to thank Karina Smits who helped produce the bibliography and index.

The editors

The Importance of Literature and Cultural Transfer – Redefining Minority and Migrant Cultures[1]

Petra Broomans

In many works on nationality, ethnicity and identity by scholars such as Benedict Anderson, Miroslav Hroch and Ernest Gellner we learn that the expression of our identity is connected with language and the place we are born. In our lives we are continuously taking positions, as individuals and as part of a family or a social group. Over time people have migrated or were forced to migrate; others have become part of new nation-states while remaining in the same place. Over time people have lost their mother tongue, learned a new one and/or regained the old one. This is a process that can be observed among minorities, migrants, refugees, people in exile and expats. These processes are not bound to one single area but can be regarded as a global phenomenon. While this volume focuses on such minority and migrant groups in northwestern Europe, their experiences, positions and strategies can be compared with minority and migrant groups in other parts of the world, and the reflections here might also offer a point of departure for theoretical thinking on this topic in other regions.

The contributions in this volume discuss the many positions and decisions of minorities and migrants in northwestern Europe over the last 200 years. These groups have created new identities, learned new languages, or attempted to preserve and reconstruct lost languages. In this introduction, I will firstly reconsider the concepts of 'minority' and 'migrant' cultures and literatures in the past and the present, locating the contributions to this volume within the context of a variety of perspectives, such as nationalism studies, literary history and cultural transfer. Secondly, I will deal with how literature and cultural transfer have been used as

1 I am grateful for the comments and suggestions made by co-editor Janke Klok and by Jeanette den Toonder, my co-coordinator of the theme group Beyond Horizons in Cultural Transfer (Research Centre Arts in Society, University of Groningen).

important tools for expressing identity, as well as how writers within small groups acted on the institutional level. Finally, the third part will present the eight papers in this volume. As will become apparent, both this introduction and the contributions point towards a new topic for further study – the differences between the various categories of minorities and the importance of literature and cultural transfer for minorities as well as for migrant groups, whether or not they are in the diaspora, writing in new languages or creating new identities.

Positioning the question

How should we define minorities and migrants? Should the concept of 'minority' literatures and cultures be distinguished from 'migrant' literatures and cultures? In addition to these questions, there are also various types of small language communities. 'Small' does not necessarily mean having less influence, as the Czech historian Miroslav Hroch argues in his seminal study, *Social Preconditions of National Revival in Europe. A Comparative Analysis of Patriotic Groups among the Smaller European Nations* (1985).[2] A small group may also gain power due to historical developments. Moreover, sometimes a group of people speaking a 'major' language lives in an area or a state where it has a minority position. Thus, a small language community with a certain language, culture and ethnicity may have various positions. Over time, states, institutions and organisations may take different approaches and have different attitudes towards both minority and migrant groups. In the following, I will position minority and migrant groups in the context of historical studies on nationalism before examining the institutional dimension. I will then move towards a definition of migrant and minority groups.

The historical dimension

Hroch, mentioned above, is one of the scholars who have discussed the rise of small groups with nationalistic tendencies in Europe in the nineteenth and beginning of the twentieth century and – relevant to our topic – how the gathering of literary texts was used in this process. He formulated

2 Originally written in German with the title *Die Vorkämpfer der nationalen Bewegung bei den kleinen Völkern Europas*, published in 1968.

three main phases in the development of national movements: Phase A. A period of scholarly interest, or as Bruno de Wever put it aptly, 'a small group of passionate intellectuals shows interest in the culture of the small nation';[3] Phase B. A period of patriotic agitation, illustrated by the founding of institutions such as publishing houses, journals and associations; and Phase C. The rise of a mass national movement. The working class also becomes involved and starts to strive for political independence or autonomy.

Hroch calls this movement a 'national transformation process', a process that he links to three stages of social transformation: the first concerns the battle against the old regime, entailing civil and social revolutions and the rise of industrial capitalism; a second stage sees the breakthrough of industrial capitalism and the rise of a working class; and the third stage involves economic rescaling and increasing mass communication. The precise synergy between the national transformation process and the social transformation stages allows for four types of national movements: 1. an integrated movement, 2. a late movement, 3. an insurrection movement, and 4. a disintegrated movement. According to Hroch, not every national movement results in the formation of a state. A disintegrated movement, for example, does not reach Phase C. Examples of such movements are the Flemish movement in Belgium[4] and the Frisian minority in the Netherlands.[5]

Hroch does not give a specific definition of a small community or minority, but uses the notions of 'Patriotic Group' and 'Small Nation'. It is evident that Hroch takes the 'nation' as a point of departure and thus we need to explore his definition of nation before we can define what a minority is. In the following description of the 'nation', Hroch speaks explicitly of a 'large social group':

3 Bruno de Wever, 'From Language to Nationality. The Case of the Dutch-speaking Belgians in the Nineteenth Century', in: Petra Broomans, Goffe Jensma, Hans Vandevoorde and Maarten Van Ginderachter, eds., *The Beloved Mothertongue. Ethnolinguistic Nationalism in Small Nations: Inventories and Reflections* (Louvain, 2008), p. 53. De Wever gives a useful and clear summary of Hroch's description.

4 See De Wever, 'From Language to Nationality', pp. 49-61.

5 Goffe Jensma, 'Minorities and Kinships. The Case of Ethnolinguistic Nationalism in Friesland', in: Petra Broomans, Goffe Jensma, Hans Vandevoorde and Maarten Van Ginderachter, eds., *The Beloved Mothertongue. Ethnolinguistic Nationalism in Small Nations: Inventories and Reflections* (Leuven, 2008), pp. 63-78.

> Now the nation is not, of course, an eternal category, but was the product of a long and complicated process of historical development in Europe. For our purposes, let us define it at the outset as a large social group integrated not by one but by a combination of several kinds of objective relationships (economic, political, linguistic, cultural, religious, geographical, historical), and their subjective reflection in collective consciousness. Many of these ties could be mutually substitutable – some playing a particularly important role in one nation-building process, and no more than a subsidiary part in others. But among them, three stand out as irreplaceable: (1) a 'memory' of some common past, treated as a 'destiny' of the group – or at least of its core constituents; (2) a density of linguistic or cultural ties enabling a higher degree of social communication within the group than beyond it; (3) a conception of the equality of all members of the group organized as a civil society.[6]

We can observe that Hroch remarks that the 'nation' is a product of a historical process and not something that unites people from the beginning. While the notions of 'the self' and 'the other' are only implicit in his description, they are discernable and can be linked to the ideas of *Éd*ouard Glissant, who is more explicit, stating that the nation is the 'root' that excludes 'the other', whereas humankind is rooted in migration and nomadism.[7] Both Hroch and Glissant consider the 'nation' to be a product of historical development; however, Glissant has a more negative conception of the 'nation'. I will discuss Glissant's perspective further below. Nevertheless, Hroch's three 'irreplaceable' ties, collective memory, linguistic and cultural cohesion, and the notion of the equality of all citizens, which are the conditions for nation-building, are elements that, in my opinion, can be transferred to small social and other groups.

In his work, Hroch also gives a historical and teleological dimension to the phenomenon of small groups and the phases they undergo within a larger political context. His thinking is endorsed by many scholars within the field of history and nationalism studies, including Eric Hobsbawm. In

---

6 Miroslav Hroch, 'From National Movement to the Fully-formed Nation: The Nation-building Process in Europe', in: Gopal Balakrishnan, ed., *Mapping the Nation* (New York/London, 1996), pp. 78-97. See especially, p. 79.

7 Édouard Glissant, *Poetics of Relation* (Ann Arbor, 1997).

his study, *Nations and Nationalism since 1780. Programme, Myth, Reality* (1990), Hobsbawm even regards Hroch's work as opening a 'new era in the analysis of the composition of national liberation movements'.[8]

Hroch is one of the many scholars who have reflected upon the question: What is a nation?, or as Ernest Renan put it in his classic lecture, 'Qu'est-ce qu'une nation?' (1882). Ernest Gellner and Benedict Anderson have also addressed this question. Gellner's study *Nations and Nationalism* (1983) is regarded as one of the seminal scholarly works on nationalism, while Benedict Anderson presents a compelling idea of the nation as a construction in *Imagined Communities. Reflections on the Origin and Spread of Nationalism,* published in the same year as Gellner's book (1983). For Anderson, the nation is 'an imagined community':

> It is *imagined* because the members of even the smallest nation will never know most of their fellow-members, meet them, or even hear of them, yet in the minds of each lives the image of their communion. Renan referred to this imagining in his suavely back-handed way when he wrote that 'Or l'essence d'une nation est que tons les individus aient beaucoup de choses en commun, et aussi que tous aient oublié bien des choses.'[9]

It goes without saying that this mechanism, imagining the nation, could also be applied to small nations and minority groups.

Hroch further elaborated his theories on small nations and nationalism in the European context in his study *Das Europa der Nationen. Die modern Nationsbildung im europäischen Vergleich* (2005). Hroch starts with with a state of research and discusses the problem of defining the nation. Some characteristics of the 'nation' that Hroch describes are of relevance to my argument here.[10] Most importantly, the nation is linked to its history, ethnicity, language identity, the beginnings of modernity, literacy and the printing press, the role of conflicts of interest of different kinds, such

8 Eric Hobsbawm, *Nations and Nationalism since 1780. Programme, Myth, Reality* (Cambridge, 1990), p. 4.

9 Benedict Anderson, *Imagined Communities: Reflections on the Origin and Spread of Nationalism* (London, 1983), p. 49.

10 Miroslav Hroch, *Das Europa der Nationen. Die moderne Nationsbildung im europäischen Vergleich* (Göttingen, 2005), p. 38.

as inequality, social status, etc., and the question of cultural and social-psychological cohesion. Furthermore, Hroch discusses various types of nations: nation-states as unifying states and nation-states that split from supranational larger states.[11] Most small nations developed in the latter manner. Another type that can be linked to small language communities is that of not ruling ethnic groups that began national movements in the nineteenth century. Hroch sees this kind of nation-building and these types of nation-states, often already developed in mediaeval times, as the two most important types of small nations in Europe.[12] Another central issue that Hroch describes is the importance of nations being regarded as such, with or without a history.[13] The importance of language, culture and education in the construction of a nation is also dealt with.

The gathering of literary texts is also used in the mobilisation of a people. Hroch mentions several genres that are of relevance: journalistic texts, educational texts, folklore and folk poetry, as well as translations and adaptations of literary texts from more developed literatures.[14] The production of novels usually occurs later in the process, although short stories might be published in journals and newspapers. According to Hroch, drama is also a genre that develops early in the process.[15] With respect to the development of academic literature, this often depends on the number of people who receive a higher education in the young nation and how many of them participate in the major institutions of the state.[16]

The construction of a common history and the creation of a common culture and language also occur within minority groups. In my opinion, the process that occurred in the nineteenth century as described by Hroch can be observed in more recent modern history in new minority groups that appeared after the Second World War, for example the Tornedalians in Sweden.

11 Hroch, *Das Europa der Nationen*, p. 41.
12 Hroch, *Das Europa der Nationen*, p. 42.
13 Hroch, *Das Europa der Nationen*, p. 145.
14 Hroch, *Das Europa der Nationen*, p. 185.
15 *Ibidem.*
16 Hroch, *Das Europa der Nationen*, p. 186.

The institutional dimension

In addition to the historical dimension, there is an institutional dimension to any understanding of minority and migrant groups. In particular, we should look at how European political and other institutions defined minority and migrant groups after the Second World War.

The *European Charter for Regional or Minority Languages* uses the following definition:

A. 'regional or minority languages' means languages that are:
   i. traditionally used within a given territory of a State by nationals of that State who form a group numerically smaller than the rest of the State's population
   ii. different from the official language(s) of that State
   iii. do not include either dialects of the official language(s) of the State or the languages of migrants

B. 'territory in which the regional or minority language is used' means the geographical area in which the said language is the mode of expression of a number of people justifying the adoption of the various protective and promotional measures provided for in this Charter

C. 'non-territorial languages' means languages used by nationals of the State which differ from the language or languages used by the rest of the State's population but which, although traditionally used within the territory of the State, cannot be identified with a particular area thereof.[17]

Some observations can be made here. Firstly, the point of departure is the 'State', thus we are dealing with a political border that is presented as relatively fixed. Secondly, the notion of 'territory' is fundamental both for regional (hence the notion of territory) and minority languages in a given area and for 'non-territorial languages' that cannot be linked to a specific area. A description of the difference between a regional or a minority language and the dialect of a part of the majority is not given, nor is a reason why the languages of migrant groups are not included. Is this because, over time, migrant groups have become minorities? As one example, the Moluccan

17 http://languagecharter.coe.int/docs/Translations/authentic_2c.pdf http://languagecharter.coe.int/byLanguage.htm (accessed October 15 2015).

minority in the Netherlands can be mentioned here. This group was brought to the Netherlands by the Dutch government in 1951 because they had served in the Koninklijk Nederlandsch-Indisch Leger (KNIL, the Royal Netherlands East Indies Army), which was dissolved after Indonesian independence. Their position in the new Republic of Indonesia was complicated, with the Christian Moluccans, especially, regarded with suspicion by their compatriots and the new Indonesian government. Not only were many of them former KNIL soldiers, but they had also proclaimed the Republic of the South Moluccans (Republik Maluku Selatan, RMS) on the island of Ambon in April 1950. As a result of the political circumstances, this group of approximately 3,800 ex-soldiers was evacuated to the Netherlands in 1951 with their families – a total of 12,582 people.[18] The Dutch government promised the Moluccans that their stay in the Netherlands would be temporary and that they would be able to return home after a short period, but for several reasons this never occurred, thus the Moluccans became a minority in Dutch society.

The *European Charter for Regional or Minority Languages* was adopted by the Committee of Ministers of the Council of Europe in 1992 and became effective in 1998. In 2015, the Charter was ratified by 25 states.[19] The language of the Moluccans is not listed in the Charter. This is also the case for Eurasians in the Netherlands, descendants of Dutch colonial men and Indonesian women, another group that migrated to the Netherlands after the Second World War.

In another definition, which can be found on the Eurominority website for Stateless Nations and Minority Peoples in Europe – which also has the motto 'Think Europe differently' – the description of the differences is more specific.[20] This definition includes 'national, cultural and linguistic minorities, native peoples, ethnic groups, areas with strong identity and autonomist, independantist (sic) or separatist tendencies'. The website allows the visitor to search for a minority on the basis of several positions: within a state, thus the notion of territory is used here as well; by type of conflict; and by type of claim, here political circumstances are taken as a frame of reference. In both of the latter two categories, minorities not facing conflicts (e.g. the Frisians)

18 See, for example, the study by Hans Meijer, *Indische rekening. Indië, Nederland en de backpay-kwestie 1945-2005* (Amsterdam, 2005), p. 195.

19 See: http://www.coe.int/t/dg4/education/minlang/aboutcharter/default_en.asp (accessed October 15 2015).

20 See: http://www.eurominority.eu/version/eng/ (accessed October 15 2015).

or making claims (e.g. the Åland Islands) are also listed. In relation to our discussion of how to define a minority, the types listed are of interest:

- Stateless Nation/People (accomplished, with political institutions or a high degree of autonomy)
- Stateless Nation/People (mature and aware of its cultural specificities)
- Stateless Nation/People (revival of the cultural identity)
- Stateless Nation/People (in danger of dissolution of the cultural specificity)
- Native people (specific community, sharing its area with other communities)
- National minority (community of an eponymic State)
- Nomadic or scattered people[21]

This overview has several features that remind us of Hroch. It also reflects a hierarchy. At the top is the nation or people that has obtained autonomy and has built institutions. One could compare this with Phase C of Hroch's division, but without a political state. The second category can be compared with Phase B, when more people are mobilised, after the first Phase, A, in which a small group of intellectuals, writers and artists start to define/redefine the cultural identity of the group by gathering or constructing/reconstructing a literary canon, among other activities. The third category, peoples whose cultural specificity is in danger, could be compared with the communities whose language is in danger, such as those mapped by UNESCO in the *UNESCO Atlas of the World's Languages in Danger*.[22] Native peoples are in a category of their own, the only indigenous people in Europe, are the Sámi in Scandinavia and on the Kola peninsula in Russia.[23] After the native peoples, national minorities are listed. The notion of an 'eponymic state' is used here. Examples are the Danes (Denmark) in the north of Germany and the Germans in Denmark. The lowest in the hierarchy are the nomadic or scattered peoples, with no institutions or any apparent awareness of their own cultural specificity. The latter, it should be noted, is not always the case, as in several countries, Sweden for example, the Roma are aware of their

21 http://www.eurominority.eu/version/eng/minority-type.asp (accessed October 15 2015).

22 http://www.unesco.org/culture/ (accessed October 15 2015).

23 The Inuit, an indigenous people from Greenland, forms a minority in Denmark. Greenland is an autonomous part of the Kingdom of Denmark.

cultural identity. Writers, artists and activists such as the sisters Rosa Taikon (1926) and Katarina Taikon-Langhammer (1932-1995) in Sweden could to some extent be compared with the cultural actors of Hroch's Phase A.[24]

The description on the Eurominority website also overlaps to a certain extent with the definition of the Charter. In the former, the state is also the point of departure, but the notion of 'native' is added and the state of awareness and the existence or lack of institutions is included. This implies a political contextualisation from the perspective of the minorities, whereas the Charter implies a fixed European border system, with states involved, and it has an institutional approach. While EU institutions do not include migrants in their political documents, it is obvious when speaking of minorities that one should include migrants in the discussion.

Towards a definition of migrants and minorities

In her introduction to the seminal book, *Litteraturens gränsland. Invandrar- och minoritetslitteratur i nordiskt perspektiv* (2002), the editor, Satu Gröndahl, makes a distinction between 'invandrar' (migrant) literature and minority literature. She proposes the following categories of ethnic groups: migrant groups, more specifically the new migrants after 1945; and historical or territorial minority groups.[25] According to Gröndahl, migrant groups are in a phase of cultural encounter with the majority group, while historical groups are in a phase of negotiating their identity and position over and against the major group. Gröndahl also depicts migrant groups as minority groups.[26] In the Nordic region, minor language groups, whether or not they are migrants or belong to historical or territorial minority groups, are fewer in number than what is regarded as the major language community. However, either kind of group may hold power, as did the white minority, the Afrikaners, in South Africa until the 1990s. Historically speaking, one could call the Swedish-speaking minority in Finland a dominant group that lost its status only after Finland became a grand duchy of Russia in 1809.

24 See: http://www.varromskahistoria.se/en/what-happened-sweden/activism (accessed October 15 2015) and Lowen Mohtadi, *Den dag jag blir fri. En bok om Katarina Taikon* (Stockholm, 2012).

25 Gröndahl, ed., *Litteraturens gränsland. Invandrar- och minoritetslitteratur i nordiskt perspektiv* (Uppsala, 2002), p. 13.

26 *Ibidem.*

Furthermore, Gröndahl regards another category of migrant literature, exile literature, as part of a global literary community, or as a 'partial' culture of Sweden. She also mentions the Kurds, a community that has been scattered over many countries and that has a strong cultural community in Sweden. The same can be said of Estonians who fled to Sweden and Canada.[27] In some cases, state borders are no longer important. However, when a migrant author starts to write in the language of the majority, the category of 'exile literature' might no longer apply. In my opinion, one could characterise this as language assimilation, with the literary works no longer exploring themes and/or motives that deal with the position of the ethnic group. However, if the ethnic theme is still apparent, such works might be regarded as undertaking the cultural transfer of the migrant/minority literature into the major literature, bringing about an awareness of the position of the minority community. In this case, the negotiation strategy, as Gröndahl calls it, can begin.

Multiculturality, interculturality and transculturality

Along with the study of migrants, movements such as nomadism and migration have also been studied and discussed. This development demands new approaches and perspectives that go beyond nationalism studies. One such approach has been proposed by Wolfgang Welsch, who developed the concept of 'transculturality', arguing against Herder's 'traditional concept of single cultures' and the modern concepts of 'interculturality' and 'multiculturality'.[28] Is this new concept of relevance here? According to Welsch, both from an intercultural and multicultural perspective, culture is still regarded as folk-bound. One might correlate such a notion of a single and folk-bound culture with the notion of the nation as a singular entity: 'It still proceeds from a conception of cultures as islands or spheres'.[29] Interculturality, however, reflects another understanding of cultures and how they interact with each other. For Welsch, cultures are never isolated or in simple conflict with each other but are in fact

27 Gröndahl, pp. 17-18.

28 Wolfgang Welsch, 'Transculturality – the Puzzling Form of Cultures Today', in: Mike Featherstone and Scott Lash, eds., *Spaces of Culture: City, Nation, World* (London, 1999), pp. 194-213.

29 Welsch, 'Transculturality', p. 3.

entangled. Furthermore, Welsch argues that in modern cultures, both globalisation and local affiliation can be handled within the framework of transculturality: 'Transcultural people combine both'.[30] While this idea of 'transculturality' is of interest and we will return to it below, Welsch does not take into consideration the importance of language for migrants and minorities, even in modern times, with the terms 'language' and 'speech' not mentioned at all.

Homelands, migration, nomadism

Up to this point, I have not mentioned the place of origin of migrants. For territorial and historical minorities, the homeland is a given, even when it is situated in a different state and there are different major languages used by the minority apart from its own language. The Swedish scholar Harald Runblom discusses the concept of homeland and the relationship between migrants and their homelands, both the old and the new, making some interesting observations.[31] Here, I will also discuss Charles Westin's contribution to the volume edited by Runblom in an attempt to define 'homeland' and the concepts of migration, migrant and minority groups.[32]

Runblom states that it is impossible to give a fixed definition of homeland, as it depends on the position of the migrant and how they perceive their homeland. Thus, various aspects have to be dealt with. It can have connotations relating to 'fatherland' (i.e. related to territory and later to the nation-state) or 'motherland' (i.e. blood relationship).[33] Although Runblom does not mention it, one could compare the word 'nation' with the Latin *nasci*, to be born.[34] The word refers to the place where a child is born

30 Welsch, 'Transculturality', p. 10.

31 Harald Runblom, 'Introduction. Homeland As Imagination and Reality', in: Harald Runblom, ed., *Migrants and the Homeland. Images, Symbols, and Realities*, Uppsala Multiethnic Papers 44 (Uppsala, 2000), pp. 9-30.

32 Charles Westin, 'Migration, Time, and Space', in: Harald Runblom, ed., *Migrants and the Homeland. Images, Symbols, and Realities*, Uppsala Multiethnic Papers 44 (Uppsala, 2000), pp. 33-42.

33 Runblom, 'Introduction', p. 11.

34 Flemming Lundgreen-Nielsen, 'Danskhed – hvorfor og hvorledes?', in: Flemming Lundgreen-Nielsen, ed., *På sporet af dansk identitet. Syv humanistiske forskere fortæller historien om hvordan vi gennem tiderne er blevet os bevidste som dansk* (Copenhagen, 1992), p. 7.

and thus intrinsically connects this place to motherhood.[35] This is the place of youth and where the child is raised but it does not need to be positioned in a state. Thus, the notion of a 'fatherland' might be considered as a symbol for the state – a political entity – while 'motherland' could be connected to the mother tongue and the ethnic group to which one belongs.

States change over time, and how the old and the new homelands are remembered and perceived depends on the position of the migrant, their phase of life, or why they migrated, for example for economic or political reasons. Runblom argues that a multigenerational perspective is needed here. First generation migrants have different memories and perceptions of the homeland to second or third generation migrants. The question of whether or not a migrant can integrate into the new homeland and whether or not the group itself has established strong associations and institutions in the new homeland is also important. The strength of the migrant group also depends to a great extent on the strength of their sense of homeland. Successful migrant groups manage to contribute their own elements to the canon of the new homeland and thus come to be included in the new homeland ideology.[36]

Migration is thus a two-way process, migrants have images of their homeland and carry these images with them to the new homeland, and they also create images of the new homeland after migrating.[37] Migration includes movement. Migrants travel by train, boat, plane, etc. to the new homeland and also cross borders. However, there are also migrants who move within a state, for example Italians moving from the south to the

35 See also Petra Broomans, 'I fadershuset. Om kön och nationell identitet i nordisk litteraturhistorieskrivning', in: Malan Marnersdóttir and Jens Cramer, eds., *Nordisk litteratur og mentalitet.* Foredrag fra den 22. Studiekongres i International Association for Scandinavian Studies (IASS) arrangeret af Føroyamálsdeid, Fróskaparsetur Føroya, Færøernes Universitet 3-9 August 1998. Annales Societatis Scientiarum Færoensis. Supplementum XXV, 2000, p. 41.

36 Runblom, 'Introduction', p. 17.

37 Here imagology, as it is developed by Joep Leerssen, could be applied as well. Texts on travelling from one place (territory) to another or travelling in other countries (fictional or not) are excellent resources for studying the images that cultures have of each other. See, for example, Manfred Beller and Joep Leerssen, eds., *Imagology: The Cultural Construction and Literary Representation of National Characters – A Critical Survey.* Series: *Studia Imagologica,* Vol. 13; Series editors: Hugo Dyserinck and Joep Leerssen (Amsterdam/New York, 2007).

north of Italy, or Sámi from the north of Scandinavia to the cities in the south. While Westin states that international migration and the crossing of borders means crossing linguistic and cultural borders, this can also be said for migrants within state borders. For example, the Sámi left their rural territory for an urban environment and also crossed cultural and, in some cases, linguistic boundaries.

Thus, whether international or internal, the movement associated with migration has both spatial and temporal dimensions. Westin defines migration as a movement that is definitive, 'unidirectional', and that takes place over a 'significant length of time' and a 'significant stretch of space, across *significant boundaries*, or away from home. The national or state boundary is the most significant boundary to be crossed, the boundary of the *homeland*'.[38] Thus, after the physical crossing there is a temporal crossing. After arrival and settlement, time is required for psychological adjustment to the new situation, to the new culture, learning to communicate in the new language, acquiring a repertoire of social skills that are appropriate to the new environment, and a basic understanding of how things operate in the new context so as to provide for oneself and for one's family.[39]

As we have observed, the notion of the state is the point of departure for scholars such as Hroch and in the institutional definitions discussed above. In the studies on migration, the state is also a strong factor. In contrast, Welsch's concept of transculturality, as shown above, challenges the notion of a single and folk-bound culture that correlates with the nation or state. Another scholar who challenges the notion of a single culture and 'state thinking' is *Éd*ouard Glissant, briefly mentioned above. Inspired by Gilles Deleuze and Félix Guattari, Glissant discusses nomadism and migration, arguing that a strong belief in the state has to be abandoned. Rather than thinking of identity in terms of taking root, Deleuze and Guattari propose the metaphor of the rhizome, 'an enmeshed root system', designating a network in the ground or in the air. In contrast to the unique or singular root which tends to kill everything around it, the notion of the 'rhizome' propagates the idea of a multiple, non-hierarchical rootedness that challenges the 'totalitarian root'. Glissant calls this rhizomatic thought the 'Poetics of Relation', in which every identity is 'extended through the relationship with the other'.[40]

38 Westin, 'Migration, Time, and Space', p. 41.

39 Westin, 'Migration, Time, and Space', p. 38.

40 Édouard Glissant, *Poetics of Relation* (Ann Arbor, 1997), p. 11.

Glissant also refers to Kant, who opposed the settled way of life, truth and society to nomads, scepticism and anarchy.[41] Glissant describes different forms of nomadism: circular nomadism and invading nomadism. The latter is more aggressive than the former.[42] On the other hand Glissant also defines arrowlike nomadism, a variant of invading nomadism. As an example he mentions the Visigoths, who gradually settled down in a new area and thus ended their existence as a nomadic people.[43] Before the modern notion of a nation arose, people in exile did not feel deprived of a nation or state, but rather disconnected from their culture, within the notion of civilisation. Glissant remarks that Greek philosophers, such as Plato and Aristotle, regarded exile and voyaging as 'necessary for a being's complete fulfilment'.[44]

The idea of civilisation – Plato regarded the city as a centre of civilisation – was opposed to the non-civilised, opposed to the Other, the barbarian. During the traveling and conquering, emperors established empires and new cities, thus according to Glissant at that time roots were not yet important. The centre and the periphery were equal.[45] However, when the idea of the nation arose in the Western world, the roots of culture became fixed in one place and intolerant towards other groups.

Unlike Welsch, Glissant discusses the importance of language in this process: 'The root is monolingual'.[46] The individual in exile is not able to speak the own language and lacks the ability to communicate. Founding books such as the Bible are in fact books about errantry and the basis on which to propagate one's own roots. 'My root is the strongest'.[47] Moreover, conquerors from the Western world exported their languages (French, English, Spanish, Portuguese, Dutch, Danish), which became 'vehicular' languages. They took the centre to the periphery. As we well know, some of these languages, such as English today, became international. According to Glissant, 'Relation is spoken multilingually'.[48] Uprooting can be seen as enabling identity, and exile can be seen as beneficial, as Glissant states, but

41 *Ibidem.*

42 Glissant, *Poetics of Relation*, p. 12.

43 *Ibidem.*

44 Glissant, *Poetics of Relation*, p. 13.

45 Glissant, *Poetics of Relation*, p. 14.

46 Glissant, *Poetics of Relation*, p. 15.

47 Glissant, *Poetics of Relation*, p. 17.

48 Glissant, *Poetics of Relation*, p. 19.

it has to be experienced as a search for the Other through a benign circular nomadism and not by a violent invasive nomadism.

After these reflections on nomadism as a fundamental first phase in the lives and being of humankind, through the development of the state in the nineteenth century (thus, in fact, a relatively recent phenomenon) to migration, which we could call a new form of nomadism – a form of movement that can be straightforward, from the old homeland to the new, or a circulating nomadism, where the periphery becomes the centre – we need to ask – whether or not we are concerned with crossing borders or migrating within a state – how we should define minorities, migrants, nomads and people in exile.

As the state is still the reality in global political negotiations, and the political state is still seen as representative of the people, whether or not they are of the same ethnicity and/or share the same culture, I have chosen to maintain the state as my point of departure. The existence of small communities is paradoxical evidence of the fact that state borders can change and inhabitants/nations change and build new states or autonomous areas.

Definition of minority and migrant groups

On the basis of the definitions above, from a historical, political and/or an institutional perspective, as well on the basis of the studies discussed, I propose the following working definition of minority and migrant groups, which includes five categories relevant to Europe:

1. Historical, ethnic and territorial minorities: the Sámi (the Lapps) and the Tornedalians in Scandinavia, and, if we apply the concept of geopolitical ties, the Inuit in Greenland, part of the Danish Monarchy.[49] The Sámi and the Inuit are indigenous peoples.
2. National minorities: for example, the Danes in Northern Germany (Holstein), the Germans in Southern Denmark (Schleswig or Southern Jutland).

49 The term used in Canada and the US for the American Indians (excl. Inuit) is 'First Nations'. In 2013, the Metis, descendants of Indians and colonisers from Europe, also obtained the status of First Nations, although this remains controversial. See also: http://www.metisnation.ca/wp-content/uploads/2015/08/PST-LLP-Summary-Daniels-Case-July-2015-Update.pdf (accessed October 15 2015).

3. Migrants: historical, for example, the Germans in Sweden in the fifteenth century, the Walloons in the sixteenth century, the Chilean political refugees in the 1980s; ethnic minorities, for example, people from Morocco or Syria in the suburbs of the big cities of northwestern Europe. People in the first category might also be migrants as soon as they start to migrate across borders or within the state borders and leave their own cultural environment, such as the Sámi and the Tornedalians, who were originally migrants, moving from southeast Finland to the north in the fourteenth century. Minorities of the second category can also be migrants.
4. Minorities in the diaspora and in exile (e.g. refugees from the Balkans, the Jews, the Kurds). Within this category there is a differentiation between minorities who have lost their homeland (e.g. it no longer exists) and those who have a territory they regard as their homeland, but where they cannot live for political reasons.
5. Nomadic minorities (e.g. Roma). While Glissant would probably call them circulating nomads who want to get to know the Other, in reality they function as the Other in Western countries, in which the majority population does not want to establish any relationship.

These definitions of various categories of minorities and migrants reveal the historical complexity and dynamics of small communities. In the next section of my theoretical framing I will deal with the literature of minorities and the strategies of using literature and cultural transfer for self-expression.

Language, literature, cultural transfer

As Hroch mentioned, literature plays an important role in Phase A of nation-building. Actors such as scholars, writers and priests collect literary texts and other cultural products to demonstrate that the small community concerned has a literature in its own language. In their book, *Kafka. Towards a Minor Literature,* Deleuze and Guattari point out three characteristics of a minor literature,[50] although they do not link these to a minor language as such. This idea can also be linked to Hroch's notion that

50 Gilles Deleuze and Felix Guattari, 'What is a Minor Literature?', in: Gilles Deleuze and Felix Guattari, *Kafka. Towards a Minor Literature* (Minneapolis/London, 1986), pp. 16-27.

a majority language can be a minority language in a given geographical and political context. What may be defined as a minority literature is what a minority 'constructs within a major language'.[51] According to Deleuze and Guattari, and this is the first characteristic they attribute to minor literature, language is influenced by deterritorialisation. As I will show below, this is not the case for all minority literatures. In the twentieth and twenty-first centuries, one of the important topics in minor literature written by authors belonging to what I have called historical, ethnic and territorial minorities – who lost their own language in the process of assimilation to the major culture, even if this took place in their own territory – is relearning the mother tongue. In this case, a reterritorialisation of language takes place.

The second characteristic defined by Deleuze and Guattari is the connection of the individual to politics. They argue that major literatures tend to be more connected to the individual than to the political sphere. Hippolyte Taine's idea that the author is influenced by environment, race and moment is adapted here. Minor literatures have limited space, according Deleuze and Guattari: 'its cramped space forces each individual intrigue to connect immediately to politics'.[52] The individual thus serves a greater purpose. Thus, the family triangle is embedded in other triangles, such as commercial, economic, bureaucratic and juridical triangles. To these triangles I would like to add language, politics and ethnicity. One might also want to discuss whether politics is important for every minor or migrant writer. In Sweden, various migrant writers do not want to be categorised as such. The Swedish scholar Magnus Nilsson has even suggested that the category of the migrant writer in Sweden no longer exits.[53] It is a mechanism that could be regarded as an aesthetic assimilation.

A logical third characteristic is the collective value of minor literature. Because of its limited space, there are few great authors, and thus the minority literature is dependent on the collective statement; its value and function lies in a 'collective, even revolutionary, enunciation'.[54] Again, one might wonder if this can be applied to every minority situation.

51 Deleuze and Guattari, 'What is a Minor Literature?', p. 16.

52 Deleuze and Guattari, 'What is a Minor Literature?', p. 17.

53 Magnus Nilsson, 'Literature in Multicultural and Multilingual Sweden: The Birth and Death of the Immigrant Writer', in: Wolfgang Behschnitt, Sarah De Mul, Liesbeth Minnaard, eds., *Literature, Language, and Multiculturalism in Scandinavia and the Low Countries* (Amsterdam, 2013), pp. 41-61.

54 *Ibidem.*

Deleuze and Guattari offer an interesting bridge to a postcolonial perspective in their description of minority status as a revolutionary force. When a minority writer produces literature within the context of a major or established literature, he or she has to find their 'own *patois*', their 'own third world', and their 'own desert'.[55] This enables us to define marginal literature. If we adapt Homi K. Bhabha's concept of the 'third space',[56] it is possible to map the phases of assimilation (mimicry) with the deterritorialisation of language, ambivalence (revolution?) towards shaping a collective, and the third possibility, of a minor literature that rediscovers its own language.

'Reterritorialisation' – understood in the sense that an author wants to rediscover a lost language, a close connection between the individual and politics, to make a collective statement, as well as demonstrating some ambivalence towards the major literature – requires decisions and strategic choices.

As mentioned above, many minority writers have lost their own language (or perhaps never learned it) and thus write in the major language. Others have insufficient skills to write in their own language. Nevertheless, minority writers have to make important decisions about their position as an individual and as a writer. This is described in detail by Iban Zaldua, a Basque writer, in his intriguing article, 'Eight Crucial Decisions (A Basque Writer is Obliged to Face)'.[57] I have formulated Zaldua's questions below:

1. The first is related to language: In which language is the author going to write? In the minority language or the dominant language? Zaldua mentions several possibilities: writing in the dominant language and then moving to one's own language, or writing first in one's own language and then moving to the dominant language, or even self-translation. Zaldua does not mention that there are writers who cannot write in their own minority language and have to learn this first (writing skills are not usually sufficient).
2. The second is the position a writer wants to take within the institutions and their attitude regarding their own literature. There are three

55 Deleuze and Guattari, 'What is a Minor Literature?', p. 18.

56 Homi K. Bhabha, *The Location of Culture* (London/New York, 1994/2004), p. XX

57 Iban Zaldua, 'Eight Crucial Decisions (A Basque Writer is Obliged to Face)', in: Mari Jose Olaziregi, ed., *Writers In Between Languages: Minority Literatures in the Global Scene* (Reno, 2009), pp. 89-112.

positions: 'pathetic speakers' (who are pessimistic about the future of the language), 'sympathizers' (who do not speak the language) and 'non-sympathizers' (who reject the language). Zaldua claims that writers are usually pathetic speakers and argues for more open critique and debate, and even cultural irony.[58]

3. The third decision is whether or not to become a nationalist. This is, of course, an important issue in the Basque region, but this decision may also be relevant to minority writers in Nordic countries. I will come back to this later. Zaldua states that race and religion were important in the first nationalist movements. With the ETA movement that started in the 1950s, the Basque language became a basic element of Basque identity.[59] According to Zaldua and others, language and nationalism should not be so closely tied together as they are now. Although things have changed in the last decade, Basque nationalism is still reflected in Basque literature.
4. The fourth decision a Basque writer has to face is whether or not to write about 'The Thing', Zaldua's name for the Basque conflict, which reveals its traumatic character. Some authors regard writing about such events as an opportunity to add something new to European literature and to gain visibility 'in the global literary market'. However, this kind of committed literature should not be regarded as a political manifesto or as approving of terrorism.
5. The fifth decision is whether or not to bypass Spanish when a writer wants to conquer the literary world, and here we are entering the field of cultural transfer. For political reasons, some writers ignore Spanish and translate their works, or have them translated, into French or English. However, there are also other views: 'Our literature must first be known in our country, if anywhere. In the end, Basque literature has been written for Basques to read. The basis for a living and healthy literature is strongly linked with language and culture. To be known abroad comes later'.[60] Zaldua made the choice to also write in Spanish – the Spanish readers are neighbours after all.
6. The sixth decision concerns the fact that Basque writers have to rely on their own literary tradition, but that tradition, in this instance, was

58 Iban Zaldua, 'Eight Crucial Decisions', p. 93.
59 Iban Zaldua, 'Eight Crucial Decisions', p. 94.
60 Iban Zaldua, 'Eight Crucial Decisions', p. 100.

poor and started as late as the 1960s. This resulted in the need to invent a tradition. Zaldua makes the ironic comment that we now know that Shakespeare merely rewrote the works of a Basque.

7. A writer must also decide whether to be an ironical writer or not. Zaldua calls irony 'a witty form of literature free from dogmatism'.[61] In Basque literature there are various kinds of plots, such as the tragic (the lost battle plot) or the naive plot (a kind of escapism in literature). One problem with irony is that it is in fact the reader who must understand the intention of the author. Zaldua believes that the dramatic (tragic) plot or the 'naive' plot are more effective than the ironic. Irony also requires self-irony, but are minorities able to laugh at themselves?
8. The last decision is what you want to achieve at conferences: Do you want to bring the literature to the attention of others or to make yourself known as a universal writer? In choosing the native line, in talking about the few speakers of the language, reflecting a sort of exoticism, Zaldua himself takes a practical position. He sees language as an instrument and regards both Basque and Spanish as his literary languages. Moreover, he does not believe in the concept of 'universal literature', which is very much oriented to the West.

In addition to the decisions a minority writer has to face, the keyword in Zaldua's text is 'language'. When taking positions in the literary field it is clear that the attitude towards language is important.

With respect to the first decision, whether to write in the minority language or in the dominant language, it is possible to delineate three levels. Firstly, one has to consider whether a writer belonging to a minority has the skills to speak and/or to write in the minority language. This is an *individual act and decision*. Secondly, there is decision at an *institutional* level. What position will the writer take within the institutions? Are they active or passive? Thirdly, there is the *supra-territorial* level, concerning the position of the minority writer as a cultural transmitter and the possibility of entering the national and international literary fields.

Decisions five and eight deal with this issue of cultural transfer. Cultural transfer can be used in the process of defining or redefining identity. Many minority writers act as cultural transmitters, literary historians and critics. The profile and position of the writer/transmitter, both in the area of

61 Iban Zaldua, 'Eight Crucial Decisions', p. 105.

transmission and in the literary system of their own minority culture, as well as the receiving major culture, need to be discussed. Cultural transfer can be considered an important instrument for minority communities and for language survival. Instruments such as literary histories, multilingual children's books, small publishing houses and the use of the internet are essential for the survival of a minority language.

Examples of the kinds of decisions that authors make

Here, I will briefly discuss four minority and migrant authors against the backdrop of my working definition of minority communities, the nation-oriented thinking as explored by Hroch and Zaldua's decisions as discussed above.

The authors Mikael Niemi and Bengt Pohjanen belong to the Tornedal Finns, a historical minority in the north of Sweden. Meänkieli, which means 'our language', was recognised as an official minority language in Sweden in 2000. Both authors were and are active in promoting the Torne Valley area and its culture but in very different ways, taking very different positions.

Mikael Niemi made his breakthrough with *Populärmusik från Vittula* (*Popular Music from Vittula*, 2000), a novel written in Swedish that made the Torne Valley visible to the rest of Sweden, as well other countries. The novel was also translated into many languages, including minority languages. Niemi cannot be regarded as a pathetic speaker, although he is quite pessimistic about the survival of Meänkieli. Niemi is an author who decided to be realistic and pragmatic; he was one of the advocates of theatre in Meänkieli, wrote his novels in Swedish and entered the global literary market with the success of *Popular Music from Vittula*. He decided to take an ironic approach in making his own region and his own literary work visible. He cannot be regarded as a nationalistic author.

Bengt Pohjanen made other decisions. He is a multilingual writer, publishing in Swedish, Finnish and Meänkieli. He is also very active within the institutions, having established a foundation, one of the activities of which is the awarding of a literary prize for minority literature. He is also active as a translator. His novels have a more satirical than ironic tone. Pohjanen is a language activist and Zaldua would call him a pathetic speaker.

Pohjanen has also co-written literary histories with Kirsti Johansson: *Den tornedalsfinska litteraturen I. Från Kexi till Liksom* (2007) and *Den tornedalsfinska litteraturen II. Från Kalkkimaa till Hilja Byström* (2009).

Anne Heith has written about this new literary history in this volume so I will not go any further into this except to mention that the second volume begins with a chapter entitled: 'Vår identitet *är* i språket' (Our identity lies in the language).[62] Here we encounter the revival of a romantic nation-building perspective à la Hroch. In my opinion, Pohjanen conceives of himself as a typical intellectual from Hroch's Phase A. He collects literary texts, writes literary history and uses phrases such as 'even if we do not (yet) have our own state, we are a nation with our own language'.[63] Following Deleuze and Guattari, Bengt Pohjanen could be called a typical political writer, but not one concerned with deterritorialisation. On the contrary, Pohjanen can be regarded as a transcultural writer, using various languages, and with a homeland he denotes as a nation without a state.

Two examples of writers belonging to a historical, ethnic and territorial minority category are Ann-Hélen Laestadius and Annica Wennström, both of whom write about young Sámi girls and women who are searching for identity. They do not speak the Sámi language because their mothers did not teach them or could no longer speak the mother tongue themselves. Here, I will briefly discuss Laestadius and compare her decisions and positions with those of the writer Alejandro Leiva Wenger.

Ann-Helén Laestadius was born in Kiruna in 1971, leaving her home town in 1999 to work in Stockholm as a crime reporter. She could not write in the Sámi language, but published her first work in Swedish in 2007, *Sms från Soppero* (Sms from Soppero), followed by *Hej vacker* (Hello Cutie, 2010), *Ingen annan är som du* (Nobody is Like You, 2011) and *Hitta hem* (Coming Home, 2012). Her books are about young Sámi people today, demonstrating the importance of Sámi language and presenting Sámi culture in a positive way. They tell the story of assimilation and the denial of Sámi roots. Her books for adolescent readers were also well received by adults, especially those with the same background: many children born in the 1960s and 1970s did not learn Sámi and thus lost a part of their identity.

Laestadius's books are also autobiographical. Her mother belonged to the Sámi and had to attend a 'nomad school' and become Swedish.

62 Bengt Pohjanen, 'Vår identitet är i språket', in: Bengt Pohjanen and Kirsti Johansson, eds., *Den tornedalsfinska litteraturen II. Från Kalkkimaa till Hilja Byström* (2009), pp. 9-14.

63 'Fast vi inte har en egen stat (ännu) är vi ett folk, som har ett eget språk' (transl. from Swedish by PB), Pohjanen, 'Vår identitet är i språket', p. 13.

She was brought up to be ashamed of belonging to the Sámi people and speaking the language and so she did not speak Sámi with her children. Laestadius thus grew up with the notion that one should not be or feel Sámi, but nevertheless harboured the dream of becoming a real Sámi. Her mother's trauma and her own search for identity and an understanding of her mother tongue are the points of departure for her books.

Laestadius started learning Sámi at university and noticed that there were many Sámi people who were in the same situation, having lost their knowledge of their mother tongue. Writing about her own search and her struggle to learn Sámi gave her a sense of pride and a feeling of being part of a collectivity once again – part of a people with a history. To be able to speak Sámi is important for her sense of identity. She writes her books in Swedish but includes Sámi words and phrases. The stories, in fact, contain a mix of languages: Swedish, Sámi and sometimes Finnish or Meänkieli. Language also seems to be a marker of identity: 'And maybe identities, Agnes thought. She could tell that their grandparents sounded different when they talked in Sámi'.[64]

To be able to speak Sámi is to be able to speak from your heart, a feeling that Vuokko Hirvonen also describes in the study *Voices from Sápmi. Sámi Women's Path to Authorship* (2008).[65] Hirvonen defined four generations of women writers in Sámi literary history: 1. Great-grandmothers, born in the late 1800s, 2. Grandmothers, born between 1900 and 1939, 3. Mothers, born between 1940 and 1960 and 4. Daughters, born after 1960 (Laestadius). For all of the generations, the literature is connected with ethno-politics, a struggle to regain esteem and the right to keep and use their own language. However, Laestadius's mother, and also Laestadius herself as a teenager, denied their Sámi roots, so she cannot be called a 'daughter' according Hirvonen's definition. Perhaps we should call Laestadius a lost daughter who had to learn the language and accept her Sámi identity.

Alejandro Leiva Wenger, born in 1976 in Concepción, Chile, migrated with his mother and brother from Chile to Stockholm when he was nine years old. Although Laestadius and Leiva Wenger are from different cultures, some themes in their work are the same: language and ethnicity. Does this mean that the concepts of 'minority' and 'migrant' are interchangeable?

64 Laestadius, *Ingen annan* är *som du* (Nobody is Like You), p. 84.

65 Vuokko Hirvonen, *Voices from Sápmi. Sámi Women's Path to Authorship* (1998, 2008).

Leiva Wenger was the first writer in Sweden to use the migrant language, known as 'Rinkebyswedish', which is a street language, a mix of Swedish, Spanish, Finnish, Arabic, Turkish, Kurdish, Greek, Persian and English loanwords. His first work was published in 2001, a collection of short stories called *Till vår ära* (In Our Honour). While in some of these stories he does not use street language, the theme is the homeland. Others are very much influenced by hip hop music, especially the Swedish band The Latin Kings. In other stories, for example in 'Borta i tankar' (Lost in Thoughts), he uses a mix of languages connected to identity, class and ethnicity. Leiva Wenger received very good reviews, with positive comments about a migrant writer who was finally using the migrant language.

The breakthrough of new migrant literature actually came with Jonas Hassen Khemeri's *Ett öga rött* (One Eye Red) in 2003. Interestingly, both Leiva Wenger and Hassen Khemeri actually use an artificial migrant language. According to Magnus Nilsson, migrant literature in Sweden has deconstructed itself; there is a denial of the label 'migrant literature'. After his first book, Leiva Wenger became active as a playwright. In 2011, he wrote *127* (a monologue) and in 2013, *Författarna* (The Authors), both of which are about integration and racism. Leiva Wenger does not want to be regarded as a 'migrant writer', a position he shares with many of his colleagues who are second-generation migrants. Nevertheless, their literature deals with language and identity, racism and integration.

When we compare the two authors we can observe some similarities but also some differences. Laestadius rejected her Sámi identity in the beginning, but as a writer she now embraces it and promotes literature in Sámi. She lost her language and wants it back. Leiva Wenger did not want to be regarded as a migrant writer, and stopped writing for a time, returning with plays about racism in Swedish society. As a child he had to learn another language, and perhaps we can see his reluctance to be labelled a migrant writer as reflecting a desire for a more hybrid identity. Nevertheless, language, identity and ethnicity are essential topics in the works of both writers. Their differences lie in the positions they have taken and the decisions they have made.

Overview of contributions

This volume comprises four parts, each containing two articles. The first part 'Borders/Nation/Language: the case of Denmark and Germany' begins with a contribution by Nikolaj Bijleveld. In 'Germans Making Danes:

Germans and the German Language in Copenhagen and the Construction of Danish Culture, 1750-1880', Bijleveld discusses how Copenhagen lost its multicultural and international character in the nineteenth century, using various studies on nationalism, ethnolinguistic nationalism and literary history as his theoretical framework. There was a plurality of cultures and languages in eighteenth-century Copenhagen, and a large German minority, for example. Paradoxically enough, the process of cultural transfer was one cause of the cultural change in Copenhagen. German philosophers and authors imported ideas on language and nationality that led to the development of a national identity in which the Danish language became the single language. In this sense, German ideas transformed the Danes with their international outlook into 'real' Danes.

In 'Language as cultural metaphor: the creation of a national identity in the German-Danish border area', Andrea Graw-Teebken discusses whether language was an important factor in ideas on national identity in Schleswig, the 'Danish' part of Schleswig-Holstein. An analysis of documents written in the period 1830 to 1880 by bureaucrats and politicians from this border region reveals that from around 1850 the idea of language as an important medium for national 'awakening' was quickly gaining traction. This correlates with Bijleveld's observations. The document analysis makes it clear that the border between Denmark and Germany was problematic. Graw-Teebken defines a 'border area' as an area 'where there are intersections of a cultural, linguistic or political nature'. Is the border determined by language or is it a natural, geographical border? Graw-Teebken uses classic historical source analysis to reach the conclusion that national identity is based on an illusion of homogeneity. It is particularly in border areas that the ambivalence and variability of options for national identification, such as language, come clearly to the forefront.

The second part of the volume is entitled 'Cultural Transfer, Language Frontiers, Across Borders'. In 'The Discovery of Finland – Patterns in Cultural Transfer', Adriaan van der Hoeven examines changing attitudes towards the Finnish and Swedish languages in nineteenth-century and turn-of-the-century Finland, studying the effect this had on the reception of Finnish culture and literature in the Dutch-speaking area. Van der Hoeven uses Hroch's phases and A.D. Smith's conclusions to describe the process of national awakening. Finland was discovered by the Dutch-speaking regions through foreign sources at the start of the nineteenth century. The first direct translations from Finnish appeared after 1850; one of the most important was the translation of the Finnish national epic *Kalevala*. The political situation in Finland gained more attention in the period 1880-1900, with Finland, since 1809 a grand duchy of Russia, increasingly confronted with Russification. After Finnish independence in 1917, the number of translations increased, but the translated literature no longer reflected the Finnish canon. The picture became more varied, and in the first half of the twentieth century mainly popular novels were translated. Sally Salminen's novel *Katrina* (1936) is a good example of this.

Salminen's novel takes centre stage in Roger Holmström's contribution 'Against all odds. Sally Salminen's *Katrina* and the possibilities of cultural transfer'. *Katrina* was translated into many languages, including Dutch. Holmström describes how cultural transfer made an international success of a debut novel from the periphery. Holmström also relates this to the question of whether or not international bestseller status justifies a place in the Fenno-Swedish canon. Holmström sets 'Sally's fairy tale' against the backdrop of the linguo-political situation in Finland. With Fenno-Swedish literature likely to be relegated to marginal status in the 1930s, Salminen's success came at just the right time. Salminen combines ethnographic description with eco-criticism and universality. Holmström argues that the plot and language, which conjure up associations with the Icelandic sagas, had a significant influence on its worldwide success. He goes on to claim that the book's successful cultural transfer was due to its ethnographic content and the universal portrait of the female main character. The novel describes a form of farming life that has vanished, but a life in which modern people can recognise general human phenomena.

The third part of the volume, 'Minor Languages and Literary History/ Within Borders', includes two case studies about minority languages within state borders. In 'The rise, dispersal and stabilisation of New Norwegian literature', Idar Stegane describes how New Norwegian came into being in the nineteenth century together with the role of literature written in New Norwegian, the second language in Norway. The aim of this article is to show that New Norwegian can be considered a counter-hegemonic cultural movement. Stegane discusses some nineteenth-century 'pioneers' and key twentieth-century figures, institutions and genres. The first nineteenth-century pioneer was a farmer's son, Ivar Aasen (1813–1896), whose achievements included the creation of a new language based on Norwegian dialects. Other pioneers were Aasmund Vinje, who wrote literary criticism in New Norwegian, Arne Garborg, who was to develop literary New Norwegian to the full, and his wife Hulda Garborg, who wrote plays in New Norwegian. Stegane places his study of the development of

New Norwegian in a Habermasian tradition that claims that the growth of a culture can only be understood by studying less formal institutions. A New Norwegian literary field was created in Norway, although this was not without some conflict with what is known as the Bokmål literary field.

The Faroe Islands are an autonomous region within the Kingdom of Denmark, but due to their geographical location they have more of a virtual position within the borders of the country, in contrast to New Norwegian. As in other Scandinavian countries, there are two languages, one of which – Danish – from the fifteenth century onwards, was for a long time the only official and written language.

In 'Towards a Monolingual Canon – Faroese and Danish on the Faroe Islands', Malan Marnersdóttir describes the change in status of these two languages. After the implementation of home rule in 1948, Faroese became the first language and Danish the second. Language became an important tool in the construction of a national identity and a literary canon. Marnersdóttir uses postcolonial theories and the term 'mimicry' to demonstrate the ambivalence and complexity of the situation on the Faroe Islands. The rejection of Danish meant that Faroese writers who wrote in Danish were only included in the Faroese canon in 1975 once their work had been translated into Faroese. Danish literature was excluded from the canon. This exclusion process is reminiscent of developments in Copenhagen as described by Bijleveld. However, Marnersdóttir suggests that crossing linguistic frontiers, also by means of cultural transfer, was of essential importance to the emergence of Faroese literature and that it caused new 'hybrid' forms and ideas to arise. This complicated the selection process for a Faroese literary history, the first volume of which was published in 2011.

The last part of this volume, 'Literary History/Within Borders/Without Borders', starts with Anne Heith's 'Reconstructing National Archives – Ethnonational Mobilisation in Meänmaa'. Heith explores the concept of the nation in her analysis of the discourse in *Den tornedalsfinska litteraturen. Från Kexi to Liksom* (Tornedalian Literary History: From Kexi to Liksom, 2007). This literary history by Bengt Pohjanen and Kirsti Johansson is the first to be written in Meänkieli, the language spoken in the Torne Valley. Heith takes Homi K. Bhabha's postcolonial studies approach, which focuses on the problem of how to narrate the nation in the context of 'top-down' narration by state institutions and the discourse of minorities. Heith demonstrates that Pohjanen and Johansson's literary history is a 'performative deconstruction of a Swedish homogenising discourse of the modern nation-state'. She also compares the experience of the Sámi with the cultural mobilisation of the Tornedalians, emphasising the importance of cultural archives and Foucault's arguments about establishing hierarchies. National literary histories have been used as instruments to strengthen the national identity of nation-states, and allow no space for linguistic or other minorities. This can also apply to internal colonisation. Writers such as Pohjanen and Mikael Niemi have shown that there was cultural mobilisation in the Swedish Torne Valley.

The final contribution, 'Cultural Transmission. Diaspora Writing from the Balkans', by Elka Agoston-Nikolova, is about how to include authors in cultural transfer studies who transcend borders and write in the new environment. Do these writers express other experiences of individual, national or cultural identity? Agoston-Nikolova discusses the history of emigration from the Balkans – historically a geopolitical region with multicultural and multilingual communities – and defines three waves: first, the establishment of Communist regimes; second, the fall of Communism and the conflict in the Balkans in the 1990s; and third, what Agoston-Nikolova calls the wave of the intellectual nomad, who moves abroad and starts writing in a new language or more than one language. Agoston-Nikolova states that the literature of the third wave is neither that of the exile nor part of a national canon but a 'creative, experimental, self-reflexive individual writing which transcends national borders', a transnational literature. This is also expressed in the language. Agoston-Nikolova illustrates this with the beautiful poem *Ein unbekanntes Wort* from 2008 by Tzveta Sofronieva. The poem is written in a mix of Bulgarian, English and German. The Bulgarian words, the 'unknown' words, stand for a metonymic gap, and the writer uses them to remind us of the mother tongue. Mixing languages and cultures is nothing special for young, global readers. Agoston-Nikolova believes that this new development requires new approaches to cultural transfer and cultural translation.

In conclusion, this introduction has redefined the concepts of minority and migrant groups against a background of the historical and institutional dimensions and we have seen the different positions that minority and migrant groups can take. Concepts such as state, homeland, transculturality, migration and nomadism were also discussed. In the second part, I demonstrated how literature and cultural transfer have been used as important tools in expressing identity. This survey made it possible to present a new perspective on minority and migrant groups. As examples, I presented four writers belonging to various minority and migrant groups:

Mikael Niemi, Bengt Pohjanen, Ann Hélen Laestadius and Alejandro Leiva Wenger. In this light, in combination with the eight contributions to this volume, a new topic has become apparent: the differences between the various categories of minorities and the importance of literature and cultural transfer for minorities as well as for migrant groups. This will be an issue for further investigation in the future.

Part I

Borders/Nation/Language, case Denmark/Germany

Monument erected in 1810 for the sailors fallen during the Battle of Odden (1808) with an early romantic inscription by the theologian N.F.S. Grundtvig (1783-1872):

Here I am raised as a monument / to witness for families in the North / Danish they were whose tender bones / crumble beneath me in the earth / Danish of tongue of birth and of soul / for they shall be mentioned for ever / worthy sons of their fathers.

Germans making Danes

Germans and the German Language in Copenhagen and the Construction of Danish Culture 1750-1880

« Nikolaj Bijleveld »

The formal introduction of Romantic thought in Denmark is dated quite precisely to November 11, 1802, when the philosopher Henrich Steffens (1773-1845) gave his first lecture at Elers College in Copenhagen. The lectures lasted until spring 1803 and introduced the higher social strata of Danish society to the Romantic ideas that Steffens had become acquainted with during his stays and studies in Kiel, Jena, Halle and Berlin.[1] There he had met and even worked with a number of prominent German poets and philosophers including Schlegel, Goethe, Schelling, Fichte, Schiller and Schleiermacher. Steffens' ideas were quite the talk of the day and were debated – often with Steffens – in the salons of contemporary Copenhagen. Many of the men who were inspired by the philosopher became leading figures in nineteenth-century Danish culture.

Steffens' programme was, for instance, decisive for the poet Adam Oehlenschläger (1779-1850), who, as the tale goes, after a sixteen-hour-long discussion with the philosopher, conceived the first and highly influential manifestation of German romanticism in Danish literature: the poem *Guldhornene* [The Golden Horns].[2] In the period 1805-1806 Oehlenschläger travelled to Germany and stayed with Steffens in Halle, met Humboldt and Fichte in Berlin and later Goethe in Weimar. The theologian N.F.S. Grundtvig (1783-1872) had attended the lectures at the age of nineteen. Grundtvig wrote in his diary that he had initially not understood Steffens at all, but gradually came to understand the themes and defined his own historical and poetical work – seminal in the formation and dissemination of Danish culture – as a continuation of the philosopher's ideas.[3]

1 Later published as Steffens, H., *Indledning til philosophiske Forelæsninger* (Copenhagen, 1803).

2 Fischer Hansen, I. et al., eds., *Litteraturhåndbogen* (Copenhagen, 1994), p. 471.

3 Koch, C.H., 'Forfatterportræt Henrich Steffens. Inledning', http://www.adl.dk/adl_pub/fportraet/cv/ShowFpItem.xsql?ff_id=64&p_fpkat_id=indl&nnoc= (accessed April 29, 2011.

Adam Oehlenschläger (1779-1850) reads his poem ***Guldhornene*** *aloud for Heinrich Steffens (1773-1845).*

Source: Drawing by Carl Thomsen from 1896.

It would be quite a superficial analysis to causally relate the creation of Danish culture to these lectures. Nevertheless, the person Steffens is a good introduction to the theme of this article. The philosopher's mother came from Denmark, his father originated from the duchy of Holstein but was born in South America, while Henrich Steffens himself was born in Stavanger, now

Norway. He received his education in Denmark, but was inspired during a long stay in Germany.[4] In 1804 he moved to Germany and became a professor at the University of Halle, after which he only occasionally visited Denmark. Steffens was quite an international person who played a prominent role in the formative phase of a Danish national movement. That is no coincidence. It was only in the eighteenth and nineteenth century that the ideal of the nation-state succeeded the reality of the culturally open and internationally oriented (multinational) states of early modern times. The possibility of the transfer of ideas across what later came to be known as national borders particularly contributed to the formation of national culture.

Whereas the latter statement seems applicable to all countries and to transfers of political, personal and cultural nature, this contribution is mainly concerned with the situation in Copenhagen. Here we can trace the transfer of German culture as a result of its high social status, of individuals travelling and of personal and institutional contacts. This article focuses on the position and influence of a German-speaking community in Copenhagen in the eighteenth century, its relationship with the increasing sense of nationhood in the capital and the deterioration of its position when the Danish nation-state and culture emerged in the nineteenth century.

Copenhagen in the eighteenth century

Copenhagen was an international city, being the royal residence and administrative centre of the Oldenburg monarchy. In the eighteenth century, this dynasty ruled over the kingdoms of Denmark and Norway, the duchies of Schleswig and Holstein bordering Germany, and the so-called *bilandene* of Greenland, Iceland and the Faeroe Islands, as well as some minor colonies in Africa and India. Already in the sixteenth century, the monarchy had embarked upon a fierce policy of centralization. The loss of the eastern Scanian Provinces to the Swedish Crown in the seventeenth century, suddenly leaving Copenhagen in the periphery, was an extra incentive in the process of state formation. The administration of the regions was

4 I use the term Germany for the countries which were part of the Holy Roman Empire – from 1806 the German League. Hence, the word German primarily refers to a region in this paper.

concentrated in Copenhagen.[5] Consequently, the capital, which numbered about 100,000 inhabitants around 1800, was a multilingual city. In the streets, not only Danish dialects, but also other Nordic languages, French, Dutch, *Plattdeutsch* and *Hochdeutsch* could be heard. The Dutch diplomat and scientist Johan Meerman (1753-1815) described the linguistic conditions in Copenhagen around 1800: 'people from the higher classes speak English, French and German almost as often as Danish. German is also common among the masses and there is hardly a shop in Copenhagen where this language is not understood and used in reply'.[6]

In her dissertation *Dänische Deutsche – deutsche Dänen*, the scholar Vibeke Winge provides an overview of the position of the German language in eighteenth-century Copenhagen.[7] Using German and understanding it was quite common in daily life. During a large part of the century about 25 percent of civil servants and an even larger percentage of craftsmen had German as their first language.[8] The Saxon traveller Küttner wrote:

> Wenn ich auf den Dänischen Inseln wegen Unkenntniß der Landessprache [ein] wenig in Verlegenheit war, so war ich es in Kopenhagen ganz und gar nicht. Ich glaube, in dieser Rücksicht ist die Stadt einzig in ihrer Art! [In Kopenhagen] verstehen und reden ungefähr alle (...) Einwohner die Sprach eeines Landes, das denn doch in einer ziemlichen Ferne von dem ihrigen liegt, und noch überdieß durch ein Meer davon getrennt ist. Ich hatte mich in wenig Tagen so sehr daran gewöhnt, daß fast jedermann Deutsch versteht, daß ich, wenn ich jemanden anreden wollte, gar nicht mehr die Frage auffwarf. Ich mochte in einen Laden gehen, oder

5 Østergård, U., *Europa. Identitet og identitetspolitik* (Copenhagen, 2000 (1998), pp. 301-302.

6 Meerman, J., *Eenige berichten omtrent het Noorden en Noord-Oosten van Europa*, vol. 1 (The Hague, 1804), p. 179. [Engels, Fransch, Hoogduitsch wordt er onder de lieden, die iets boven den burgerstaat zijn, bijna zoo veel als Deensch gesproken; het Hoogduitsch is aan verscheiden van eene geringere Classe dikwijls gemeenzaam; en er is nauwelijks een winkel in de stad, waar men in hetzelve niet verstaan en beäntwoord wordt.]

7 Winge, V., *Dänische Deutsche – deutsche Dänen. Geschichte der deutschen Sprache in Dänemark 1300-1800 mit einem Ausblick auf das 19. Jahrhundert* (Heidelberg, 1992), pp. 185-324; Cf. Winge, V., 'Dansk og tysk 1790-1848', in: Feldbæk, O., ed., *Dansk identitetshistorie*, vol. II (Copenhagen, 1991), pp. 110-149; Feldbæk, O. and Winge, V., 'Tyskerfejden 1789-1790. Den første nationale konfrontation', in: *ibidem*, pp. 9-109.

8 Østergård, *Europa*, pp. 300-301.

> Früchte in der Gasse kaufen, irgendwo etwas besehen, oder den ersten besten Menschen auf der Straße nach einem Wege fragen, man ist mir nie Antwort schuldig geblieben.[9]

Given the international character of the Oldenburg monarchy, this multilingual state of affairs was only to be expected. However, it was also the result of a relatively high percentage of the population of Copenhagen originating in Germany. As a consequence, the German-speaking community had its own social environment in the capital. German books could be bought in several bookshops. Most books translated into Danish actually originated from the German cultural area as well, being translations of texts written in German. Germans owned the majority of the twelve publishers in Copenhagen in the mid-eighteenth century. Furthermore, Copenhagen counted a number of churches where the German language was used and even more schools where German was the language of instruction. These institutions were popular among the other inhabitants of the capital. They were renowned for their quality and the German language enjoyed high status.

The social status of the German language was closely related to its role in politics. The German language dominated the royal court, the army and the state administration. Proficiency in Danish and German was required for a successful career.[10] In a sense, the German language was the *lingua franca* of the Oldenburg realm and the first language of the ruling class. This was partly a result of the centralization of power in Copenhagen, which induced the aristocracy to move from the countryside and take up semi-permanent residence in Copenhagen.[11] The members of this international and internationally-oriented elite were employed in the highest functions and provided the closest advisors of the king. The nobility, where political and much economical power was concentrated, usually had German linguistic, cultural or even geographical backgrounds.

9 Küttner, K.G., *Reise durch Deutschland, Dänemark, Schweden, Norwegen und einen Theil von Italien in den Jahren 1797, 1798, 1799* (Leipzig, 1801), quoted in: Winge, V., *Dänische Deutsche – deutsche Dänen. Geschichte der deutschen Sprache in Dänemark 1300-1800 mit einem Ausblick auf das 19. Jahrhundert* (Heidelberg, 1992), p. 317.

10 Winge, *Dänische Deutsche – deutsche Dänen*, p. 201.

11 Heiberg, S., 'Herskab gennem tiderne', in: Heiberg, S. and Venborg Pedersen, M., eds., *Herregården*, vol. I (Copenhagen, 2004), pp. 37-118.

This German connection gave important cultural impulses to Danish society. The German-speaking and oriented noblemen Christian Ditlev Reventlow (1748-1827), Johan Ludvig Reventlow (1751-1801) and Ernst Schimmelmann (1747-1831), for instance, were greatly inspired by enlightened educational principles in Germany and France. Given their close bond with the Danish king, they received royal approval to found schools on their large estates. There the children of their farmers were educated as diligent, law-abiding and good citizens. As these noblemen were prominent members of the board for school reforms (*Den store Skolekommission*), their ideas and work laid the foundation for primary schools across Denmark in 1814.[12]

Personal contacts between Copenhagen and Germany also existed. Schimmelmann and Count Frederik Christian II of Augustenborg were so relieved that the announced death of the intellectual Friedrich Schiller (1759-1805) in 1791 proved only to be a rumour that they offered the German intellectual a three-year grant from Denmark. In the following years Schiller wrote a series of letters to the Duke of Augustenburg as a sign of gratitude.[13] These letters were edited and published in 1793-1795 as *Über die ästhetische Erziehung des Menschen in einer Reihe von Briefen*. Whereas Schiller declined an offer by the Duke to seek refuge in Copenhagen, other prominent men like Johan Elias Schlegel (1719-1749) and Friedrich Gottlieb Klopstock (1724-1803) accepted similar invitations and stayed in Copenhagen for some time.[14] The German-born and educated Schlegel lived in Copenhagen between 1743 and 1749 and profoundly influenced the Danish market for journals with his aesthetic theories. The German poet Klopstock received support from the Danish king Christian V during the period 1751-1770, enabling him to live a prosperous life in the Danish capital. There he influenced one of the prominent forerunners of Danish Romanticism, Johannes Ewald (1743-1781). Another prominent German scholar, Johann Gottlieb Fichte (1762-1814), found a safe haven in Copenhagen in 1807 from the French occupiers of Prussia. The Danish ethnologist Inge Adriansen considers it likely that it was there that Fichte

12 Feldbæk, O., 'Skole og identitet 1789-1848. Lovgivning og lærebøger', in Feldbæk, O., ed., *Dansk identitetshistorie*, vol. II, pp. 268-269.

13 Venborg Pedersen, M., 'Gevormd tot het juiste karakter. Adellijke mentaliteit en de hertogen van Augustenborg aan het einde van de achttiende eeuw', *Virtus. Yearbook of the History of the Nobility* 15 (2008), pp. 121-141.

14 Winge, *Dänische Deutsche – deutsche Dänen*, p. 280.

became acquainted with the nationalist thoughts of the Danish professor of history, Laurits Engelstoft (1774-1851). She even sees clear parallels between Engelstoft's ideas and the thoughts put forward by Fichte in his *Reden an die deutsche Nation* from 1808.[15] Nevertheless, though here we may have an indication of a cultural transfer from Denmark to Germany,[16] the transfer was more prominent the other way around.

Meerman observed around 1800 that the close connection with the German empire 'removes (...) much of the typical, every other nation otherwise, and nations living on islands even more, always retain (...) and Denmark appears to me in all respects as merely a continued Germany. In the Capital it is even harder to discern between a Dane and a Stranger, if one has not talked to him in advance.'[17]

Meerman also observed that the Danish literature of the eighteenth century, 'in poetry as well as in prose has completely incorporated the German spirit'.[18] The descriptions by the Dutchman contain a moral judgement that was shared by many Danes. They illustrate, however, the international contacts of the social elite and their cultural openness, which constituted a prominent, cultural gateway from intellectual and higher social circles in Germany to Copenhagen.

Social and national conflicts in Copenhagen

In the course of the eighteenth century, opposition to the sociolinguistic division in Copenhagen grew. The upcoming Danish well-educated middle class claimed political power and criticised the elite, since their position was based on birth and descent and not on the enlightened ideals of

15 Adriansen, I., *Nationale symboler i Det Danske Rige 1830-2000*, vol. II (Copenhagen, 2003), pp. 31-32.

16 For other examples concerning music, literature, mythology and art, cf. some of the contributions in Henningsen, B., Klein, J., Müssener, H. and Söderlind, S., eds., *Skandinavien och Tyskland 1800-1914. Möten och vänskabsband* (Berlin, 1997).

17 Meerman, *Eenige berichten*, p. 179. [beneemt (...) veel van het characteristique, 't welk anders iedere Natie, en Eilanders nog meer dan anderen, steeds behouden; en Denemarken heeft mij schier in alle opzichten een voortgezet Duitschland toegeschenen. In de Hoofdstad is het nog moeijelijker dan elders den Deen uit den Vreemdeling uit te kippen, zo men niet eerst met hem gesproken heeft.]

18 *Ibidem*, p. 180. [in Poësie zoo wel als in Prosa den gantschen Duitschen geest tot zich overgenomen]

deeds and virtues. The opposition was partly formulated in terms of the differences between the bourgeoisie and the aristocracy. This placed critique on expressions of German culture and language at the heart of the dispute.[19] The animosity was articulated especially after the fall of Johan Friedrich Struensee (1737-1772) in 1772.[20] This enlightened medical doctor was the royal physician of the mentally ill Danish King Christian VII. By 1771 this doctor had gained so much power that he was *de facto* regent of Denmark. One year later he lost his governing position as the result of a coup organised by a number of aristocrats who had the most to lose from Strensee's enlightened policy. The physician was sentenced to lose his right hand, to be beheaded and quartered. His remains were displayed for some time in public. During his reign, popular opinion shifted from support to protest, contributing to anti-German sentiments. These sentiments persisted and culminated in what is now known as the Holger Feud and the German Feud in 1789-1790.[21]

The Holger Feud derives its name from the opera *Holger Danske* [Holger Danish] which had its première in March 1789. The libretto was by the Danish poet Jens Baggesen (1764-1826) and the music by the German composer Friedrich Ludwig Æmilius Kunzen (1761-1817), who lived in Copenhagen in the 1780s and from 1795 until his death. Initially the opera was well received; however, the literary Danish elite of Copenhagen began criticising the opera as an art form and the depiction of Holger Danske as a romantic hero. A feud was triggered when C.F. Cramer, professor in Kiel and known for his critique of the anti-German sentiments of his time, translated the opera into German and in the preface praised the poet Baggesen, to the detriment of Johannes Ewald (1743-1781) who was much esteemed by the Danes. A fierce reaction from literary Copenhagen followed. P.A. Heiberg (1758-1841) questioned Baggesen's qualities partly because of his relationship to the German aristocracy and stated that in his experience, all who spoke German identified with the Holy German Empire and looked down on Denmark and the Danish language. He even wrote a parody of the opera, called *Holger Tydske* [Holger German] in which the main character constantly boasts about his German origins.

19 Cf. Winge, 'Dansk og tysk 1790-1848'; Feldbæk and Winge, 'Tyskerfejden 1789-1790'.

20 Struensee is known to a wider public through the eminent historical novel *The Royal Physician's Visit* by Per Olov Enquist, translated into English in 2001 (first published in Swedish in 1999).

21 Based on Feldbæk and Winge, 'Tyskerfejden 1789-1790', pp. 56-104.

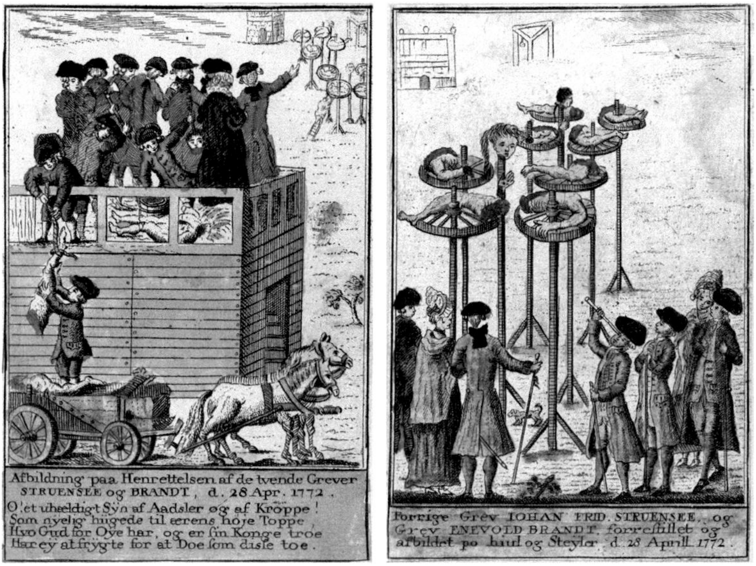

Johan Friedrich Struensee (1737-1772) was found guilty of 'lèse majesté' and usurpation of the royal authority and executed together with his friend and accomplice Enevold Brandt (1738-1772) on April 28, 1772. Struensee's right hand was first cut of. After the third attempt he was succesfully beheaded. His body was afterwards drawn and quartered and put on wheels. His head was stuck on a spear and presented to all the people gathered.

Source: Department of Maps, Prints and Photographs – The Royal Library of Denmark.

Although the Holger Feud revolved especially around the Danish bourgeois elite, the *Holger Tydske* piece provoked an important reaction from the nobility. In 1789, Ernst Philip Kirstein (1759-1834) anonymously published *Ausrufungen veranlasst durch Holger Danske und Holger Tydske.* Kirstein originated from Prussia and was closely connected to the international aristocratic elite. He had worked as the secretary of Count Schimmelmann, to whom he was related, and was a friend of Count Ludvig Reventlow. His piece criticised Danish provincialism and cultural mediocrity and warned of the demise of the conglomerate state. Many pieces followed, all centring around questions of language, national loyalty and national borders. In the summer of 1790, however, pens were downed and the public debate ended temporarily.

Anti-German sentiments posed a threat to the Oldenburger realm and the government took measures in order to contain this animosity. The state government under Ove Høegh-Guldberg (1731-1808), who had brought down Struensee and was in power until 1784, changed the formal relations between the Danish and German languages. In 1772 it was decided that only Danish was to be used – at the cost of the position of German – in political and administrative matters concerning Denmark and Norway. Danish became the language of command in the army, instead of German, and Danish was introduced as an independent subject in Latin schools.[22] In 1776 the so-called Indfødsretten [The Law of Indigenous Rights] followed, which gave – with exceptions – only indigenous people living under the Oldenburgers the right to acquire a position in the state administration. A balance between the different areas was aimed at. Høegh-Guldberg even commissioned a new history book that was to be used in Latin schools, which ordered:

> Love your Country above all Things. And what is your Country? All the king's Countries in Denmark, Norway, Holstein and Iceland, none excluded. Let the evil Difference between being Danish, Norwegian, Holsteinian end. Off course there are some Differences between your Languages; but God understands you all, one King rules over you all. Fear God, honour the King![23]

Ole Feldbæk, editor of an impressive four-volume study of the history of Danish identity, argues that a nationalism, or proto-nationalism had already developed in the late eighteenth century among the bourgeoisie in Denmark. Many elements of the bourgeois programme recurred in nineteenth-century nationalism. Nevertheless, whether the 'nationalism' label is appropriate has been questioned. As the movement had not taken root in large parts of the population and since the conflict centred on the bourgeoisie opposing the aristocracy, the focus should perhaps be on the social dimension of the conflict instead.[24] The ethnologist Tine Damsholt profoundly influenced the Danish academic dispute by taking a fierce stand against Feldbæk, stating

22 Feldbæk, O., *Danmarks historien*, vol. IX (Copenhagen, 2003, 1990), pp. 332-333.

23 Suhm, P.F., *Danmarks, Norges og Holstens Historie udi tvende Udtog til brug for den studerende Ungdom* (Copenhagen, 1776), quoted in: Feldbæk, O., 'Fædreland og Indfødsret. 1700-tallets danske identitet', in: Feldbæk, O., ed., *Dansk identitetshistorie*, vol. I (Copenhagen, 1991), p. 196. [Elsker eders Fædreneland over allt Ting. Og hvad er eders Fædreneland? Alle Kongens Lande i Danmark, Norge, Holsten og Island, intet undtaget. Lad den daarlige Forskel imellem at være dansk, norsk og holsteensk ophøre. Vel er der nogen Forskel imellem eders Sprog; men Gud forstaaer eder alle, een Konge behersker eder alle. Frygter Gud, ærer Kongen!]

24 Winge, 'Dansk og tysk 1790-1848', pp. 110-111.

that the term 'nationalism' should not be used for the eighteenth century.[25] In her research, Damsholt stresses that the main discussion in the eighteenth century did not concern the borders of the *patria*, but rather the love for the country insofar as it stood as a decisive factor in good citizenship. She defines this patriotism, or civic nationalism, in contrast to Maarten Van Ginderachter, as distinct from the nationalistic perspective.[26] Despite a possible watershed, we see that the themes of national belonging and anti-German sentiments became more important and that the support they received grew in the first half of the nineteenth century.

Cultural and political nationalism in Copenhagen

German language and culture gradually lost its grip in Denmark. The market for German newspapers had already disappeared in 1790. The last journal in the German language was printed in 1830. In this period we see a decreasing number of books printed in German or translated from German into Danish. German theatre became less important and the position of the German language in the churches and in the schools in Copenhagen worsened. The old generation of German and German-speaking purveyors of culture died out or moved around 1820. Those remaining in the capital lived more withdrawn lives.[27]

The deteriorating position of German in Copenhagen was closely connected to the growing cultural interest of the bourgeoisie in what was perceived as their own, Danish history, language, mythology, etc. Notably, the thoughts of the German romantic philosopher Johann Gottfried Herder (1744-1803) influenced this developing national and introspective perspective.

In an appraisal of the importance of the author Ludvig Holberg (1684-1754) for Danishness, the Danish poet and translator Christian Wilster wrote the following lines in 1827:

---

25 Most elaborate in Damsholt, T., *Fædrelandskærlighed og Borgerdyd. Patriotisk diskurs og militære reformer i Danmark i sidste del af 1700-tallet* (Copenhagen, 2000).

26 Van Ginderachter, M., 'How Useful is the Concept of Ethnolinguistic Nationalism? On imagined Communities, the Ethnic-Civic Dichotomy and Banal Nationalism', in: Broomans, P., Jensma, G., Vandevoorde, H. and Van Ginderachter, M., eds., *The Beloved Mothertongue. Ethnolinguistic Nationalism in Small Nations: Inventories and Reflections* (Louvain, Paris, Dudley, MA, 2008), pp. 1-13.

27 Cf. Winge, 'Dansk og tysk 1790-1848', pp. 136, 143.

> Before [Holberg] there was hardly a book written in Danish
> that people could remember,
> only fairytales told around the fire,
> only songs for in the spinning room.
>
> Every man who was well educated,
> only wrote Latin on paper,
> French with the ladies, and German with his dog
> and Danish with his servant he spoke.[28]

The poem criticises the low social status of the Danish language and regards this, furthermore, as a neglect of Danish identity. Interestingly, hardly any attention is paid to the fact that Holberg originated from the town of Bergen in Norway.

Despite the romantic inspiration from the South, the developing national culture coincided with a recurring anti-German sentiment. As the meaning of national symbols can change, they may serve to elucidate what preoccupied society. In the middle of the nineteenth century, Niels Ebbesen (1308-1340) was one of the most important Danish national symbols.[29] According to historians this nobleman from Jutland saved the kingdom of Denmark by defeating Count Gerhard of Holstein in 1340. At the end of the eighteenth century, Niels Ebbesen, in conformity with contemporary civic values, was depicted as a man of virtue who had shown exemplary bravery.[30] From the 1840s onward though, new meaning was attached to the symbol. In the song 'On Denmark's distress' from 1839, Niels Ebbesen was presented as a man who had liberated Denmark, Danish identity and Danish language from German oppression.[31] The last verse notes that the 500th anniversary of Ebbesen's deed was approaching and, in honour of the event, calls upon all to unite again.

28 Wilster, C., 'Ludvig Holberg', quoted in: *Folkehøjskolens sangbog no. 187* (Odense, 1986), vv. 1-2 [Før var der knap skrevet på dansk en bog, / som ret kunne hjerterne hue, / kun eventyr brugbart i kakkelovnskrog, / kun vise til spinderskens stur. / Hver mand, som med kløgt gik i lærdom til bund, / latin på papiret kun malte, / med fruerne fransk, og tysk med sin hund / og dansk med sin tjener han talte.]

29 Adriansen, *Nationale symboler*, vol. II, pp. 481-500.

30 Malling, O., *Store og gode Handlinger af Danske, Norske og Holstenere, samlede ved Ove Malling,* Hansen, E., ed.] (Copenhagen, 1992).

31 Grundtvig, N.F.S., *Om Danemarks kvide der lød en sang* (1839), quoted in: Folkehøjskolens sangbog, no. 183.]

In the formation of their self-image, nationalistic movements tend to relate to other cultures. In the introduction to a collection of folk tales, the collector Just Mathias Thiele stated in 1820 that the tales illustrated that Denmark 'is not backward compared to other nations'.[32] Like others of his contemporaries, he referred especially to the Germans. Grundtvig, for example, elaborated on his opinion in an article from 1848 called *Sommeandres og mit Tyskerhad* [Some others' and my hate of Germans].[33] He stated that his hate of Germans was limited to the Germans living north of the river Ejder (more or less the border between Schleswig and Holstein). Those Germans in Danish-denoted parts were regarded as threats to the country, the Danish language and the Danish way of thinking. As Hobsbawm observed, collective identity formation is more effective when uniting against the Other.[34] In Denmark the Other was the German – also depicted as 'the old arch-enemy of Danishness and Denmark'.[35]

By the 1830s, the liberal middle-class movement had triggered the question of the preservation of Danish language in the duchy of Schleswig.[36] The conflict in this duchy over the border between Danish and non-Danish gave language a prominent role in the national battle. The vernacular became a criterion for one's national identity, and as a consequence, language was a means of imposing a national identity upon the people. Consequently, in popular opinion, language was not only a means of communication but first and foremost represented nationality. Popularising the question of the nationality of the inhabitants of Schleswig proved to be a good means of mobilising the people. In the 1840s, several meetings about this topic headed by intellectuals mainly from Copenhagen were able to attract more

32 Thiele, J.M., *Danske Folkesagn*, vol. III (Copenhagen, 1820), p. iii.

33 Grundtvig, N.F.S., 'Sommeandres og mit Tyskerhad', in: Christensen, G. and Koch, H., eds., N.F.S. *Grundtvig. Værker i Udvalg*, vol. V (Copenhagen, 1943), pp. 276-278.

34 Hobsbawm, E.J., *Nations and Nationalism since 1780. Programme, Myth, Reality* (Cambridge, 2000 (1990), p. 91. For a discussion on the dependence of identity on alterity: Baumann, G. and Gingrich, A., eds., *Grammars of Identity/Alterity: A Structural Approach* (New York, 2004).

35 Viborg, K.F., *Folkeforsyndelsen og Folketugtelsen. Prædiken på Almindelig Bededag 1864* (Slagelse, 1864), p. 10. [Danskhedens og Danmarks gamle dødsfjende]

36 For the following see, Bijleveld, N., 'Language, National Culture and the Clergy in Nineteenth-Century Denmark', in: Broomans, P., Jensma, G., Vandevoorde, H. and Van Ginderachter, M., eds., *The Beloved Mothertongue*, pp. 93-107; and Andrea Teebken's contribution in this volume.

than 10,000 people in the countryside. The potential for mobilising these numbers gave the citizenry political influence.

During most of the years of his reign (1839-1848), King Christian VIII persevered with language politics that aimed at a balance between the spoken languages in order to keep the conglomerate state together. However, as a result of pressure from the Danish middle class, the formal position of the German language had already been declining since the end of the eighteenth century. This process was given a boost in 1848, when absolutism was abolished. From then on, national parties partook in government and supported a new language policy contributing to the formation of a Danish nation-state by imposing a language upon the people. For instance, between the wars over Schleswig in 1848-1851 – won by Denmark – and in 1864 – won by Germany – the state aimed at the complete Danification of the region by improving the position of the Danish language at the expense of German. Hence Denmark not only had an historical anti-German ideology as a means of constructing a national culture, but also a highly tangible enemy, the Germans, who had to be forced out of the Danish nation.

Constructing national homogeneity

By the mid-nineteenth century the cultural, political and administrative role of the German language in Copenhagen had been reduced significantly. Even though social contacts between Germany and Denmark persisted, many of the old cultural bonds had been cut and the memory of them excised. A new social and cultural dominant class had emerged focusing on Denmark and Scandinavia, and a new cultural canon was constructed.

This construction becomes manifest in the writing of the history of literature. Flemming Conrad points out that despite some early attempts, the Danish history of literature as a discipline emerged at the beginning of the nineteenth century. Initial discussions – interestingly enough, similar to some in present-day discussions in the field[37] – included whether or not to include texts in languages other than Danish or written by non-native authors (e.g. translations). By the 1820s, the discipline had become closely connected to cultural and political nationalism, since it supported the view that the bourgeoisie in Denmark was the foundation

37 Cf. some of the other contributions in this volume.

of Danish culture, reflected a national ideology and aimed at contributing to the process of nation-building in all educational institutions. A literary canon was constructed based not solely on aesthetic criteria, but also on nationalistic principles, excluding elements that had previously belonged to the conglomerate state by defining them as foreign.[38]

These processes of exclusion and inclusion recur in the humanities in all countries, as becomes manifest in the main character of our introduction: Henrich Steffens. Through tentative research on the internet we encounter interesting, almost national appropriations. In Wikipedia, the lemma Steffens in the Danish version defines the philosopher as Danish-German, in the Norwegian version he is a Norwegian-born German philosopher, whereas the *Biographisch-Bibliographisches Kirchenlexikon* stresses that Steffens was the son of a German physician.[39] Another example, now from art history, would be the painter Louis Gurlitt (1812-1897) from Altona, Germany. He received his formal education in Copenhagen 1832-1833, worked closely with leading Danish painters and painted motives and scenes, and reached an artistic level similar to still famous Danish painters like Johan Thomas Lundbye (1818-1848) and Martinus Rørbye (1803-1848).[40] It was, however, only at the end of the twentieth century that he was rediscovered in Denmark, thoroughly removed from the cultural canon as he was. Turning now to an exhibition catalogue of The Danish National Gallery [Statens Museum for Kunst] from 2001, he is even depicted as a Danish artist (from Holstein).[41] Finally, I would like to point out that for all the upheaval it caused, the excellent opera *Holger Danske* disappeared from collective memory for some two hundred years. Only in the 1980s

38 Conrad, F., 'Den nationale litteraturhistorieskrivning 1800-1861', in: Feldbæk, *Dansk identitetshistorie*, vol. II pp. 391-468.

39 See http://da.wikipedia.org/wiki/Heinrich_Steffens; http://no.wikipedia.org/wiki/Henrik_Steffens; and http://www.bbkl.de/s/s4/steffens_h.shtml (all accessed April 29, 2011).

40 Kaufman, G., Ohrt, N. and Schulte-Wülwer, U., 'Vorwort', in: Schulte-Wülwer, U. and Hedinger, B., eds., *Louis Gurlitt 1812-1897. Porträts europäischer Landschaften in Gemälden und Zeichnungen* (München, 1997), pp. 7-8; Schulte-Wülwer, U., 'Louis Gurlitt – Leben und Werk', in: *ibidem*, pp. 27-144.

41 Monrad, K., 'De Hollandse dimensie in de landschapschilderkunst van de Deense Gouden Eeuw', in: Bøgh Rønberg, L., Monrad, K. and Linnet, R., eds., *Twee Gouden eeuwen. Schilderkunst uit Nederland en Denemarken* (Zwolle, 2001), p. 51; 'Catalogus', in: *ibidem*, p. 165, no. 26.

was the piece performed again in Denmark. Then in 2006 the Danish committee responsible for constructing a national cultural canon even chose *Holger Danske* as a unique part of the Danish cultural heritage.[42]

The international background of many of our main characters from the nineteenth century was the result of the Oldenburger realm lacking national borders. This situation lasted until 1864 when Denmark lost the duchies to Germany. Now, the new borders of the kingdom contained a primarily Danish-speaking group. The loss of Schleswig in particular in 1864 became a seminal event in Danish culture. Many national symbols refer to the war and to the separation of Denmark and Schleswig.[43] Herman Bang (1857-1812) drew in his novel *Tine* from 1899 an impressive picture of its impact. Even as late as 2008, the politician Hanne Reintoft published a historical novel about a Danish family in Schleswig trying to retain its bonds with Denmark after the separation.[44]

The anti-German sentiments and the physical struggle against Germany contributed strongly to the nationalisation of Danish culture. In 1864 the pastor Karsten Friis Viborg (1813-1885) advocated cultural cleansing, which by that time had already partially been realised: 'we put our enemies' language and thereby their way of thinking everywhere from throne to living room; German thoughts and German education we put on the desk in our schools, on the pulpit and in court, even in parliament, which was to ensure our Danishness' and what he called for was a return to 'the Danish nature (...), our way of living, thinking, speaking and feeling, our language, our country'.[45]

---

42 Viking, M. and Høvring, E., *Kulturkanon* (Copenhagen, 2006), pp. 168-169.

43 Cf. Adriansen, I., *Nationale symboler i Det Danske Rige 1830-2000*, vol. I-II (Copenhagen, 2003)

44 Bang, H., *Tine* (Copenhagen, 1989, 1909); Reintoft, H., *Nu er det længe siden* (Copenhagen, 2008).

45 Viborg, K.F., *Folkeforsyndelsen og Folketugtelsen. Prædiken på Almindelige Bededag 1864* (Slagelse, 1864), pp. 12, 9 [have vi sat vore fjenders sprog og dermed deres tankesæt ind i alle vore forhold lige fra tronen til borgerstuen; tydsk tankegang og tydsk åndsdannelse have vis at på lærerstolen i vore landsbyskoler og lærde skoler, på prædikestolen og på dommersædet, ja selv i den lovgivende forsamling, der skulle sikkre vor danskhed]; [den danske natur (...), vor måde at leve, at tænke, at tale og føle på, vort modersmål, vort fædreland]

Conclusion

If we recall the situation in the mid-eighteenth century, the German language and the German minority had a prominent position in daily life and in the political and cultural fields in Copenhagen. Looking at their influence, it is probably correct – despite the numerical differences – to consider this a majority position. This German connection contributed to the importance of the existing gateway to the South, enabling the transfer of ideas, language and people from Germany to Denmark.[46] Indeed, Germans contributed to the making of the Danes. The transparency of the border between Germany and Denmark had most influence on the latter country. However, we must be aware that this cultural transfer can be established for many other countries and other periods as well.[47]

Ironically, in the case presented here, the processes of cultural transfer contributed to the declining importance of international cultural ties. In eighteenth-century Denmark, the gateway provided the bourgeoisie with many important elements of romantic thought from Germany that contributed to the formation of Danish culture. As such, the concept of cultural transfer may serve to elucidate why the nationalistic movements in the nineteenth century were such an international phenomenon. In Denmark, this movement was rooted in the eighteenth century as an opposition between the bourgeoisie and the political elite: the latter, the aristocratic class having especially deep international ties. The opposition was articulated in national terms and with strong anti-German sentiments. In the early nineteenth century, romanticism strengthened the search for national uniqueness in Denmark and – strongly influenced by the struggle for Schleswig – alien elements denoted as foreign or specifically German were removed.

By the mid-nineteenth century, the international character of Copenhagen had been reduced, not to say eliminated. The dominant language was now Danish, leaving few German educational and ecclesiastic institutions and increasingly degrading the German language to the private sphere. The Danish language had changed places with the German language, which by the 1870s was a foreign language in the Danish nation state. In the new cultural canon the German influence was depicted as negative or had even been removed.

46 The duchies also formed an important means of cultural transfer, cf. Frandsen, S.B., *Holsten i Helstaten. Hertugdømmer inden for og uden for det danske monarki i første halvdel af 1800-tallet* (Copenhagen, 2008); Schultz Hansen, H., Henningsen, L.N. and Porskrog Rasmussen, C., *Sønderjyllands historie*, vol. I (Aabenraa, 2008).

47 E.g. Leerssen, J., *National Thought in Europe. A Cultural History* (Amsterdam, 2008), p. 95.

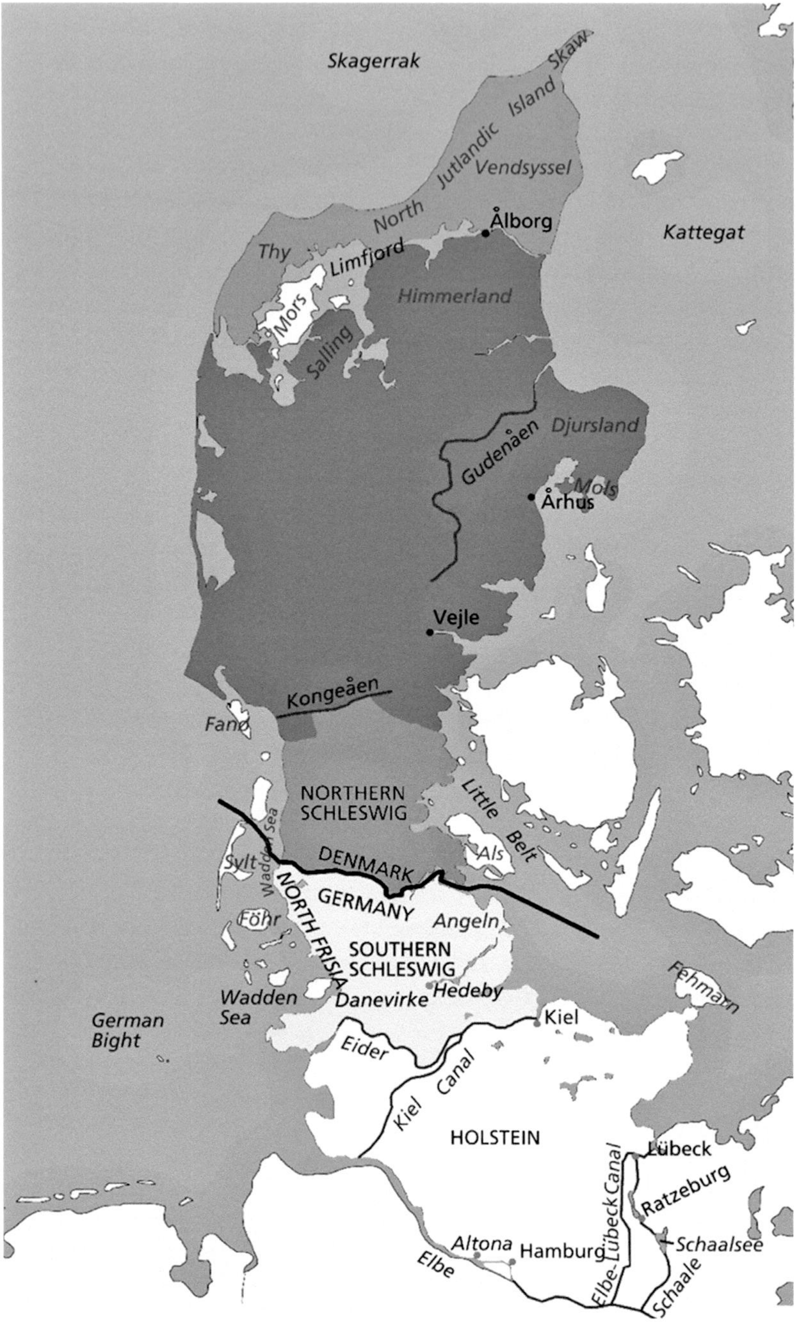

Skagerrak
Skaw
North Jutlandic Island
Vendsyssel
Kattegat
Ålborg
Thy
Limfjord
Himmerland
Mors
Salling
Djursland
Gudenåen
Mols
Århus
Vejle
Kongeåen
Fanø
NORTHERN SCHLESWIG
Little Belt
Wadden Sea
Sylt
DENMARK
Als
GERMANY
NORTH FRISIA
Föhr
Angeln
SOUTHERN SCHLESWIG
Fehmarn
Wadden Sea
Danevirke
Hedeby
German Bight
Kiel
Eider
Kiel Canal
HOLSTEIN
Lübeck
Ratzeburg
Elbe-Lübeck Canal
Altona
Hamburg
Schaalsee
Elbe
Schaale

Language as cultural metaphor:

The creation of a national identity in the German-Danish border area

« Andrea Graw-Teebken »

Denmark is the only Scandinavian country that directly borders on Germany. Yet where precisely the border between southern Scandinavia and the German territories ran was a matter of dispute for a long time. The border area became the site of military conflict in the nineteenth century, when the question of nationalities turned increasingly from a purely cultural into a highly sensitive political issue. The idea of German philosopher Johann Gottfried von Herder (1744–1803) that language and nationality were insolubly linked did not fit well with the conditions that applied to the periphery of the German states – be it in Alsace-Lorraine, the German-Polish areas or, as here, Schleswig-Holstein. Here, at the northernmost edge of the German nation, the nation state had not only to form, but at the same time demarcate itself from the Danish composite state. This article will deal with the attempts at demarcation and the creation of identity which occurred in the first half of the nineteenth century in the multilingual Duchy of Schleswig.

Language and nationality – these themes had played a major role in the history of the Duchies of Schleswig and Holstein since the Napoleonic Wars. They continue in their historiography: the border question and the language issue dominated the historiography of both German Schleswig-Holstein and of Denmark for a long time. However, the interpretative patterns on which these issues were based can already be found in writings and pamphlets, and in historical works and academic dissertations from the early nineteenth century. However, as will be argued here, language did and does not have a specific independent importance.

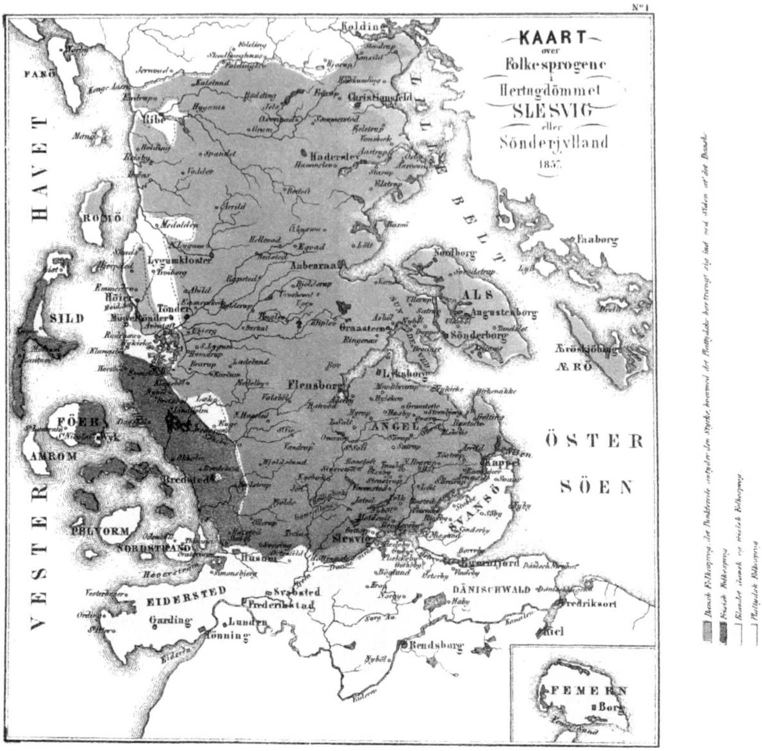

Language is a cultural metaphor and its importance arises from its context.[1] The national development of the Duchy of Schleswig in the nineteenth century is a good example of this. Until the mid-nineteenth century, many of the citizens of Flensburg had no difficulty in combining loyalty to the Danish king with the use of German in everyday life.[2] This only changed after the nationalist political conflicts around 1848, and many families who crossed over to the Danish side as a result only learned Danish at that time.

Such pragmatism was possible precisely because language does not have natural, intrinsic importance. It is people who attach a certain meaning to language; often they use it for political purposes. National language as a construct thus played a fundamental role in the geopolitical ideas of nineteenth-century political visionaries longing for a unified nation-state.

1 Joseph, J.E., *Language and Identity: National, Ethnic, Religious* (London, 2004).

2 Schultz Hansen, H., *Danskheden i Sydslesvig, 1840-1918* (Flensburg, 1990). See also the contribution by Nikolaj Bijleveld in this volume.

Philosophers and poets like Ernst Moritz Arndt (1769–1860) wrote about a German nation, spreading as far as where the 'German tongue is spoken'.[3]

After the war of 1848-1851, this process was initially pragmatic, but later nationalist and cultural reasons were used to justify it. At the same time, Denmark's hands were tied with regard to the further integration of the Duchy into a Danish nation state: this was impossible while the major European powers watched with eagle eyes the preservation of the Metternich restoration.

3 'Soweit die deutsche Zunge klingt' from the song 'Was ist des Deutschen Vaterland', written by Ernst Moritz Arndt in 1813, became – not only in Schleswig-Holstein – well known through the quickly spreading network of the so-called 'Sängerbünde' [singing clubs]. See Holzapfel, O., 'Deutsch-dänische Grenz– und Anpassungsschwierigkeiten. Patriotismus und Nationalismus im Spiegel einiger schleswig-holsteinischer Liederbücher von 1802 bis 1864', *Jahrbuch für Volksliedforschung*, vol. 27/28, 1982/1983, pp. 225-234.

The period between c. 1830 and 1920 is a time in German-Danish history that can be described as a phase of demarcation. Probably the most important date in that century was 1864 – not as a year of war but as the symbolic end of the composite state. Of course, the Prussian-Danish War of 1864 had a huge impact not only upon Denmark, but also on Europe as a whole. For a long time, therefore, the war dominated views of the period. Recent studies tend to put a greater focus on the structural changes around and after 1864, especially on the composite state model. After 1864, the composite state became history and was quietly buried. No-one lamented its passing and only later was this model of the state interpreted as a potential alternative to the nation state.[4]

This negative picture of the composite state was linked to the fact that from 1850 onwards, the Danish composite state ignored arts of its domestic policy. Debates about nationality and language shifted increasingly into civil society as a result. Some of these debates will be discussed here. In conclusion, there will be some consideration of the subject of the discursive creation of a border area in the interplay between these two levels – the state and politics and the intellectually discursive. I shall start with a few words on the methodological and theoretical starting point.

Sources

The instrumentalization of the use of language will be approached by looking both at how language was instrumentalized at the state level and at a lower level, which we will refer to as the discursive level of intellectual debate in the public space. The Danish state endeavoured to achieve a uniform language settlement for the Duchy of Schleswig from the start of the nineteenth century onwards. Parallel to this political development, the mental mapping took shape through Danish-German debates and arguments in book reviews and small booklets, articles, discussion papers and pamphlets, to name but a few sources. This material has hardly ever been used for analytical purposes. The same applies to the use of

4 Frandsen, S.B., 'Det nya Norden efter Napoleon. Den dansk-tyske helstat 1814-1864', in: Engman, M. and Sandstrøm, Å., eds., *Det nya Norden efter Napoleon. 25de Nordiska Historikermøtet* (Stockholm, 2004), pp. 19-54.

newspapers.[5] For a long time, statements about the language border or 'the right place' for a future national Danish-German border have mostly been taken as something that should be proven right or wrong. In this sense, my research seeks to not only present new material, but also to focus on the language question as a discourse.[6]

These small booklets were produced in Copenhagen, Leipzig or Hamburg. Anonymous or non-anonymous writers elaborated on their political ideas and on their visions of the future. They discussed, often quite emotionally, whether the Duchy of Schleswig belonged to the German or the Danish nation. Book reviews were used for spreading personal ideas, and responses to those book reviews could include a great many footnotes. Who were the writers? Respected citizens, politically interested officials and politicians of the assembly of estates published texts and pamphlets that set out the linguistic and nationality situation in the Duchy of Schleswig from their perspective. A number of these writings were published anonymously.

It would take a lifetime to read – or even find – all the texts dealing with the language and border issue in Schleswig. I have read 40 to 50 of them, choosing those texts which explicitly – through their titles – or implicitly – by cross-reading a few pages – deal with the issue. The local libraries and archives in Flensburg and Aabenraa are not the only places holding these sometimes uncategorized booklets. Specialized bookshops can also be quite helpful.

Even though there is such a great variety of texts, the writings I have chosen display a number of common characteristics and repetitions. The Schleswig-Holstein question was a matter which was also of supra-regional importance, and from about 1845 onwards was also debated south of Altona as part of the 'German question'. Nevertheless, key words kept recurring and the arguments remained similar. Each author referred in turn to previous writings by political friends and opponents. I have limited myself to texts from around 1830 to 1880.

5 A newly published study systematically uses newspapers and political writings from the 1830s onwards, especially from Holstein: Frandsen, S.B., *Holsten i Helstaten. Hertugdømmer inden for og uden for det danske monarki i første halvdel af 1800-tallet* (Copenhagen, 2008).

6 Even though my study has been inspired by discourse analysis, I would rather use the term text analysis or classical historical source analysis for the method used.

The texts acquired a wider impact through their quantity – some of them were published in large numbers. Their low price was also significant – a text could be acquired for a few pennies and the publisher on many occasions recommended other texts in the same genre on the back page. In other words, for their contemporaries these short texts – usually about 25 pages long – with frequently sensational titles and daring hypotheses were probably significantly more accessible than the writings of the German philosophers Herder or Johann Gottlieb Fichte (1762-1814). They thus contributed to the spread of nationalist ideas among the population.

In the following, I will discuss the concept of a border region. I will then outline the development of language policy in the Duchy of Schleswig in the nineteenth century. Afterwards, the connection between language policy and language discourse will be made, based on the aforementioned source material.

Theoretical approaches: border and nation in the Duchy of Schleswig

The national idea was hard to implement in regions, particularly those situated between two powers, because the national discourse had to adapt itself to the regional circumstances. While the nationalisation processes in border areas took a different form to those in centrally located regions, i.e. the nation state had to 'bend' to local requirements, the regions were also called upon to make compromises – they first had to grow into their new position as areas on the periphery of a nation.

The Duchy of Schleswig is designated here as a border area. The concept of border area comes from interdisciplinary border studies, which aid in understanding the way that borders function.[7] Accordingly, this study seeks to contribute a further aspect to the history of the interpretation of the region beyond the traditional 'regional history'. Regional history, including that of Schleswig-Holstein until some years ago, mostly restricted its scope to the regions of a nation state. In contrast, border studies see their area of investigation precisely where there are intersections of a cultural, linguistic or political nature.

A cross-border perspective is connected with an idea of nation and nation state that can be described as constructivist.[8] In my view, the modern

7 Hastings, D. and Wilson, T.M., *Borders: Frontiers of Identity, Nation and State* (Oxford/New York, 1999).

8 For a pragmatic interpretation see Langewiesche, D., 'Was heißt "Erfindung der Nation"? Nationalgeschichte als Artefakt – oder Geschichtsdeutung als Machtkampf', *Historische Zeitschrift*, vol. 277 (2003), pp. 593-617.

nation state can be regarded as an example of a spatial division limited in time: 'Territorial units are historical products (...). Hence territories are not eternal units but, as manifestations of various institutional practices, emerge, exist for some time and disappear in the transformation of the world system'.[9] In political history, borders were generally ascribed a passive role: in connection with wars or the dynastic ceding of territory it was merely their demarcating function that was perceived. This aspect is not wrong but it is only part of the picture. Accordingly, this study seeks to determine who gave language its importance and what influence was accorded to the border area in this respect. This approach is quite new in connection to the history of the Danish-German border area and its language debates. Most monographs and articles since the 1950s which have dealt with the language debates tend to discuss the right-sizing of the border and the validity of the arguments. It should also be added that until the mid-1990s, scientific discourse was divided into Danish and German studies, where it was common not to quote or read studies produced by the 'others'. Nevertheless, viewed in retrospect, it seems to me that those nineteenth-century debates and arguments still live through the scientific discourse of the latter half of the twentieth century. Therefore, for me, the discourse itself has to be studied, because looking at state-managed language policy is not sufficient to throw light on this issue. State policy always arises through the interchange with social realities and neither area can necessarily be placed in the cause-effect matrix. Their focus thus lies at two levels: state policy and public debate.

Language policy as an instrument of integration

The Danish composite state around 1800 was anything but centralist, which of course contradicted the new ideal of a modern and effective state administration.[10] Until 1814, Norway was also part of this pre-nation state construct. From 1815, the German Confederation lay at the southern border of Denmark, to which Holstein also belonged. In addition, there was an extremely complicated administrative structure. It became clear to those in charge in the state administration in Copenhagen that a number

9 Paasi, A., *Territories, Boundaries and Consciousness: The Changing Geographies of the Finnish-Russian Border* (Oulu, 1996), p. 3.

10 Gustafsson, H., 'The Conglomerate State: A Perspective on State Formation in Early Modern Europe', *Scandinavian Journal of History*, vol. 23, no. 3-4 (1998), pp. 189-213.

of things had to change in the structure of the composite state if the connection – also in economic terms – to Europe was not to be lost.

State and later also national unity was desired: language policy was one of the means to achieve this aim. It is, by the way, astonishing for how long it had been possible to get along with parallel German and Danish language administration, schools and churches. It was only with the Prussian-Austrian administration from 1864 onwards that these circumstances changed for the last time. The first attempts in about 1810 to actively influence linguistic practice are certainly described in the specialist literature as language policy. However, the policy as it was conducted was only vaguely based on clear-cut politics.[11] The further development of this area occurred in the course of the century and reached its culmination in the Prussian language policy following the annexation of the duchies of Schleswig and Holstein to the Prussian state in 1867. However, this phase is not what we are looking at here.

At the same time (c. 1834), the wish arose for greater political autonomy in the duchies of Schleswig and Holstein. The government in Copenhagen was concerned about the consequences of a regional political conflict, which eventually became reality. Whatever the scale of the responsibilities of the assemblies of estates that the duchies demanded, they would have been a symbol of the autonomy of Schleswig and Holstein and would, it was feared, lead to secession in the long term – which in fact they did. That the assemblies of estates were nevertheless called in 1834 is due largely to the growing pressure from abroad. These regional parliaments did not have a great deal of power, nor was there any kind of general suffrage. However, they increased in importance through political debates and often very emotional speeches on the language problem.

The government in Copenhagen attempted to avoid the most heated debates and at the same time find solutions to some practical problems. Thus Frederik VI attempted in 1810 to decree that from then on the Danish language would be the administrative language in North and Central

11 Bracker, J., 'Die dänische Sprachpolitik 1850-1864 und die Bevölkerung Mittel schleswigs', *Zeitschrift der Gesellschaft für Schleswig-Holsteinische Geschichte* (1972), pp. 127-225 and (1973), pp. 87-213; Rohweder, J., *Sprache und Nationalität: Nordschleswig und die Anfänge der dänischen Sprachpolitik in der ersten Hälfte des 19. Jahrhunderts* (Glückstadt, 1976); Olsen, S.T., *Die Dänenpolitik im deutschen Kaiserreich: Preußisch-deutsche Nationalitätenpolitik in der Region Nordschleswig/Sønderjylland 1864-1914* (Hamburg, 1999).

Schleswig. By this means an attempt was made in 1810 to define the area – an area that was linguistically completely mixed to the extent that the language differed from village to village and from family to family.

These so-called language rescripts of 1810 might be interpreted as an attempt to achieve a unified administration and thereby a closer integration between the Kingdom north of the Königsau/Kongeåen and the duchies. Frederik VI 'saw language as the vehicle for the centralisation of his state', for him the important matter was to modernise his state.[12] He ventured to tackle the unresolved language problem and soon after issuing the order, he sent a circular to his officials in the part of Schleswig north of the Husum-Schleswig line. They were asked about their views on the language decree and its practicability.

The general tenor was one of rejection. Most of the officials were of the opinion that the introduction of the Danish language as the administrative, school and church language was neither desirable nor practicable, certainly not in those parts of Schleswig in which High or Low Danish/Sønderjysk was the vernacular. German should retain its traditional role as the educated language. As a result, the situation did not change and the effect of the rescript vanished into thin air.

While the language rescript of 1810 came in a period when the monarchy in Copenhagen gave little thought to the nationalist issue, the situation 40 years later was completely different.[13] In the course of the 1830s, a Schleswig-Holstein movement developed in the duchies, which became increasingly more radical in the 1840s. The spark caught fire in 1848, when the Danish king was declared to be 'not free' in his decisions and an independent government for the two duchies was formed. The revolutionaries in Kiel soon received support from other German states that saw the 'matter of Schleswig-Holstein' as a *pars pro toto* of the German question.[14] The war of 1848-1850 has been judged differently in Danish and German research, but however the war is regarded, it is determined by the fact that it failed.

In this climate, the government of the composite state made a further attempt at language policy. The background was completely different from

12 Rohweder, *Sprache und Nationalität*, p. 24.

13 Langewiesche, D., *Nation, Nationalismus, Nationalstaat in Europa und Deutschland* (München, 2000).

14 Bjørn, C., *1848: Borgerkrig og revolution* (Copenhagen, 1998); Siemann, W., *Die deutsche Revolution von 1848/49* (Frankfurt a.M., 1985).

1810. When in 1851 another attempt was made to intervene in the linguistic practice in the Duchy of Schleswig, the government already had sufficient experience of the explosive nature of the nationalist idea.

The language rescript of 1851, named after the departmental chief August Regenburg, was the first example of a nationally motivated language policy in the German-Danish border area. Even if later political actions such as the Prussian restrictions in around 1900 went further in their endeavours, the approach could already be seen in 1851. Now it was no longer a matter of rationalising the state. The attempt was to be made for the first time to appeal to the inhabitants of Schleswig directly as citizens and as members of the Danish nation.

The intention was to build on the concept of 'Central Schleswig' – a so-called 'mixed district' which coincided with the area described above. The Regenburg department here endeavoured not only to unify the language situation but tried to turn the hybrid language area completely to Danish. Henceforth, Danish was to be the administrative language. Official church activities such as confirmations were given a deadline of 1864 to be performed exclusively in Danish, and Danish was also to be introduced in schools as quickly as possible.[15]

Regenburg would not be deterred. Although only a short time previously, in 1846 and again in 1850, a large number of vicars in Central Schleswig had been questioned about the linguistic conditions in their communities, the results were not included in the new regulations. Regenburg was driven by his strong national conviction and his wish to turn the hybrid language area to Danish. He thought that he could achieve this through a language policy imposed from above – an error that the Prussian government repeated in 1867.

Regenburg's attempts to impose Danish as the language broke with all the language traditions of the Duchy of Schleswig. It was not just that the language policy angered those with German leanings, 'the attempt to enforce ways of thinking which underlay the language rescripts was also criticised by a Danish group in North Schleswig'.[16] In this sense, the Danish language policy in about 1850 is a good example of a policy that damages itself through its restrictions.

After 1851 there were no further attempts to unify the language used in the administration or schools until 1863. Instead, however, the government

15 Lange, U., ed., *Geschichte Schleswig-Holsteins: Von den Anfängen bis zur Gegenwart* (Neumünster, 2003).

16 *Ibidem*, p. 452, translations Graw-Teebken.

of the composite Danish state pursued a policy of low level conflict. Not until 1863, with the proclamation of the November constitution and the attempt to create a future Danish nation state up to the Eider, the so-called Eider programme, were the debates moved to civil society. We will consider these debates in the following section.

Discourse of partition and community

In 1840, intellectuals, academics and the politically engaged inside and outside the duchies of Schleswig and Holstein started to concern themselves with the issues of political and linguistic demarcation. Let us begin with the Danish National Liberal Carl Ferdinand Allen (1811–1871), whose study of the linguistic conditions in the duchies is often quoted. The ideas underlying Allen's main work from 1857-1858 can already be found in one of his articles from 1848. In 'Ueber die Sprache und Volksthümlichkeit im Herzogthum Schleswig oder Süderjütland', Allen combines an analysis of the linguistic situation in the duchy with the idea of geopolitical affiliation.[17]

Allen's ideas incorporated key points from the romantic nationalist ideas of his time. They included the idea that the 'folk spirit' is revealed most clearly in the national language. Dialects only develop very slowly and it is precisely in them that traditional culture is preserved the longest. Allen applied this idea to Central Schleswig, where there is a hybrid form of the language.[18] An idea of daily language practice in Central Schleswig can be formed from reports by village teachers and pastors from the early 1850s.[19] The southern Jutland national language on the peninsula of Anglia was suffused with high and low German expressions, a hybrid language of German and Danish.

17 Allen, C.F., 'Ueber die Sprache und Volksthümlichkeit im Herzogthum Schleswig oder Süderjütland', *Anti-Schleswig-Holsteinische Fragmente*, 6 (Copenhagen, 1848).

18 Nielsen, N.Å., 'Sprogpolitik og dialektforskning i Slesvig 1851-64', *Sønderjysk Månedsskrif*, vol. 58, no. 10 (1982), pp. 283-290.

19 See also Bijleveld, N., 'Language, National Culture and the Clergy in Nineteenth-Century Denmark', in: Broomans, P., Jensma, G., Vandevoorde, H. and Van Ginderachter, M., eds., *The Beloved Mothertongue. Ethnolinguistic Nationalism in Small Nations: Inventories and Reflections* (Louvain, Paris, Dudley, MA, 2008), pp. 93-107; Bracker, 'Die dänische Sprachpolitik'; Henriksen, S.H., 'Det blandede sprogdistrikt mellem krigene', *Sønderjysk Månedsskrift* vol. 28 (Aabenraa, 1952), pp. 136-143.

Carl Ferdinand Allen

Photo: Budtz Müller & Co, Royal Library, Copenhagen

However, this contradicted Allen's idea of a uniform Danish national culture and led him, as demonstrated by Anders Bjerrum, to change the original language reports in his quotes. Selected Low German expressions were replaced with pure sønderjysk and this changed their content. As Bjerrum summed up: 'Allen must have recognised that he was faced here with a real hybrid language and that if he wanted to rescue his thesis of the uniformity of the southern Jutland dialects he would have to thoroughly change the text. And that is what he did.'[20] Anders Bjerrum's discovery in 1953 was noted with astonishment.[21] The forgery shows to what extent 'language was instrumentalised in the area in the political battle' and how a 'linguistic contact was changed into a linguistic conflict'.[22] It is therefore very difficult to acquire an 'objective picture of the linguistic circumstances in the duchies' in the nineteenth century.[23]

Very quickly there was considerable resistance to Allen's writings on the German side. We can use a review of Allen's article as an example. The author of the review, Knut Jungbohn Clement (1803–1873), published his comprehensive publication 'Das Wahre Verhältnis der süderjütischen Nationalität und Sprache zur deutschen und frisischen im Herzogthum Schleswig' in Hamburg

20 Bjerrum, A., 'De danske sprogprøver hos C.F. Allen', *Festskrift til Peter Skautrup 21. januar 1956* (Aarhus, 1956), p. 306.

21 Nielsen, *'Sprogpolitik'*, p. 286.

22 Winge, V., 'Dansk og Tysk i Slesvig', in: Jørgensen, S.A. , *Meddelelser fra Thorvaldsens Museum 2001* (Copenhagen, 2001), p. 57.

23 *Ibidem.*

in 1849.[24] It is dedicated to the German National Assembly in Frankfurt's St Paul's Church, which the author used to clearly position himself. On the one hand, his work is a response to Allen's article; on the other hand, his remarks show the central position which the connection between region and language set out above also took on the German side.[25]

Clement begins by commenting that Allen's historical and cultural arguments in favour of Danish dominance in Schleswig are simply untrue. On the contrary, this could not have been more thoroughly German territory. At the time of the migration of the peoples, Clement says, the western and eastern Germanic tribes encountered one another there. The eastern Germanic tribesmen, direct ancestors of the Germans, were even at that time clearly superior to the western Germanic tribesman, the original Dane. Making pseudo references to history is a well-known argument. The nation is dated back to a vague original age and it is claimed that there lies the origin of the nation that is superior today. The next step is the awakening of this original identity.

A particular thorn in Clement's eye was a remark by Allen about Denmark's border: 'Denmark's borders for a thousand years have been the Schlei and Eider – that is the main argument on which all should rest. (...) The Danewirke also bears witness. The Danish nation and Danish language extended to here and to the Schlei'.[26] The Eider frontier as the southern border of the Danish nation and the Danish language – this view was rejected by Clement. For him the original borders of language and nation lay much further north, namely at the Königsau.[27] He argued that the whole of Schleswig was archetypal German territory.[28] He takes language and place names as evidence for his thesis. He also devoted many pages to linguistic analysis in order thus to prove the origins of the Germans.

24 Clement, K.J., *Das wahre Verhältnis der süderjütischen Nationalität und Sprache zur deutschen und frisischen im Herzogthum Schleswig: Eine historische und ethnographische Beleuchtung des 6ten Hefts der anti-schleswig-holsteinischen Fragmente von Dr. K.J. Clement* (Hamburg, 1849).

25 Riecken, C., 'Zwischen Wissenschaft und politischem Erwachen: Nordfriesische Sprachforschung im 19. Jahrhundert', *Nordfriesland* (2001), pp. 24-27.

26 Clement, *Das wahre Verhältnis*, p. 6.

27 *Ibidem*, p. 7.

28 This argumentation must be seen in the context of German cultural nationalism and geopolitical visions in the time period discussed. See also Leerssen, J., 'Linguistic Geopolitics and the Problem of Cultural Nationalism', in: Broomans et al., *The Beloved Mothertongue*, pp. 15-36.

Clement concluded his remarks with these words:

Thus I have disproved the sixth volume of the anti-Schleswig-Holstein fragments, whose immodest tendency it was to prove that the present Duchy of Schleswig had extended from primeval time to the Schlei and the Danewirke, indeed to the Eider, in all its parts, impartially, thoroughly and as appropriate from an academic standpoint.[29]

Clement here aligned himself with a discourse adopting an apparently factual approach to given linguistic circumstances that could not be integrated into the pattern of ideas of a primordial theory of nationality. It is indicative that even an author like Knut Jungbohn Clement allowed himself to be drawn into the discourse of 'either-or', even though it would be precisely a person like him, a North Frisian by birth, who would be no stranger to the idea of a 'third way' in Schleswig-Holstein: 'Indeed it does not seem quite right to talk of exclusively Danish, German and Frisian nationality in Schleswig because such does not really exist'.[30]

Clement and Allen wrote their texts at a time of political change. On the Danish side, the border at the Eider was propagated as a living geopolitical vision. On the Schleswig-Holstein side there was increasing agitation in favour of the annexation of the duchies to an – as yet nonexistent– German national state. In Clement in particular a specific strategy becomes evident which can be noticed again and again in subsequent writings: the attempt to appear objective and neutral, which can be described as a strategy of neutrality. Repeatedly, an appeal is made to the facts and an attempt is made to describe his own position as objective. This technique is used by both discourse types, which will be presented below using the example of two selected texts: the discourse of community and partition.

The subject of language is a central point in a short text from 1856 entitled 'Actenstücke zur Geschichte des Hochdeutschen im Herzogtum Schleswig'.[31] The anonymously published text (probably by P. Njort) is 34 pages long. The anonymous author remarks that there are 'many misunderstandings

29 *Ibidem*, p. 121.

30 *Ibidem*, p. 119.

31 N.N., *Actenstücke zur Geschichte des Hochdeutschen im Herzogtum Schleswig* (Copenhagen, 1856). The author is anonymous although 'P. Hjort' is noted in pencil on the cover page.

about the true linguistic and political circumstances in Schleswig'.[32] He is concerned to discover when and where the German language was introduced in Central Schleswig. He attempts to prove, using the example of a number of specific words, that the population of this area has always been Danish: 'The word "Nysted" is pure Danish, as is well known; even the pronunciation of the soft d as j is a true Danish provincialism and again provides evidence of the Danish nationality of the Angles (...).'[33]
How far south Low Danish truly dominated in the mid-nineteenth century will not be discussed here. The point here is to highlight the strategy of neutrality, proclaimed by the anonymous author. This is the central message of this text – only facts are dealt with and they are supported by credible, factually neutral investigations. The author implies that those with German leanings were largely one-sided, while those with Danish leanings were balanced and neutral.

Another type of argumentation can be found in a text published only a few years later.[34] Moritz Busch published 'Schmerzenschrei von der Eider' in 1860. Whereas the previous anonymous text deals exclusively with the Schleswig-Holstein question and the linguistic conditions as a regional issue, Busch is interested in embedding the problem within current European events.

One of the main subjects in Europe at that time was the 'German question' and the establishment of an Italian nation state. A cry of pain from the Eider is how Busch describes an address sent by the Schleswig-Holstein assembly of estates to the Danish king in response to the policy of the day, which Busch describes as Danish tyranny.[35] This cry, Busch says, is addressed to the 'kith and kin on the far side of the Eider'.[36] This might be described as the discourse of community. The affiliation with Germany is underpinned by the idea of a kind of ethnic community.

Busch was impressed by the Italian endeavours to establish a nation state. He criticised the German inclination towards 'moderation' – 'we lack the offensive spirit', he complained. Where this offensive was heading only becomes clear towards the end of the booklet. Here the author calls

32 *Ibidem*, p. 3.

33 *Ibidem*, footnote *).

34 Busch, M., *Der Schmerzensschrei von der Eider. Ein Nachtrag zu den 'Schleswig-Holsteinischen Briefen' von Moritz Busch* (Leipzig, 1860).

35 *Ibidem*, p. 10.

36 *Ibidem*, p. 3.

on Prussia to settle the Schleswig-Holstein question by military action: Prussian troops should move 'to the Eider and across the Eider' because the matter of the 'German duchies' lies close to the heart of the German national soul, a military strike against the Danish composite state was desired by 'public opinion'.[37] Indeed, the Danish composite state was an unhealthy structure in the view of the author: a disease that could only be cured by means of an 'incision'.[38] Here the author uses the image of the nation as a body, as an organic whole. The idea of a precise and smooth demarcation of the nation also enters the picture because the incision to which Busch refers can only be interpreted as the drawing of a clear border for the nation state. The border question in the north is compared to Italian nation-building. Busch accords central importance with regard to the German question to the issue of the national affiliation of the duchies of Schleswig and Holstein. He describes both duchies as German, although Schleswig had never been part of a German confederation of states.

Both texts are aimed primarily at a German or German-speaking public. Whereas the 'Actenstücke' deal with the unsettled linguistic and national circumstances as a regional problem, it is clear in Busch that there were also contemporary writers who viewed the Schleswig-Holstein question as significant with regard to the formation of the German nation state, and who drew comparisons to similar cases such as the formation of the Italian nation state. He makes clear that the German-Danish border area is not an isolated case but a case of ambivalent national affiliation, which certainly bears comparison.

Another text which dealt with the linguistic and national questions in the Duchy of Schleswig shortly before the start of the Prussian-Danish war in 1864 is Carl Bollmann's 30-page 'Eine Verschwörung'.[39] Published in 1862 by a Flensburg publishing house called Sundby and Jespersen, it is easy to assume that it is a text loyal to the King. However, it too has more to offer than mere criticism of Prussia or the German movement.

Carl Bollmann writes about the period before the first Schleswig war from 1848-1851 and attempts to present it from a contemporary historical perspective. The text claims to be historical in approach but is political in

37 *Ibidem*, p. 86.

38 *Ibidem*, p. 13.

39 Bollmann, C., *Eine Verschwörung: Von Carl Bollmann, ehemaligem Kabinetssecretair Sr. Hoheit des regierenden Herzogs von Koburg* (Flensburg, 1862).

execution. Bollmann addresses the German public, which he wishes to inform about the 'true circumstances' in the north, and positions himself as a Danish Liberal. The objects of his fulminations include the aristocrats, who in his view have damaged the democratic idea, they:

> (...) were concerned to bring the duchies into opposition against the other parts of the Danish monarchy (...) and that is why the national question (...) had to be placed in the foreground in order to distort the true situation such as if the province of Schleswig were a German land.[40]

Bollmann here builds on the discourse of neutrality which can already be found in the 'Actenstücke(n)' of 1852. Here he draws on a tradition in the German-Danish debate which presents the opponent as being partial while praising his favoured debaters as objective and 'truthful'. If Carl Bollmann is similar in this discourse of neutrality to other contemporary authors writing about the Schleswig-Holstein question, he is quite different from them in another respect: he adopts a critical attitude towards nationalism and recognises the national principle as an 'invention'. He explains this in numerous parts of the text, for example when he writes: '(...) in what was most willingly sacrificed for the so-called Schleswig-Holsteiners one must regret all the more that all this was given for a hollow, political invention'.[41] He relates this 'invention' to Schleswig and Holstein as German provinces and to the process of nationalist influence.

According to Bollmann, an important role is played by the nationalisation of the past: 'In the meantime, the "political and dialectical" campaign had been commenced, but there were no victories.'[42] In another part, he writes that indeed, 'weapons which had been sought in historical arsenals had not been ineffective in giving the political plans a historical base'.[43] The passages quoted here are quite surprising because it is rare that an author in the middle of the nineteenth century moves beyond the nationalist discourse and clearly recognises the process of historization – the writing of the nation back into the past – as a construct.

40 *Ibidem*, p. 12.
41 *Ibidem*, p. 3.
42 *Ibidem*, p. 14.
43 *Ibidem*, p. 4.

Because of the linguistic conditions, both sides could politically adopt Schleswig: both sides have historical, cultural and political arguments for their vision of the future geopolitical affiliation of Schleswig. Moreover, although both sides were vocal in advocating an 'integrated solution', there already appears to have been a widespread idea at the time that Bollmann published his text that a possible solution was the partition of Schleswig. He describes this as follows:

> Most recently, these Schleswig-Holstein Gothaers or Gotha Schleswig-Holsteiners have already aired the idea of a division of Schleswig in the petit bourgeois German press, thus themselves uncovering the falseness and hollowness of Schleswig-Holsteinism. Because either Schleswig-Holsteinism is a truth and then cannot be divided or it is what it has indeed turned out to be, a lie (...). Previously people said 'Op ewig ungedeelt' (...), today they say Schleswig should be partitioned (...).[44]

Bollmann refers here to a discourse of partition: he refers to circles which at that time already considered the partition of Schleswig to be possible and worth doing. Although Carl Bollmann fell prey to a polemical style in certain sections, his account in particular of the idea of a partition of Schleswig – 58 years before the idea became reality through the 1920 border – provides support for the view argued here of the slowness of geopolitical visions.

In conclusion, we can say that the debate before the Prussian-Danish war of 1864 was characterised by great diversity. There were recurring elements but it was quite possible for a broad discussion of the Schleswig-Holstein question to be had from a regional or international perspective. This also makes categorization difficult. We can state, though, that there were three to four main discourses on the language and border issues: one discourse was based on the idea that the Danish conglomerate state was the ideal state of being and should be held or re-established. Another argument saw the possibility of a Schleswig-Holstein construct connected to the Danish state, but more politically and economically independent. Those ideas increasingly became threatened by ideas of 'pure' Danish or German regions, divided by a line, cutting the mixed language areas into two halves. The idea that an ideal line could be found and then transformed

44 *Ibidem*, p. 25.

from being merely a linguistic-historical division of space into an actual border led to attempts to find the appropriate location for a future border.

During the mid-1860s it is possible to trace this shift from a certain openness of discourse to a closed one. It is no coincidence that by this time the aforementioned political tensions became quite intense, culminating in the 1864 war. The more the nineteenth century progressed, the more the positions in the German-Danish language conflict hardened. Arguments kept recurring, divisive elements gained precedence over what brought people together and political opponents were defamed. Furthermore, the battle metaphors increased the closer the next military conflict with Prussia came.

In this atmosphere, M. F. Blaunfeldt published 'Das Schleswigsche Sprachrescript vertheidigt wider die Angriffe des Herrn Conferenzraths Raaslöff', which was a good fifty pages long.[45] As its title already indicates, this text does two things: it is a defence of Danish language policy, specifically the language rescripts of 1851, and a direct response to a previous text.

Blaunfeldt expressly addressed a readership in the German regions south of the duchies. They were to be educated about the true linguistic circumstances in the Duchy of Schleswig, which 'for centuries has been a bone of contention between the mighty Germany and the small kingdom of Denmark'.[46] Blaunfeldt mainly refers back to the period before 1848 in his defence of Danish language policy. The role that he ascribes to language in this context is remarkable.

The German language had been the most important 'means of conquest' of German nationality while the 'toughness of the Danish nationality from the Schlei to the Königsaue' had resisted it.[47] The vernacular in particular is an important moment in the politicisation of language. Danish was still overwhelmingly spoken in Central Schleswig because:

> all steps aimed at introducing the German language as the popular and colloquial language of the population, at enforcing it on the individual families (...) have failed due to the toughness of Danish nationality.[48]

45 Blaunfeldt, M.F., *Das Schleswigsche Sprachrescript vertheidigt wider die Angriffe des Herrn Conferenzraths Raaslöff von M.F. Blaunfeldt, Hardesvogt in der Hüttener Harde im Herzogthum Schleswig* (Copenhagen, 1863).

46 *Ibidem*, p. 1.

47 *Ibidem*.

48 *Ibidem*, p. 21.

The discourse of conflict thrives on opposition and black-and-white representation. Thus, the political opponents of Blaunfeldt are all described negatively. The German press had thrust itself to the forefront 'howling and yelling' and was placing its hopes on a small part of the population 'which is, however, making the loudest noise'. On one side order and reasoned, factual arguments; on the other side playing up and defiance. The author keeps to this division throughout when discussing the language conflict. Even though Blaunfeldt presents his own arguments as objective, factual and correct, he does not always succeed in remaining factual – 'But let us stay with the matter of language' he reminds himself and the reader. The reason for this inability lies, in my view, in the fact that an objective and factual description of the linguistic conditions was no longer possible at that time. The national interpretation dominated the debate.

So what is the geopolitical vision of the author, where for him does the border between German and Danish language and nationality lie? He writes about this:

> Even today the inhabitants on both banks of the Schlei consider it to be the border between the German and the Danish-speaking parts of Schleswig. (...) (Thus) clearly the Schlei reveals itself as the linguistic border in the life of the people, in individual words and in the outer appearance of the personality of the inhabitants of both banks of the Schlei.[49]

The author thereby draws the border between German and Danish at the Dan(n)ewerk border, also mythologised in other writings, even if he does not mention it but makes the Schlei the 'natural border'.[50] The description is remarkable for the clear way in which the border is drawn wholly in the spirit of nationalist ideology.

Although shortly before the outbreak of the second Schleswig war the conflict-laden rhetoric seemed to be increasing, there was no longer any trace of a conciliatory element between German and Danish after the war. Prussia's annexation of the two duchies led to demonstrations and agitation north of the Königsau, while at the same time the resistance

49 *Ibidem*, pp. 24-25.

50 Sahlins, P., 'Natural Frontiers Revisited: France's Boundaries in the 17th Century', *American Historical Review* vol. 95, no. 5 (1990), pp. 1423-1451.

in Sønderjylland was supported by the considerably reduced kingdom. The text by the Danish National Liberal Orla Lehmann can be used as an example of the tone of those years. In 1865 he published the text 'Det Tydske i Danmark'.[51]

Orla Lehmann found it difficult to come to terms with the loss of the duchies of Schleswig and Holstein, but he was also able to see the benefits of the new structure. In 1864 limbs were cut off the body of the Danish nation but at the same time the disease was also cut out.[52] The diseased structure – the Danish composite state – had now been excised and the primary defect, which had burdened Danish history, had been rectified: a stable external border had been created. It should be emphasised here how the geopolitical image of Denmark in terms of an 'awakening' and 'healing' of the national body is integrated into and interpreted as part of the national concept. He draws a comparison with England: '(...) the English kingdom only acquired its identity in that it grew smaller and only because it acquired and accepted its identity was it able to grow.'[53]

After all, this also corresponds to the policy of national unity which was conducted in Denmark after 1864.[54]

Conclusions

As we have seen, the Duchy of Schleswig became strongly politicised from the mid-nineteenth century onwards. Short and long texts concerned themselves with the role of language and national 'awakening'. They also connected the subject of language with the subject of German and Danish state building. What should the German nation state look like and how far north would it extend? Which parts of the Danish composite state were a 'natural' part of the Danish nation and where did the border lie?

In summary, the political debates about language and nationality were greatly exacerbated in the course of the nineteenth century. Opinions and differences about which there had been reflection were replaced by a

51 Lehmann, O., *Det tydske i Danmark: Et foredrag i arbejderforeningen af 1860 af Orla Lehmann* (Copenhagen, 1865).

52 *Ibidem*, p. 23.

53 *Ibidem*: '(...) at det engelske Rige først ved at blive *mindre*, blev *sig selv*, og først ved at blive sig selv, kunde blive stort.'

54 O'Leary, B., ed., *Right-Sizing the State: The Politics of Moving Borders* (Oxford, 2000).

harder tone, particularly around the time of the year of war. It is apparent in these debates how German-Danish antagonism became more intense.

The geographical situation influenced the formation of national identity in border regions. The National idea was consolidated through the interaction between state and society, where the state provided a modern communication network, implemented the standardisation of language and culture and where, on the other hand, the citizen tied himself to the state through solidarity with the nation.

This feeling of community is the glue that holds the nation state together. The state had to react to the special conditions in the border regions, either through special dispensations or tighter regulations aimed at standardisation. Nationalisation policy in border regions had to be adapted to the special conditions of the interior and border regions.

The assignment of importance to language in the texts and pamphlets from Schleswig quoted here was controversial. Whether the discourse was of partition or community, everything was aimed at occupying this space within various patterns of interpretation. Whether language was seen and interpreted as a dividing or unifying element depended on the standpoint of the speaker or writer. A monopoly on interpretation was marked out in the discourse but was never immutable. From 1864 onwards, the nationalist interpretation increasingly gained ground while the composite state idea was declined. The discourse of neutrality attempted to defame the opponent and present opinions as neutral and free of prejudice. The Dan(n)ewerk was mythologized as the natural border and a geopolitical vision of a Denmark to the Eider arose. It can be concluded that the linguistic border was never seen as free of value judgements but was always part of the political discourse about the affiliation of the region.

Language and nationality are not connected *per se* but are combined through patterns of interpretation. The often ambivalent cultural affiliation of border populations is one of the greatest challenges that developing nation states have to confront. Those who fail to integrate their border regions lose. The homogeneity of nation states spreads not only from the centre to the periphery but must at the same time be anchored in the periphery.
National identity is based on an illusion of homogeneity. In border regions the ambivalence and changeability of national identifiers is revealed with particular clarity.

Part II

Cultural Transfer,

Language Frontiers, Across Borders

The Discovery of Finland

Patterns in Cultural Transfer

« Adriaan van der Hoeven »

When Zacharias Topelius (1818-1898) was appointed the first professor of Finnish history in 1863, he felt that his field only covered the previous half a century. He believed that as an independent entity with its own history, Finland only came into being as late as 1809, the year it became an autonomous grand duchy with the Russian tsar as grand duke. However, when he began lecturing he did not adhere to this theoretical principle, as he understood only too well the importance of a respectable history for a young nation in the making. Thus, when the authority of scholarship fell short, he made use of the arts, writing a historical novel in six parts, entitled *Fältskärns berättelser* (The Stories of a Surgeon) (1851-1866), which was about the Thirty Years' War of the first half of the seventeenth century. Using these stories he aimed to give the Finnish people an identity by making them aware of their history.

This was also why he wrote *Boken om vårt land* (The Book about our Country) (1875), which would be used as a textbook in schools throughout the century to come. This book provided all the essential information any Finn should know about their country, culture and history; a true canon of Finland. It opens with a poem about his native country, a song of praise[1]: 'Wake up around your endless shores, my beautiful country, my fatherland!', and continues the themes of home and fatherland: 'This book deals with Finland. This book deals with our native country. What is Finland? A country amidst many other countries. What is native country? It is our Home'.[2] After some preliminary ideological remarks he gives a description of the country. He discusses the geography – in the broad sense of the word – of Finland,

1 See also the complete text of 'Morgonsång' at the end of this article.

2 'Tämä kirja kertoo Suomesta. Tämä kirja kertoo isänmaasta. Mikä on Suomi! Maa monien joukossa. Mikä on isänmaa? Se on meidän suuri kotimme', Topelius, Z., *Maamme kirja. Lukukirja Suomen alimmille oppilaitoksille* (Kolmaskymmeneskolmas, korjattu painos, Porvoo, 1929), p. 7.

not only to enhance his readers' knowledge of their country, but especially to foster their love for it. After this he deals with Finland's history, beginning with 'The pagan gods of the Finns and the heroic legends'[3], in other words, with the era before Christianisation, when Finland still had its own culture - according to the prevalent view - as laid down in the *Kalevala* (1835, 1849) by Elias Lönnrot (1802-1884). Topelius stresses the significance of Lönnrot right from the start: 'Thanks to him the Finnish people came to know their history, which was shrouded in mystery, and found the courage to exist as an independent people alongside other peoples'.[4] *Land, people* and *history* (including *cultural history*) were the three magic words for each nation, to which one should immediately add *language* as a constitutive element. However, Topelius was a Swedish speaker and this probably kept him from overly emphasising the Finnish language.

Language

At the beginning of the eighteenth century, when Finland was still the eastern buffer of the Swedish empire, Israel Nesselius (1667-1739), who had studied in Leiden in 1701-1702, suggested Finland do away with the Finnish language and replace it with Swedish: 'If, because of its oddity, it should be protected from complete disappearance, we could perhaps leave some parishes near the Lappish border Finnish-speaking'.[5] This illustrates the disdain and the self-evident sense of superiority maintained by the Swedish-speaking ruling class in those days.

It was against such prevailing attitudes that the Fennomans revolted. However, this would not have been possible without radical changes in thinking and mentality, which occurred firstly through the revolution in thought due to romanticism, and secondly in the shift of power from Stockholm to St Petersburg. The romantic movement's focus on the individual and unique character, not only of persons, but also of peoples and their cultures, opened the way for the recognition of and research

3 'Suomalaisten pakanalliset jumalat ja sankarisadut', Topelius, *Maamme*, p. 209.

4 'Hänen kauttansa Suomen kansa on oppinut tuntemaan hämärän muinaisaikansa ja saanut rohkeutta pysymään omintakeisena, itsenäisenä kansana muiden kansojen rinnalla', Topelius, *Maamme*, p. 213.

5 Tarkiainen, V. and Kauppinen, E., *Suomalaisen kirjallisuuden historia* (Neljäs painos, Helsinki, 1967), p. 96.

into Finnish language and culture. The political break with Sweden and incorporation as an autonomous region into the Russian Empire, which was very different in a social sense and in terms of its mentality, made the choice obvious: 'Swedes we are no longer, Russians we don't want to become, so let us be Finns!',[6] as the slogan went. This was exactly what happened, with language being an essential part of this process of Fennicisation because it expressed what the romanticists referred to as the soul of the people.[7] 'A people that loses its language, loses itself as well', the early Fennoman Adolf Ivar Arwidsson wrote in Åbo Morgonblad in 1821.[8] Saving the Finnish people was ultimately the objective of the activists of the nineteenth century. Today, this heroic discourse on the national project, on the construction of national identity, sounds rather pompous, but for the Fennomans it was a case of a *must*. Much more than a rational concept, it was an emotional necessity. Finnishness was something primordial to them. It was not merely situational or constructed. Nevertheless, its exact meaning was difficult to define in words; fortunately, it could be traced through such elements as history and the environment.

Patterns of a growing self-awareness

This national project of Fennicisation not only took time but also took place in phases. Miroslav Hroch has developed a model of the various phases through which national movements pass, from their genesis as a philosophical and cultural idea to the establishment of a politically independent nation-state.[9] In countries such as Finland, the movement starts with a few intellectuals interested in their own culture, literature and folklore; an interest which does not initially have specific political

6 In Swedish: 'Svenskar äro vi inte längre, ryssar vilja vi inte bli, låt oss alltså bli finnar'; in Finnish: 'Ruotsalaisia emme ole, venäläisiksi emme tahdo tulla, olkaamme siis suomalaisia'

7 Herder, for example, held the opinion that the soul of the people, the national character, is embodied in the national language, Herder, J.G., *Sämtliche Werke*, Suphan, B., ed., vol. XIII (Berlin, 1877-1913), p. 363.

8 'Kielensä kadotettuaan, kansa itsekin on kadonnut'. Quote from Krohn, J., *Suomalaisen kirjallisuuden vaiheet* (=SKS Toimituksia 86 Osa) (Helsinki, 1897), p. 186.

9 Hroch, M., *Social Preconditions of National Revival in Europe. A Comparative Analysis of the Social Composition of Patriotic Groups among the Smaller European Nations* (Cambridge, 1985), pp. 22-24.

implications or aims. A period of patriotic agitation then follows, when advocates of a national idea become politically active, and the third phase encompasses the rise of a national mass movement. While the first two phases occur before the industrial revolution, the transition to a popular movement coincides more or less with the industrial and bourgeois revolution. In Finland, the first phase began around 1840 and continued until the years 1870-1880. After this, patriotic agitation broadened into a mass movement which culminated in the national strike of 1905 and finally ended with the realisation of the nation-state of Finland in 1917.

Politics – development nationalism	Period	Phase
Shift of power Transition of Finland from being a part of Sweden to being part of Russia (1808-09)	1800–1840	Scholarly interest
Breakthrough capitalism – industrialisation Language struggle *Kalevala* 1835, 1849 *Fänrik Ståls sägner* 1848, 1863 *Fältskärns berättelser* 1851-66 *Boken om vårt land* 1875	1840–1880	Patriotic agitation
Victory of the Fennomans Emergence of a working class Class society Threat of Russification General strike, 1905	1880-1905	Rise of national mass movement
Growing gap between elite & working class End of nineteenth-century national idealism	1905-1917	National mass movement
Independence (Civil war)	1917-1918	Realisation of nation-state

Thus, a clear and in fact logical pattern is discernable. Nationalism spread insidiously, unchecked and more or less as the communists had hoped to spread their doctrine: a small vanguard convinces a whole population, coupled with a growing self-awareness strongly based on culture. However, according to Anthony D. Smith, what is sought in culture also follows a certain pattern.[10] In the beginning, the concern is with something as general as the national character (or the soul of the people). Later, the focus shifts towards the explanation of this specific character – Why is it as it is? – moving from a historical perspective, and thus from the general

10 Smith, A.D., *National Identity* (London, 1991), pp. 87ff.

to the specific; from a hypothesis to the explanatory facts. The road then branches out, as the explanation can be found either rationally in political history or more instinctively in the vernacular literary-cultural heritage of the indigenous people. While, for example, the Swedish-speaking Topelius often made use of Finnish history, the Fennomans mostly chose the other path. The epic *Kalevala* was especially regarded as an objectification of Finnish values, as a manifestation of the unique genius of the nation – as Smith called it.[11] The soul and the heroic history of the Finns were embedded in the epic and the *Kalevala* was immediately canonised. The only Swedish-language literary work to compete with it was Runeberg's (1804-1877) *Fänrik Ståls sägner* (The Tales of Ensign Stål) which was published in 1848 – almost at the same time as the final version of the *Kalevala*. Its description of the Finnish War of 1808-1809 and its Romantic, idealistic portrayal of humanity has left clear traces in the Finnish psyche. Where the *Kalevala* was supposed to contain the history of the Finnish-speaking population, *Fänrik Ståls sägner* – along with *Fältskärns berättelser* – above all mirrored the past of the Swedish-speaking Finns.

Acerbi and Rühs – the discovery of Finland

In fact, nationalism is basically the discovery of one's country. It follows a certain pattern. In the Netherlands, the 'discovery' of Finland also followed certain lines and took some time to gain momentum.[12] At the beginning the nineteenth century, foreigners such as the Italian Giuseppe Acerbi (1773-1846) and the German historian and *Edda* translator Friedrich Rühs (1781-1820) opened the way with their travel journals, which were not bad sources at all for the Dutch public. Acerbi wrote, for instance, about folk poetry: 'There is scarcely any event, public or private, which does not find a poet amongst the Finnish peasants to celebrate it'.[13]

---

11 *Ibidem*, p. 89.

12 Cf. Figure 1.

13 Acerbi, G., *Travels through Sweden, Finland, and Lapland, to the North Cape, in the years 1798 and 1799*, vol. I (London, 1802), p. 303; in Dutch: 'Naauwlijks is 'er eene gebeurtenis, 't zij algemeene of bijzondere, of dezelve vindt onder de Finlandsche boeren een dichter, die dezelve bezingt', Acerbi, G., *Reizen door Zweeden en Finland, tot aan de uiterste grenzen van Lapland. In de jaren 1798 en 1799*, vol. II (Haarlem, 1804-1806), p. 140.

Illustration from Acerbi's Travels etc. 'Extraordinary Mode of Singing by Finlanders'.

He also described the unique manner in which they sang: 'A circle is formed of the auditors, in the midst of which stand the improvisator, and his repetitory coadjutor. Every line which the improvisator sings or delivers, is repeated in the same tune by the coadjutor, who, taking up the last word, or the last but one, finishes the line with him, and then repeats it alone'.[14] He added an illustration (see above) which greatly influenced the popular image of this tradition. Rühs's observations fit well with Acerbi's (Rühs had read Acerbi's book). However, it is highly unlikely that either personally witnessed singing bards. Rühs, conspicuously enough, took a clear stand on the language issue, which was being discussed by only a few intellectuals at the time: 'Despicable and also very preposterous was the idea, which had arisen in some brainless heads, namely that the government of this country should force its people to

14 Acerbi, *Travels*, p. 303.

lay aside its mother tongue'.[15] Later, the travel accounts of Matthew Consett (1818), Friedrich Wilhelm von Schubert (1826-1827) and Xavier Marmier (1841) were also published. Nevertheless, Finland was still far away, and what attention was paid to it occurred only now and again.

From the general to the specific

As suggested above, the discovery of Finland in the Netherlands seemed to proceed along certain lines. In addition to the fact that the Dutch had to rely on foreigners for information until the 1840s or 1850s, no matter how resourceful the writers were, the books and articles can best be characterised as very general. The preponderance of travel journals is especially striking. This did not change until the 1850s, when the *Kalevala* was first mentioned in a one page account about Sweden![16] Not very promising. However, from about 1860, attention becomes concentrated on literary works. Principally, it was Runeberg who was the object of investigation and not the *Kalevala*. Seven items, or about 15 percent of the material covering the previous century, dealt with him, as opposed to four items about the *Kalevala*. Runeberg's poem *Bonden Paavo* was translated into Dutch in 1859 by a well-known poet, although based on an English translation rather than the Swedish original, while his comedy *Kan ej* (Impossible) was published in 1884.[17] The first translation of the *Kalevala* was only published as late as 1928 – if we do not take into account the adaptation for children by Nellie van Kol (1851-1930) published in 1905.[18] It is interesting that initially the Dutch relied heavily on the existing Finnish canon, with the focus clearly on the two representatives of Finnish and Swedish-language literature who, in their own country, were above all criticism. However, in the

15 'Abscheulich und abgeschmackt war übrigens die Idee, die bisweilen in beschränkten Köpfen ausgestiegen ist, dass die Regierung dies Volk zwingen sollte, auf seine Muttersprache Verzicht zu thun', Rühs, F., *Finland und seine Bewohner* (Leipzig, 1809), p. 347; in Dutch: 'Verachtenswaardig en ten hoogste ongerijmd tevens was het denkbeeld, 't welk nu en dan in hersenlooze hoofden is opgestegen, dat namelijk de regering dit volk behoorde te noodzaken, zijne moedertaal voor altijd af te leggen', Rühs, *Finland*, vol. II, p. 167.

16 N.N., 'Zweden', *Algemeene konst- en letterbode*, LXVI, vol. 1, no. 19 (1854), p. 151.

17 For the translations of Finnish literature in the Netherlands between 1875 and 1925 see Van der Hoeven, A.M., '"So Fresh, So New and So Perfectly Healthy": The Literature of Finland in the Netherlands 1875-1925', *Scandinavica*, vol. 45, no. 1 (2006).

18 For the translations of the Kalevala in Dutch see Van der Hoeven, A.M., 'The Dutch translations of the Finnish epic *Kalevala*', in Blokland, R., and Hasselblatt, C., eds., *Finno-Ugrians and Indo-Europeans: Linguistic and Literary Contacts. Proceedings of the Symposium at the University of Groningen, November 22-24, 2001* (Maastricht, 2002), p. 112-147.

1880s, there is a clear shift to politics, cumulating in 1899 with five items. The explanation for this shift seems to be related to the tsarist politics of oppression and Russification which writers took a firm stand against.

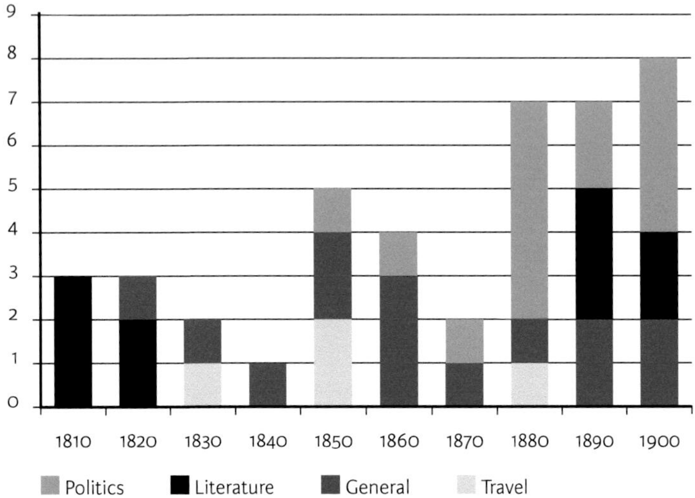

Figure 1[19] Books and articles on Finland in the 19th Century.

Hence, it appears one can discern three or perhaps four stages of development in the nineteenth century. The first runs between 1800 and 1850 to 1860, with the decade from 1850-1860 possibly a transition period. During this period, Finland remained very remote from Holland and the Dutch relied on foreigners for information. The travel books testify to a certain spirit of discovery of the unknown. The descriptions of Finland initially attempt to provide an overall view, but during the 1850s this seems to change, with more specific subjects being considered, such as Finnish sayings, collected by Matthias Alexander Castrén, and the *Kalevala*. From 1860 until roughly 1885, literary works come into focus, specifically that of Runeberg and the *Kalevala*. Obviously, there is no longer such a need for general descriptions and Finland is considered familiar enough to be dealt with in a more specific way. This trend becomes stronger in the following years, until the turn of the century. The *Kalevala* was discussed in Holland once more, while in 1895 the first translation of a Finnish

19 Based on my bibliography, see Van der Hoeven, A.M., 'Bibliografie van in het Nederlands verschenen literatuur op het gebied van de Finoegrische volken 1800-1900', in: Van der Hoeven, A.M. and Kylstra, A.D., eds., *Tien jaar Finoegristiek in Groningen 1966-1976* (Groningen, 1978), pp. 45-98.

literary work of art was published – Juhani Aho's *Papin rouva* (The vicar's wife), which had first been published in the original only two years before.[20] Again, this work can be regarded as part of the canon and one of the highest ranked novels of the day. Thus, while there was little Finnish literature available to Dutch readers, at least what they could read was of the highest possible quality.

The other works available were specifically concerned with politics. At this stage we can say that Finland had moved closer to Holland and was now regarded as part of the civilised world, with the Dutch also able to identify with the Finns. The threatening Russification perhaps reminded them of the Eighty Years War (1568-1648) in which the Dutch fought against Spanish absolutism and Catholicism; a small country fighting for independence. In any case, Dutch writers took the Finnish side against Russia, expressing compassion for them and indignation at their plight. Nevertheless, the scale on which articles on Finland were written in the Netherlands during the nineteenth century remained very small. Other publications may yet be uncovered, but generally speaking we are talking about only a few publications a decade, one a year at the most. However, in the twentieth century this changes rather suddenly:

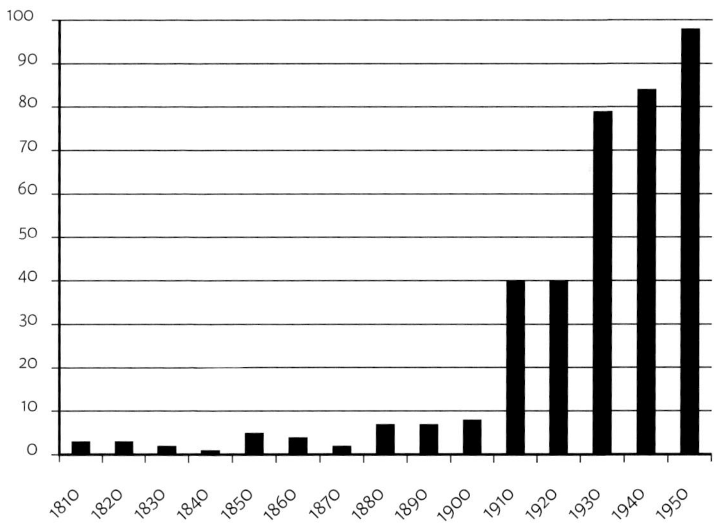

Figure 2[21] Books and articles on Finland in the 20th Century.

20 Translation by J. Visscher, not directly from the Finnish original, but through the Swedish translation published in 1893.

21 Based on the author's bibliography and other data collected by the author, as yet unpublished.

The news coverage of Finland also increased rapidly, to such an extent that it becomes difficult to record in detail. The discovery of Finland seems a fact, so to speak.

The Finnish and Dutch model

Comparing the discovery of Finland by the Finns with its discovery in the Netherlands, the resemblance between the two periods is remarkable. Hroch's period of scholarly interest coincides with the time of discovery and general description of Finland in travel books in the Netherlands. Between 1860 and the mid-1880s we notice a shift to specific subjects in the writings on Finland in the Netherlands. This again coincides more or less with Hroch's second phase of patriotic agitation and is even more striking since the specific subjects were Runeberg's *Fänrik Ståls sägner* and the *Kalevala*, the two canonical, epic literary works, both of which – in different ways – have Finnish history at their heart and played vital roles in the development of Finnish identity. While the transition occurs a little later in the Netherlands, it could still be seen as a kind of *echo effect*. The third phases also seem to coincide. The period of a rise of the mass movement against the threatening Russification or loss of autonomy in Finland is reflected in the articles on Finnish politics published in the Netherlands. The Dutch professor, Willem van der Vlugt (1853-1928), for example, wrote a pamphlet in defence of Finland, and also travelled to St Petersburg as a member of *Pro Finlandia*, a European committee of scientists and artists who presented a petition to the Tsar demanding changes to his policies with respect to Finland. The fact that the Tsar refused to receive the committee did not change Van der Vlugt's commitment to the Finnish cause and his subsequent popularity in Finland.

Even if there seems to be a certain parallel between the developments in Finland and the Netherlands it is problematical to compare the patterns. In the Netherlands, there was, of course, no emotional bond with the country and there were certainly no political implications either. Nevertheless, what took place in Finland seems to have been fundamentally reflected in the process of its reception in the Netherlands. In the beginning, one or two people interested in the issues exchanged thoughts with other kindred spirits (phase 1); subsequently, they thought their views to be important enough that others should also be informed (phase 2); and finally they convinced large parts of the population (phase 3). In other words, there was a movement from *exploration*, through *deepening of insight* to a *broader commitment* and the realisation that Finland was of equal value and standing (*recognition of an equal*). This parallel development was not the result of coincidence or sheer chance, but was due to the fact that the stream of publications in the Netherlands was guided by what happened in Finland and what was regarded to be important there, that is, the Finnish canon.

Type of publications in the Netherlands on Finland (in the nineteenth and beginning of the twentieth century)		**Development of nationalism in Finland (in the nineteenth and beginning of the twentieth century)**	
Travel General	1800-1860	1800-1840	Scholarly interest
General Literature on Runeberg on the *Kalevala* (Travel)	1860-1885	1840-1880	Patriotic agitation The *Kalevala* *Fänrik Ståls sägner* *Boken om vårt land*
Literature First translation of a Finnish novel by Aho, *Papin rouva* Adaptation of the *Kalevala* for children Politics Threat of Russification General	1880-1905	1880-1905	Rise of national mass movement
(Rapid growth in numbers of publications)	1905-	1905-1917	National mass movement
		1917-1918	Realisation nation-state

Conclusion

During the first half of the nineteenth century, after the shift of power in the north, the Finns more or less waited to see which way the wind blew. What did the new status of grand duchy mean? How far did autonomy extend? In the second half of the century, many, often dramatic changes and developments took place. This time is perhaps best described as a period of consciousness-raising; a time in which the Finns discovered

22 Cf. Figure 1

23 Cf. periodisation given above: Patterns of a growing self-awareness.

who they actually were (*Let us be Finns!*). When they finally found the answer, the Tsar threatened this newly found identity, again causing public outcry. At this time, the Finns strove to create an even more distinct image of themselves, especially in the arts. These developments followed the pattern sketched by Smith: from a concern with national character to explaining this character, or national genius, by digging through the national past, which can be purely politically driven or, alternatively, represented in artefacts and literature.

The Netherlands first became acquainted with the character of Finland by way of general travel journals, before turning to literature, that is to say the *Kalevala* and the work of Runeberg, the most important representatives of the Finnish canon. Both the *Kalevala* and Runeberg's epic poetry evoke a heroic past, which had a clear function in the ongoing national project. Without being aware of it, Dutch readers followed in the tracks of Finnish *cultural nationalism*, which fitted the strategy of the Fennomans in Finland so well. Later, when the repressive politics of Russification instigated by Nicholas II also caused indignation in the Netherlands, it was politics and a rational appeal to law and justice that set the tone for publications about Finland. This, again, was in line with the more *political form of nationalism* advocated by Finnish (usually Swedish-speaking) liberals.

By the time Finland became an independent state with its own borders, changing from a culturally defined nation into a nation-state in which the national project became a reality, the function of nationalism had changed. Its goal was no longer clear and, in any case, no longer the same for all Finns. A few months after the declaration of independence (December 6, 1917), a civil war broke out, emphasising the lack of unanimity. In the Netherlands, this division became visible in the publication of a rapidly growing stream of books and articles on a multitude of subjects, and also through a very slow increase in the number of translations. These did not mirror the Finnish canon as faithfully as before but introduced more popular contemporary novels such as *De getuige* (1926) by Hilja Haahti, *Vuur des Heeren* (1927) by Mauno Rosendal, *In adamskostuum* (1945) by Yrjö Soini, *Het ijs kruit* (1946) by Matti Hälli and *De lange lente* (1940), *Op zand gebouwd* (1943), *Lars Laurila* (1946), *Het nieuwe land* (1948), *De wijde mensenzee* (1949), *Prins Efflam* (1954), *Een spoor op aarde* (1963) and *Katrina* (1937), all by Sally Salminen.[24]

24 See the contribution by Roger Holmström in this volume.

The complete text of the song in Swedish is as follows:

Morgonsång

Vak upp kring hundramila stränder,
mitt sköna land, mitt fosterland!
Vak upp, när dagens sol sig tänder
i morgonglans vid himlens rand!
Din långa vinternatt förgår,
ditt segerglada ljus uppstår.
Vak upp kring hundramila stränder,
mitt sköna land, mitt fosterland!

Uppvakna till den nya tiden
som blommig strand i morgonväkt,
ty dödens skugga är förliden,
och livets ljusa dag har bräckt!
Väx stort i ädla minnens skygd,
väx klart i tanke, högt i dygd!
Uppvakna till den nya tiden
som blommig strand i morgonväkt!

Avtorka dina gömda tårar,
som dagg förgår i morgonvind!
Låt grönska de förfrusna vårar,
låt blomma ros på bleknad kind!
Låt vecklas ut var duven knopp!
Drick hälsa, liv och mod och hopp!
Avtorka dina gömda tårar,
som dagg förgår i morgonvind!

Än ruvar dimman över kärren;
stå upp, driv nattens spöken ut,
och väpna dig med kraft av Herren
uti din grynings livsminut!
Omgjorda dig med livets ord;
stå stark i Gud, min fosterjord!
Än ruvar dimman över kärren;
stå upp, driv nattens spöken ut!

Vak upp, mitt sköna land, mitt unga!
Vak upp, mitt hav, min insjö blå!
Hör, alla dina fåglar sjunga
och alla dina böljor slå!
Vak upp vid glada vindars brus
och bada fritt i morgonljus!
Vak upp, mitt sköna land, mitt unga!
Vak upp, mitt hav, min insjö blå!

Sally Salminen.

Source: http://www.uppslagsverket.fi/bin/view/Uppslagsverket/SalminenSally?template=highlightsearch&search=sallysalminen.

Against all odds

Sally Salminen's *Katrina* and the possibilities of cultural transfer

« Roger Holmström »

Today's fiction market is extremely globalised and focused on the same bestsellers. The same top-ten writers can be found across the world – especially in bookshops at international airports. In about nine cases out of ten the stories are originally written in English – anyone who has attended book exhibitions or browsed the new titles of fiction in the nearest bookshop will be aware of the Anglo-American influence on the book market in general. Under such centralised and in many ways monopolised conditions it seems to be almost impossible for a minor-language writer to achieve an international breakthrough. This would be even more difficult for a completely unknown newcomer to the Finnish market with no connections to the cultural establishment in the Finnish capital. The inner circle of established writers in Finland was in essence very closed before the two world wars. A newcomer from the countryside had an extremely small chance of being accepted. Nevertheless, once in a while this happened and this essay deals with just such a case – the international success of Sally Salminen's *Katrina*.

Let us go back about 70 years and have a look at the Finland-Swedish cultural situation in the mid-1930s. It was a decade of language controversies, played out between the Finnish-speaking majority and the Swedish-speaking minority in the officially bilingual Republic of Finland. Before the Second World War the native language of about 90 percent of the population was Finnish, while for the other 10 percent it was Swedish. After the acceptance and rise of Finland-Swedish modernism, the two leading Finland-Swedish publishing houses, Söderströms and Schildts, were eager to broaden the base of fiction by finding new and promising writers outside the limited intellectual circles of writers living in the Finnish capital or in the Helsinki area. At the time, literature in Sweden was well known for its school of writers called the estate workers (*statarförfattarna*), which included Ivar Lo-Johansson and Harry and Moa Martinson. Among the Finnish writers active at the time were similar storytellers such as Ilmari Kianto, Joel

Finland Swedish cover of Katrina.

Lehtonen and the subsequent Nobel Prize winner Frans Eemil Sillanpää, all of whom became very popular, especially among a growing group of readers familiar with everyday life in the countryside. In order to find more popular storytellers of this kind, the Schildts publishing house, in cooperation with the Swedish publisher Wahlström & Widstrand in Stockholm, decided to organise a novel-writing competition. In 1936, Sally Salminen (1906-1976), a completely unknown 30-year-old working as a maid in New York City was chosen as the first prize winner for her novel *Katrina*.

These are the basic facts of Salminen's achievement against all odds, which we will discuss in detail below. The main questions to be considered are: How did Sally Salminen manage to become an international bestselling writer? Which elements in her story were especially attractive? To what extent can her novel be regarded as a classic and are there any arguments in support of the novel securing a place in the Finland-Swedish canon?

Towards a personification of the American dream

Before the Second World War the situation in Finnish and Finland-Swedish literature was quite similar to the general conditions in the Scandinavian field of literature at the time. Increasing numbers of people could afford to buy books and this reduction in social differences promoted an increasing interest in working-class and middle-class surroundings. From this point of view one can say that in all essence Sally Salminen arrived on the scene at just the right moment. The fact that she literally became famous over night also contributed to the enormous interest in her personal background. Seventy years after Sally Salminen's debut, Thomas Warburton – a writer and for many years the manager of the literary division of the Finland-Swedish Schildts publishing house – wrote an article with the title 'Den välsignade damen' (The blessed lady). Here Warburton emphasised that it was precisely because Sally Salminen was completely unknown in all Scandinavian literary circles that newspapers became interested in her.[1] He also points out the importance of the laudatory reviews and states that the novel *Katrina* is a very unusual book in terms of its genre and that its ethnographic content still has considerable importance. Sally Salminen's combination of, on the one hand, an idyllic description of the beautiful Åland Islands and, on the other, many critical comments about the

1 Warburton, T., 'Den välsignade damen', *Nya Argus* 2 (2006), p. 29.

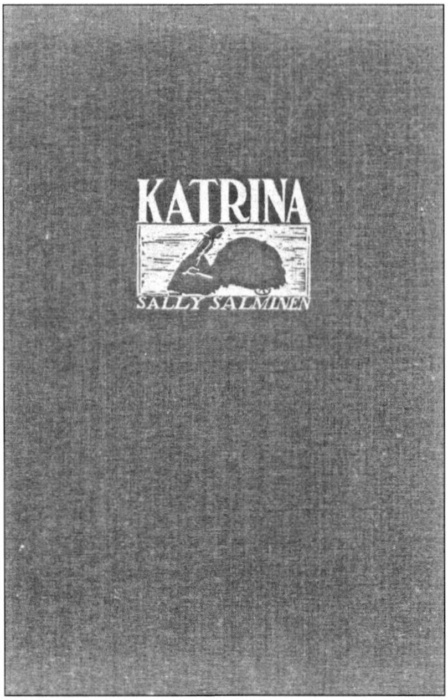

Dutch cover of **Katrina**.

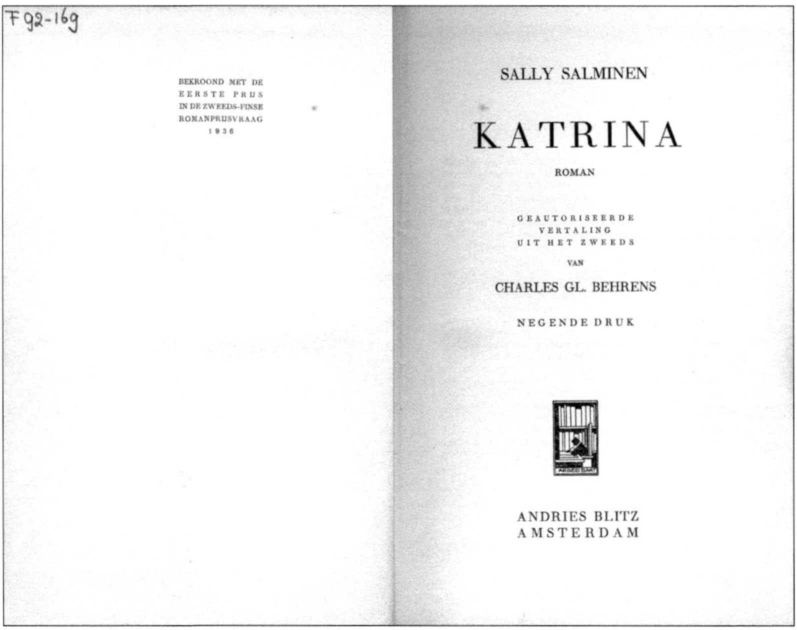

F92-169

BEKROOND MET DE
EERSTE PRIJS
IN DE ZWEEDS-FINSE
ROMANPRIJSVRAAG
1936

SALLY SALMINEN

KATRINA

ROMAN

GEAUTORISEERDE
VERTALING
UIT HET ZWEEDS
VAN
CHARLES GL. BEHRENS

NEGENDE DRUK

ANDRIES BLITZ
AMSTERDAM

Dutch inside of **Katrina**.

difficulty of life as a woman in a rural village at the beginning of the last century makes the book rather specific to its time. It is the many details of the description of everyday life within this context that gives the story an ethnographic value of increasing importance.

In her four-volume autobiography, Salminen revealed the background of her creative writing. The first volume, *Min amerikanska saga* (1968) ([My American fairy tale]), tells her life story as an example of the American Dream, or in a manner somewhat like the story of Cinderella, the fairy-tale heroine that Salminen resembles in many respects. Like so many others, Sally Salminen crossed the Atlantic in order to find a better life. She settled in New York City in 1930 and worked as a maid. In 1934 she started to write, initially to improve her English skills. In these English-language exercises Salminen explored her memories of a strong woman called Katrina who lived in a village on the Åland Islands where she had grown up herself.[2] Very soon Salminen recognised that her short story was growing beyond her control and that she had so much material that she felt that she could never manage to express what she wanted in a foreign language.[3] Therefore she reverted to her Finland-Swedish mother tongue and let the story about Katrina and her destiny blossom. To complete what she later called her life's exam, she used all her spare time as well as a number of hours at night to write.[4] In the winter of 1935 when she finally finished her story, her manuscript consisted of about 600 handwritten pages. The next step was to find a typist, after which Salminen sought her fortune by sending a chapter of her novel to the Stockholm publishing house, Bonniers. Their answer was anything but encouraging, Bonniers was not interested.

At this point Salminen began looking for a publisher in Finland. Her sister Aili Nordgren (who later also became a writer) sent her the postal addresses of the two leading Finland-Swedish publishers, Schildts and Söderströms, and at the same time told her elder sister that Schildts, in collaboration with the publishing company Wahlström & Widstrand in Sweden, had announced a competition for novelists several months earlier. Salminen asked for more details about the competition and in spite being short of time she decided to take the chance. The deadline was at the end of April 1936 but due to the surface mail conditions across the Atlantic,

2 Salminen, S., *Min amerikanska saga* (Helsingfors, 1968), p. 200.

3 *Ibidem*, p. 207.

4 *Ibidem*, p. 234.

Dutch cover of Katrina

Salminen had to carry her heavy manuscript to the post office in New York as early as the beginning of March.

The Finland-Swedish section of the competition attracted 17 entries. Among the judges were the professor of Swedish literature at the University of Helsinki, Gunnar Castrén, the modernist writer Elmer Diktonius and the Swedish literary historian and critic John Landquist. In June, Sally Salminen received a letter telling her that her manuscript had been chosen as the best of this group, with the next step being the struggle for the final and decisive position in the competition with the Swedish section of the competition.[5] Wahlström & Widstrand received 49 entries and at the end of August a joint prize committee decided that Salminen's *Katrina* was the winner. The prize (FIM 50,000; equivalent to about EUR 16,000 today) was announced in mid-October 1936, the same day that the novel arrived in the bookshops. Her debut is one of the most successful in Nordic book history, *Katrina* with fifteen editions appearing within the first three months of its publication and with the story having since been translated into more than twenty different languages. It seems to have been especially popular in Denmark, France, Germany and Italy where it has been through more than six editions, while the Finnish translation has been published more

5 *Ibidem*, p. 294.

than seven times. In addition, to commemorate the fiftieth anniversary of the prize-winning novel's first publication, an anniversary volume entitled *Sallys saga* (Sally's fairy tale) was produced. As well as the bibliography assembled by Kerstin Eriksson, upon which the information above is based, this volume also includes several essays of interest regarding both the conception and the reception of this success story.[6]

At the same time as the result of the competition was announced in Finland and Sweden, Sally Salminen appeared before the American public. The prize made it possible for her to go back to Åland in order to start a new life, but before embarking on the famous steamship Kungsholm, moored in New York harbour, she gave some interviews. On the front page of the *New York Times* of October 16, 1936 was the following headline:

> Maid spent 2 years writing prize book. Sally Salminen, winner of the Swedish award, worked on first novel in spare time. Now to revisit its scene. She depicts struggle of "Wifes [sic] who stay at home" in her native Finnish islands.[7]

Before leaving she also had the opportunity to speak on American radio, while some days later the headline of the *New York Evening Journal* announced: 'Kitchen Maid Writing Prize Novel Inspires Youth to Conquer Adversity'.[8] Such examples show how, from the beginning, Sally Salminen personified the American Dream. Her story was seen as a modern version of *Cinderella* with all of the publicity initially focused on Salminen herself. No one was interested in the book itself, let alone in the possibilities for cultural transfer it might have presented. The value of the prize in dollars was of much greater interest than the content of the novel, while the typical description by the domestically orientated American journalists was that the Åland Islands were located somewhere between Sweden and Denmark, a mistake which was repeated in several newspapers after first being published in the *New York Times*.

6 Bondestam, A., ed., *Sallys saga: En bok om Sally Salminen till 50-årsminnet av 'Katrina'* (Helsingfors, 1986), p. 164.

7 Salminen, *Min amerikanska saga*, p. 313.

8 *Ibidem*, p. 317.

Cultural transfer of *Katrina*

In retrospect, the question of the cultural transfer of *Katrina* becomes even more interesting. The concept of 'cultural transfer' is used here in the way Petra Broomans defines it in her introductory chapter to *From Darwin to Weil: Women as Transmitters of Ideas* (2009). Broomans speaks of 'a cultural transmitter' who, for example, could be a writer 'transmitting another national literature and its cultural context to one's own national literature and cultural context'.[9] From this point of view, Sally Salminen can be seen as a transmitter and her story as an active link between different generations of readers in different countries. In the following I will attempt to shed some light on this question in order to discern the most important factors behind the process of the canonisation of the book. One factor – unknown to the judges in 1936 – has already been revealed. A book written by a completely unknown woman living outside the social and cultural establishment can in itself have a considerable market value. This type of commercial value is as a rule no guarantee of a bestseller's literary qualifications. There must be other criteria behind a book's longer term position in the field of literary history. From this point of view I imagine that the question of cultural transfer may be of specific importance.

One reason for the novel's success can be found in the plot. The main character, Katrina, is a strong woman, and a woman of the people. She is apolitical but brave and honest. In Dutch terms, she could be seen as a much younger sister of Max Havelaar. Both criticise injustices arising within a class-based society. Sally Salminen is, however, considerate and unobtrusive and most of her critical comments only appear between the lines, where they are left for her readers to interpret. The main point to be made about the plot is that Salminen manages to create a protagonist who the majority of her readers can recognise and with whom they can identify.[10] Katrina is a kind of prototype of the strong and independent woman who takes care both of her children and of her simple-minded and sluggish husband. All her dreams fall apart but she is strong enough to stand on her own two feet without becoming embittered.

Another element which promotes the universal applicability of the story can be found in Salminen's use of language. The first chapter 'Österbotten'

9 Broomans, P., ed, *From Darwin to Weil: Women as Transmitters of Ideas* (Groningen, 2009), p. 2.

10 Widén, G., 'En folkbok med sällsam lyskraft', *Hufvudstadsbladet*, April 21, 1994.

(Ostrobotnia, the name of the region in the west of Finland where Katrina grows up) begins with the two following sentences:

> Katrina was the eldest of three sisters, daughters of a farmer in northern Österbotten: the prettiest, the gayest, and the proudest of the three. Her tall young body was strong; work was like play to her, whether it was timber felling in the forest, plowing and harrowing in the fields, or spinning and weaving withindoors.[11]

The simplicity, combined with the use of the epic triad, evokes associations with the Icelandic sagas or fairy tales. Another reason for the impact of the story is its frankness and lucidity. All 39 chapters are fairly short (about ten pages each) and every chapter has a memorable title (in many cases only one word) which illustrates what will happen next. The chapter titles considered together provide an overview of the straightforward story. It is a typical life story focusing on Katrina's childhood home, her marriage to Johan, the young couple's small house on the Åland Islands, their many children, their life of drudgery working on the land of the rich farmers, the death of her husband, her many grandchildren and Katrina in her old age, wilful and indefatigable to her last breath.

A striking feature of Salminen's use of language is her simple and unaffected style. Both the symbols and the metaphorical language are ordinary and the distance between reality and image is straightforward, as in August Strindberg's *Hemsöborna* (The natives of Hemsö). The linear third-person narrative contributes to the overall impression of clarity. No wonder that the novel has been characterised by so many as a picture of the life and manners of the common people, a real *folkbok* in the best sense of the word. The popularity of the story is to some extent based on the ease with which women readers in particular could and still can identify themselves with the heroine. In a postscript to an edition of *Katrina* published as part of a series of Finland-Swedish classics in paperback, Åsa Stenwall-Albjerg tells the story of a woman who possessed only one book and that book was *Katrina*. For that woman the story was 'livets roman', a novel of human life.[12] Stenwall-Albjerg states that there are thousands of women who have read and cried over Katrina. The life-long perspective

11 Salminen, S., *Katrina*, transl. by Naomi Walford (New York, 1937).

12 *Ibidem*, p. 349.

of the plot and the heroine's development and inner growth invite many levels of identification on the part of readers, and perhaps explains why the prize-winning novel is still read today.

The cultural transfer of Sally Salminen's story is in particular the result of two circumstances: its ethnographic content and its universal portrait of a woman of the people. The ethnographic value of the book grows as time passes. The many details, for example in the descriptions of the different tasks performed on a farm or the various preparations for a country wedding, present readers with fascinating knowledge about everyday life in the countryside on the Åland Islands at the beginning of the last century. The descriptions of how people lived and interacted with nature throughout the four seasons of the year provide a great deal of valuable information, the interest in which will only increase with each new generation of readers. I can even imagine that the broad overview given by this novel of a self-sufficient household in a small country village will sooner or later become the object of some type of ecocritical study. The story provides us with a glimpse of the old peasant culture, in which we can recognise so many universally shared traits, apart from any national differences.

A chapter entitled 'Apples in the Dewy Grass' tells us how Katrina attempts to realise her vision of a garden outside her own humble cottage. After a long working day she carries soil in a big woodchip basket and concentrates all her energy on filling a little space on the south side of the cabin. The story continues as follows:

> In a tin box on her windowsill were some leafy seedlings. They were tiny apple trees which she had grown from the pips of ripe apples. When they were bigger, and her soil more plentiful, she would bed them out. People would laugh at her, no doubt – but she would show them! Why might not one apple tree at least grow there in the warm sunshine, under the lee of the cabin, if she collected plenty of earth, and tended the plant well? She had heard people say that apple trees must have deep soil to thrust their roots into, but it must be with trees as it was with people: they had to adapt themselves to circumstances. She had seen pines and firs growing in the thinnest layer of moss, on the rocks above the cabin. When they could not send their roots downward they spread them out all around instead, and so must her apple trees do.[13]

13 *Ibidem*, pp. 136-137.

The quotation illustrates Katrina's fighting character, as well as her patience and optimism. No matter what the situation, she always knows what to do. From this point of view the heroine is the soul of industry and it is easy to understand why Katrina became such an encouraging female character in different translations of the book across the world.

Universal characters

It is important to emphasise strains of characterisation in the novel common to all humanity. When the book was first published, many in the small communities of the Åland Islands attempted to work out who had served as models for Salminen's story. In a symposium on the main character, held in Eckerö (one of the many Åland Islands) in the summer of 1997, the well-known Finland-Swedish writer Ulla-Lena Lundberg (1947) emphasised the fact that every author uses real conditions as a starting point. Lundberg has herself written several novels dealing with a similar subject to Sally Salminen, especially in her novels *Kungens Anna* (1982) and *Ingens Anna* (1984). Lundberg states that the characters in a story always enter into a process of transformation on their way from reality to fiction.[14] If all goes well, the characters, or at least the main ones, will come to represent universal aspects during that transformation process. This happens in the case of Katrina and is the reason why the novel became so popular in different cultures.

Sally Salminen's ability to create universal characters is the key to her marvellous success with her first novel. Katrina became – and still becomes – an encouraging female character in different translations of the book across the world.

14 Steinby, A.-G., 'Katrina är fiktion, inte verklighet', *Hufvudstadsbladet*, July 30, 1997.

Part III

Minor Languages and Literary History/Within Borders

The rise, dispersal and stabilisation of New Norwegian literature

« Idar Stegane »

The main purpose of this article is to discuss the literary situation in Norway, where there are two officially recognised written variants of the language. It examines the historical and social background to this situation, beginning in the mid-nineteenth century, and how it affected Norway's literary development as well as its broader cultural development. I will discuss the rise of a certain prejudice against the New Norwegian literature because of its rural origin, which meant that for a long time cultural conservatives regarded literature in the new language – the less used variant one might say – as more of a threat than a supplementary possibility. In this context, I argue that 'Nynorsk', or New Norwegian, can be seen as a counter-hegemonic cultural movement.

An unsettled language situation

Norway had been the second ranked nation in the Danish union or empire, which had existed since the early fourteenth century and included Denmark itself, the southern provinces (the Duchies of Schleswig and Holstein now belonging to Germany), Norway, the Faroe Islands, Iceland and Greenland. In negotiations after the Napoleonic Wars in 1814, Denmark lost Norway, which was forced into a new union, this time with Sweden. However, before accepting this, people representing different parts of Norway assembled at Eidsvoll and formed a national constitution. The constitution was accepted by the Swedish government with minor alterations, and Norway obtained a degree of self rule under the Swedish king, with the acceptance of Sweden's foreign policy.

Danish had become the official written language during the years of union with Denmark, and modern Norwegian writers of literature had to deal with a language situation which was unsettled and confusing. Soon after the dissolution of the union there were signs that this situation had to change. For example, teachers and other leading users of the written language would seldom refer to it as Danish, but rather as 'Modersmaalet' [mother tongue]. Some intellectuals and authors, however, including the leading poet and cultural activist Henrik Wergeland (1808-1845), openly articulated a need for some kind of autonomous Norwegian language. While a much altered medieval Norwegian language still existed in spoken form in dialects throughout the country, the commonly used written language had for several hundred years been Danish, as state officials were either Danish or had been educated in Denmark. Public officials and the bourgeois class spoke a form of Dano-Norwegian, a mixed language generally spoken by the 'higher class' in the urban areas.

In spite of his views, Henrik Wergeland himself did not contribute much to any practical attempt to develop an alternative language. Two of the first to move in this direction were Peter Christian Asbjørnsen (1812-1885) and Jørgen Moe (1813-1882), both collectors of fairy tales and other folkloristic prose, who found it necessary to expand written Danish and develop a style that incorporated words and phrases from the oral language of their informants. Such 'norwegisation' of Danish was continued by Henrik Ibsen (1828-1906), especially in his poetic drama *Peer Gynt*, and more so by Bjørnstjerne Bjørnson (1830-1910) in his 'Bondefortællinger' [Peasant Stories]. Through further activities of this kind the language – at first called Dano-Norwegian – gradually developed into modern Bokmål, which is still the dominant written form of Norwegian today.

A more radical approach to the creation of a modern Norwegian language was based on a common idea of 'one language, one nation', adopted from the German tradition, especially from the cultural philosopher J.G. Herder (1744-1803).[1] Although Danish was understood – more or less – throughout the country, there were voices who called for the development of a genuine Norwegian written language based on contemporary dialects. Extensive work recording words and phrases throughout the country and writing a Norwegian grammar had to be done, and this fundamental work was carried out by the son of a peasant, Ivar Aasen (1813-1896).

1 In a discussion of the factors defining the concept of 'nation' in the German tradition starting with Herder, Klaus Kriener mentions a combination of characteristics such as common language, territory, history and mentality. Kriener, K., 'Sprache – Rasse – Volk: Aspekte des deutschen nationalen Diskurses', http://www.comlink.de/cl-hh/m.blumentritt/agr128s.htm, p. 2 (accessed April 8, 2010).

Bokmål: H. Uthuslien's drawing of Ivar Aasen from 1891.

Source: http://en.wikipedia.org/wiki/File:Uthuslien_Aasen_1891.jpg.

Pioneers (1): Ivar Aasen – constructing a counter-hegemony

Ivar Aasen had no formal academic education but was a self-educated philologist and botanist. He set up a herbarium consisting of specimens from his home region and wrote a grammar of the dialect used in the region. He took both to a clergyman in Bergen, who introduced him to Jacob Neumann (1772-1848), the bishop of Bergen, whose interest in education and enlightenment was fairly common among academics educated in the spirit of the eighteenth century. The historian Halvdan Koht (1873-1965) surmises that Aasen went to the bishop because the leading scholar of Norwegian language and traditions in Bergen, W.F.K. Christie (1778-1849), was away at the time but Neumann shared the latter's interest in the Norwegian language.[2] The bishop did not pay much attention to Aasen's herbarium and was much more interested in his grammar. As a result, on the bishop's initiative, Aasen obtained official support to travel around the country, studying dialects and recording words and phrases for a grammar and a dictionary documenting the state of the people's language, a project he worked on for the rest of his life. When not travelling and collecting material, he lived and worked in Christiania (Oslo), studying and writing. The first versions of his *Det norske Folkesprogs Grammatik*

2 Koht, H., 'Ivar Aasen. Granskar og maalreisar', in: Garborg, A., Hovden, A. and Koht, H., *Ivar Aasen. Granskaren, maalreisaren, diktaren* (Kristiania, 1913), p. 66.

[Grammar of the Norwegian People's Language] and *Ordbog over det norske Folkesprog* [Dictionary of the Norwegian People's Language] were published in 1848 and 1850 respectively, the second editions were simply entitled *Norsk Grammatik* [Norwegian Grammar, 1864] and *Norsk Ordbog* [Norwegian Dictionary, 1873], the change emphasising that they concerned the language of all Norwegians. Initially the new written language was called 'Folkesproget' [the people's language], but later the official name became 'Landsmål' [the language of the country], the modern form (from the 1920s) of which is 'Nynorsk' [New Norwegian]. During the nineteenth century, an alternative linguistic and cultural movement based on New Norwegian developed alongside but in conflict and competition with the dominant language of Dano-Norwegian. Scholars who have studied this development have drawn on different theories. In *Det nynorske skriftlivet. Nynorsk heimstaddikting og den litterære institusjon*, I discuss the development of New Norwegian writing to around 1905.[3] In *Farewell the Spirit Craven*, Stephen J. Walton discusses Ivar Aasen's work and ideas in particular. The theory underlying Walton's thesis is best characterised in his own words:

> In this thesis National Romanticism in the mid-nineteenth century is seen as playing a role in a hegemony. Aasen, whose origins lay outside this hegemony, had to take it into account and exploit the possibilities it offered.[4]

Walton takes the notion of hegemony from the Italian socialist philosopher and journalist Antonio Gramsci (1891-1937), who saw a connection between the state and a so-called hegemonic apparatus within society – institutions such as the Church and the education system – the apparatus through which the ruling class is able to secure political support for and approval of its politics. Walton looks upon Norwegian National Romanticism in the mid-nineteenth century as hegemonic, claiming that the hegemony encompassed both the right and left spheres of National Romanticism.

The relationship to the peasant class, with peasants not belonging to either of the spheres of the dichotomy, seems to be of importance. The left

3 Stegane, I., *Det nynorske skriftlivet. Nynorsk heimstaddikting og den litterære institusjon* (Oslo, 1987).

4 Walton, S.J., *Farewell the Spirit Craven. Ivar Aasen and National Romanticism* (Oslo, 1987), p. 10.

sphere saw the peasantry as 'an embodiment of a national continuum that can with time be generalised across existing social barriers' while the right sphere did not accept such a fundamental role of the peasants 'as bearers of a national heritage'.[5] The point is that any affinity or possibility of the peasant language becoming the foundation for the development of a national language lay with the left sphere of National Romanticism. The question for Walton is whether Ivar Aasen, in his works as a linguist as well as a poet and cultural politician, intended to found a counter-hegemony. From Walton's references to the theoretical deliberations of Gramsci it is likely that counter-hegemony refers to a rather moderate manifestation of opposition – barely a deliberate opposition at all. He wants 'to investigate to what extent Ivar Aasen conceives of and lays the foundation for (...) a counter-hegemony'.[6]

There is no doubt that the cultural elite considered Aasen and the New Norwegian movement as a potential threat to the Dano-Norwegian hegemony. The critic Marcus Jacob Monrad (1816-1897) would only accept New Norwegian writing as a phenomenon confined to an idyllic sphere on the outskirts of the cultural field.[7] The early literary historian Lorentz Dietrichson (1834-1917) went a step further when he declared that New Norwegian writing:

> (...) could not protect Norwegian Culture from the loses it would suffer should that error become victorious that preaches that the Norwegian people's salvation lies in a linguistic separation from the cultivated brotherhood of peoples as well as the cultivated part of the Norwegian people itself.[8]

5 *Ibidem*, p. 31.

6 *Ibidem*, p. 140.

7 Monrad, M.J., 'Ervingen. Sangspil i een Akt', *Norsk Tidsskrift for Videnskab og Literatur* (1854-1855), p. 367. Cf. also Stegane, *Det nynorske skriftlivet*, p. 56. The terms cultural field and literary field throughout the article are used as defined by Bourdieu in: *The Rules of Art. Genesis and Structure of the Literary Field* (Stanford California, 1996). First published in France as *Les Règles d'art* (Paris, 1992).

8 'Dietrichson, L., *Omrids af den norske poesis historie. Literærhistoriske forelæsninger. II: Den norske literatur efter 1814* (Copenhagen, 1869), pp. 209-210. '[K]unne ikke holde den norske Kultur skadesløs for hvad den vilde miste, hvis den Fejltagelse skulde blive sejrende, der forkynder at det norske Folks Frelse ligger i at separere sig sprogligt fra de kultiverede Brødrefolk og den kultiverede Del af selve det norske Folk'.

To me it seems decisive that there is a kind of opposition embodied in Aasen's endeavours, linguistically as well as poetically. I understand that Walton is apt to define this counter-hegemony within the framework of his Gramscian selection of theoretical considerations, stating, for example, 'that Aasen's populism is permanent, inalienable and unredeemed'.[9]

My studies are concerned with the entire cultural movement connected to the growth and development of the New Norwegian language. In the 1970s and 1980s – similarly to other Nordic colleagues at the time – I was particularly influenced by impulses coming from the German philosopher and social theoretician Jürgen Habermas (1929), as well as theoretical and pragmatic studies influenced by discussions about the bourgeois public sphere ['die bürgerliche Öffentlichkeit'], as Habermas presents it in his 1962 doctoral thesis, *Strukturwandel der Öffentlichkeit. Untersuchungen zu einer Kategorie der bürgerlichen Gesellschaft.*[10] Habermas defines the public sphere as an open arena where citizens might come together as private people to converse and discuss in a free and independent atmosphere, where the best arguments would be likely to win and decisions of common interest would be made accordingly.

There were few, if any, obvious objections within the Norwegian bourgeois public sphere or the public servant class to the idea that it was of national interest to study the Norwegian dialects and their vocabularies and connections to the medieval Old Norse language. At first, therefore, it was no great problem for some scholars and public servants, as well as the bishop of Bergen, the chairman of the board of Det Kongelige Norske Videnskabers Selskab [The Royal Science Society] in Trondheim and certain others, to reach agreement on applying to the Society for money to allow Aasen to begin his studies of the rural dialects of Vestlandet [the Western regions].

Aasen himself was apparently aware that his work might in the course of time become controversial, and this may have been the reason why he hesitated to reveal his ultimate aim of constructing a new alternative language. His early plans (1836) for doing so were only published posthumously, in 1909. Reading these, one understands that Aasen was well aware of the

9 Walton, *Farewell the Spirit Craven*, p. 140.

10 Habermas, J., *Strukturwandel der Öffentlichkeit. Untersuchungen zu einer Kategorie der bürgerlichen Gesellschaft* (Neuwied, 1962), English translation: Burger, T. and Lawrence, F., *The Structural Transformation of the Public Sphere. An Inquiry into a Category of Bourgeois Society* (Cambridge, 1989).

possibilities within the liberal public sphere for the construction of a new written language and preparation for its use: 'What we want is a people's language, a language that every countryman may share; our constitution justifies our claim'.[11] Later he presented his first collection of texts in New Norwegian, *Prøver af Landsmaalet i Norge* [Samples of the Language of Norway, 1853], calling them 'prøver' [samples] probably in order to avoid provoking other citizens, despite all citizens being equal according to the self-understanding ['Selbstverständnis'] of the bourgeois public sphere.

In his writings, however, Aasen showed counter-hegemonic tendencies. The drama *Ervingen* [The Heir, 1855], the poetry collection *Symra* [Summering/The coming of summer, 1863] and some other writings express his solidarity with the rural population, especially the peasants as the bearers of the people's language. His attitudes clearly express a social as well as national character, often in one.

Pioneers (2): Aasmund Vinje – a New Norwegian writing critic rejected by the cultural elite

Aasen's efforts proved successful in that he inspired Aasmund O. Vinje (1818-1870), who combined national and social arguments in some lines of verse:

> Our people lived long in slavery,
> with sorrow and no joy.
> But just as it got its freedom back,
> so it must get its voice.[12]

Vinje, also according to the self-understanding of a general public sphere, took it for granted that this sphere was open and freely accessible to every citizen when he started his political-cultural critical weekly magazine *Dølen* [The Dalesman, 1858-1870]. However, he soon discovered that this was not the case. His critical activity, be it in the political or in the literary

11 Aasen, I., 'Om vort Skriftsprog', in: Aasen, I., *Skrifter II* (Oslo, 1926), p. 50. 'Vi ønske os just et Folkesprog, et som enhver Landsmand uden Møie kan tage Deel i; vor Statsforfatning berettiger os til dette Ønske'.

12 Vinje, A.O., 'Vaart Maalstrev', in: Vinje, A.O., *Norske Dikt* (Oslo, 1897), p. 2. 'Vaart Folk i Trældom lenge gjekk, i Sorg forutan Sæle. Og som det att sin Fridom fekk, so maa det faa sitt Mæle'.

field, was not accepted by leading critics. It was argued that literature in the new Landsmål, as spelled earlier, could not be accepted as common or *allgemein*, but only as belonging to an idyllic sphere, 'tilhører kun Idyllen', as described by Monrad, the leading critic of the time.[13] However, the stronger the opposition from the leading critics became, the sharper became the polemical tone of Vinje's critical articles and essays. The adversity no doubt contributed to him becoming one of Norway's best essayists, as well as a pioneer in creating modern Norwegian journalism.

In other words, only lyrical poems by Aasen and Vinje were accepted by the leading literary critics. As poets they were both regarded as national romanticists, as were Johan S. C. Welhaven (1807-1873) and Henrik Wergeland. However, the New Norwegian poems by Aasen and Vinje differ markedly from those of the latter poets. What Monrad thought of as idyllic because of the rural motifs, should often rather be called 'realistic' because the motifs often underlined themes from the everyday life and work of ordinary people. As Aasen wrote in his song text 'Nordmannen' [The Norwegian] in *Symra*:

> Between cliffs and the billowing breakers
> The Norwegian of old found his home
> A foundation he laid in these acres
> His own hands raised his house from the loam.[14]

Relying on his boyhood experiences as a shepherd, Vinje wrote songs and stories about goats and cows and thereby became one of the first writers of children's literature in Norway. As time went by, both Aasen and Vinje became loved by readers and listeners and even highly appreciated by critics, but often with some reluctance, especially with respect to Aasen, whose poems were said to be well written but lacking in imagination. However, in the first extensive Norwegian literary history, the naturalist Henrik Jæger praised Aasen's best poems for their down-to-earth motifs.[15] Unfortunately for the New Norwegian movement, the great contributors to the growth of Norwegian literature from the 1850s on – above all Henrik

13 Monrad, 'Ervingen', p. 367.

14 Myskja, K., 'The Norwegian', in: Myskja, K., *Ivar Aasens Poetry* (Fjærland, 2002), p. 5. 'Millom Bakkar og berg ut med Havet heve Nordmannen fenget sin Heim, der han sjølv heve Tufterna gravet og sett sjølv sine Hus uppaa deim'.

15 Jæger, H., 'Ivar Aasen', in: Jæger, H., *Illustrert norsk litteraturhistorie. Bind II* (Kristiania, 1896), p. 484.

Ibsen, the dramatist, but also the poet, novelist, playwright and all-round man of letters, Bjørnstjerne Bjørnson, the novelist Jonas Lie (1833-1908) and the novelist and short-story writer Alexander Kielland (1849-1906) – all chose to write in Dano-Norwegian and to remain within the Danish literary institution, with their works all being published in Denmark. This also hindered the development of Bokmål, a combination of Danish and urban Norwegian; however, the lack of Norwegian publishing houses made it especially complicated to publish literature written in New Norwegian.

The first two counter-hegemonic writers, Aasen and Vinje, were both from the countryside and probably had similar social and cultural experiences from their childhoods and youth. Aasen was personally modest and a self-taught linguist who did his scholarly work with the aid of official financing by the state. We know from his 1836 notes[16] that early on he had intended not only to investigate and describe the people's language, but was preparing the ground to make it possible for people to write in this language, despite still regarding it himself as primarily an alternative which might gradually become more frequently used. Vinje, in contrast, was a restless journalist who felt an eager need to break with the Danish language, not only in creating poetry – in common with Aasen – but in everyday journalistic and essayistic prose when commenting on the events of the day in politics, science, scholarly work, factories, agriculture and other topics.

Aasen and Vinje were both conservative in looking back to specific Norwegian traditions in language and folk literature. However, though they clearly differed in strategy, they were both radical in the way they used political and national independence to achieve modernisation in cultural and other spheres of life.

Pioneers (3): Arne Garborg – leading member of the counter-hegemonic movement as well as a central man of letters

A third pioneer in New Norwegian writing was Arne Garborg (1851-1924). This versatile intellectual continued the work of Vinje as a writer of both belles-lettres and critical essays concerning literature, politics and many social, even philosophical and religious questions. Like Vinje he also founded a newspaper in New Norwegian, *Fedraheimen* [The Home of our Fathers, 1877-1891), the title referring to the historical connection between New Norwegian and medieval Old Norse.

16 Aasen, 'Om vort Skriftsprog', pp. 47-50.

Arne and Hulda Garborg in their home at Låbråten, ca. 1910. (Photo: A.B. Vilse).

Garborg began his literary activities as a somewhat idealistic literary critic in Dano-Norwegian and wrote, among other things, an estimated essay on Ibsen.[17] Although he joined the struggle for the right to publish in New Norwegian, for a long time he was also actively engaged in the production of literature in Dano-Norwegian. He wrote both an 'Ibsenian' social play (*Uforsonlige* [Irreconcilable] 1888) and a fin-de-siècle epistolary novel (*Trætte Mænd* [Tired Men] 1891) in Dano-Norwegian, alongside works in New Norwegian. He became a writer partly to support his family after losing his position as a State Auditor ['statsrevisor'].

Garborg wrote some short stories and two naturalistic novels in New Norwegian, which he set in the surroundings of Kristiania – *Mannfolk* [Men, 1886] and *Hjaa ho Mor* [At Home with Mother, 1890], demonstrating that urban characters and an urban environment could also be written about in New Norwegian; in other words, that it was not just an idiom appropriate to the countryside. It is significant that Garborg wrote these works in New Norwegian, as at the time – the 1880s – he was about to become the intellectual and literary leader of the entire New Norwegian movement.

17 Garborg, A., *Henrik Ibsen's "Keiser og Galilæer". En kritisk studie* (Kristiania, 1873).

The New Norwegian literary field – a variety of genres

Garborg's production of high-brow literature, however, also proved that the dominant bourgeois public sphere had little room for the publishing of work in New Norwegian. In a retrospective essay (1913), he revealed that after his debut in the early 1880s he worked with five editors, attributing his publishing problems to the language he had chosen: 'The main reason was that I was writing Norwegian. Accordingly, the door to Denmark was locked for me and I had to find myself a Norwegian publisher'.[18] Towards the end of the century, the literary field was to a great extent still dominated by publishing houses in Denmark. To counter this dominance, various kinds of organisations arose within Norway, such as literary and cultural groups and associations.

In the Habermasian tradition it has proved fruitful to study the growth of literature, arts and other cultural phenomena in a society in terms of the development of institutions, but not as regular institutions with fixed systems of rules, such as the law, the Church and the education system, but as institutions which develop in a less regulated manner. In the case of New Norwegian, we can see that its development is clearly an attempt to create new literary institutions – a New Norwegian literary field.[19] Thus, we can see the establishment of important associations and literary societies in this light, with Det Norske Samlaget (Christiania) and Vestmannalaget (Bergen) founded as early as 1868. Both societies published books in various genres, and Vestmannalaget also published school textbooks for children. In Bergen, the pioneer Mons Litleré (1867-1895), opened his publishing house with the intention of mainly publishing books and other written material in New Norwegian, including school textbooks. During the 1890s, local communities gained the legal right to choose New Norwegian as the first language of schools, and the churches gained the same right to choose to sing hymns and conduct rites and sermons in the same language. This led to a need for school textbooks and other material for children and youth

18 Garborg, A., 'Forleggjarvanskar', *Festskrift til William Nygaard* (Kristiania, 1913), p. 204. 'Mest det serhøve at eg skreiv Norsk. Dermed var eg utestengd frå Danmark og matte finne meg Norsk forleggjar'.

19 When writing about such a field, in principle I include all forms of published texts in New Norwegian. For the last two decades of the nineteenth century there is particular reason to do this, as the field is still relatively easy to survey and because some people within the New Norwegian movement tended to see it as one consistent literary system opposed to the existing Bokmål literary field (although the word 'field' was never used).

in New Norwegian, which also often had religious and didactic purposes. Among the publications in New Norwegian were the children's magazine *Norsk Barneblad* [The Norwegian Children's Magazine, 1887-], the youth magazine *Nora* (1885-1894), the general periodical *Syn og Segn* [Seen and Said, 1894-] and the newspaper *Den 17de Mai* [The 17th of May, 1894-1932]. Moreover, by the 1880s and early 1890s a number of younger writers had begun to publish literature in New Norwegian in the naturalist style of the Modern Breakthrough.

The battle between the New Norwegian and Bokmål literary fields

A noticeable change in the literary norm around 1900 is significant because it came to influence much of New Norwegian literature for some decades.[20] The person who systematically registered and acted as a spokesman for this development was the editor of *Syn og Segn* from 1894, Rasmus Flo (1851-1905). In the late 1890s he himself wrote the annual reviews of the previous year's New Norwegian literature. In his first review in 1896 he made some remarks on what this literature ought to be like in principle. In his opinion, New Norwegian literature should not strive to copy that of Bokmål – he wanted it to 'have its own life, have something that can give some original contribution to life not only be a special costume'.[21] In this way, it was considered that New Norwegian literature would also be able to contribute to the wellbeing of the entire population. Flo acknowledged that New Norwegian writers generally had a rural background. This background, he thought, had given them experiences, feelings and knowledge of an intimate kind that might enable them to write better and more genuine peasant literature than authors from urban societies. It is evident that his ideal was a form of realistic literature rather than naturalism. He was concerned that less experienced rural readers might be negatively affected by the bad morals and shameful behaviour of some characters in novels

20 In the 1890s the norm changed, a fact which is easy to observe in more extensive articles about the literary production of one year in the periodical *Syn og Segn*. See also the chapter 'Den litterær-estetiske norma I nynorsken før 1905', in: Stegane, *Det nynorske skriftlivet*, pp. 122-153.

21 Stegane, *Det nynorske skriftlivet*, p. 139. 'Vil ein leva sit eige liv, so fær ein ogso hava noko for seg sjølv aa leva paa, noko som det er livsinnhald i, og ikkje berre ein serbunad.'; Flo, R., 'Norske bøker', *Syn og Segn* (1896), p. 373.

and short stories should they be drawn too naturalistically. At the same time, he also acknowledged the need for the characters to be well-rounded.

However, in Flo's review articles concerning the development of New Norwegian literature there was a moralistic seed, and the growth of this seed was accelerated by religious demands from the Church and schools and from several pietistic laymen's associations and activities. The Danish Grundtvigian High School movement took root within the New Norwegian movement and contributed to these dominant Christian ideological demands. The ideology had its effect, with some of the best peasant writers in New Norwegian, such as Jens Tvedt (1857-1935) and Hans Seland (1867-1949), being influenced by the events and writing some rather trivial, non-conflictual novels with happy endings which are comparable to what the Germans call *Heimatdichtung*. Even Arne Garborg became infected and wrote a peasant novel full of harmonious relationships and sentimentality (*Heimkomin Son* [The Son Who has Returned Home], 1908). Thus, in the long run, the special contribution that Flo had in mind for New Norwegian literature in 1896 lapsed into harmony-building and did not generate literary or aesthetic renewal.

The trend was not followed by everyone, for example, the pioneer of New Norwegian children's literature, Rasmus Løland (1861-1907), who also wrote novels and short stories for adult readers, criticised his New Norwegian colleagues, quoting Goethe: 'Man merkt die Absicht und wird verstimmt'. In other words, suggesting that it was obvious that everything in a certain book was meant to fulfil some didactic or religious purpose.[22]

Despite these problems, New Norwegian literature made remarkable progress, increasing in quantity during the late 1890s and around 1900. In addition to the authors mentioned above, the list also includes: Hulda Garborg (1862-1934, plays), Vetle Vislie (1858-1933, plays, novels), Bolette Pavels Larsen (1847-1904, short stories, criticism), Per Sivle (1857-1904, poems, short stories, children's texts), Anders Hovden (1860-1943, poems, novels), Kristen Stalleland (1861-1949 children's magazine, children's books), Anders Vassbotn (1868-1944, poems), Sven Moren (1871-1938, poems, novels). A book that excited great interest was Arne Garborg's epic lyrical poetry cycle *Haugtussa* (1895) about a thoughtful and clairvoyant young peasant girl, Veslemøy, whose nickname is given in the title.

22 Løland, R., 'Ei røda um bøker og andre ting', in: Løland, R., *Skrifter i samling IV* (Oslo, 1942), p. 312.

Embedded in Veslemøy's clairvoyant observations was also a certain degree of political satire. The book became highly esteemed by leading urban critics, and the famous composer Edvard Grieg wrote music to several of its poems or songs. Arild Linneberg shows that the urban Bokmål critics mostly praised the book for its fin-de-siècle atmosphere, while the New Norwegian critics were more likely to focus on its political implications.[23]

The very active combatant, writer and poet, Bjørnstjerne Bjørnson, who represented the hegemonic literary field of Bokmål, reacted in a unique way. He no doubt observed the increased quantity of New Norwegian literature and may have gained the impression that its broadening and growth might threaten the dominance of Bokmål literature. Thus, in a famous speech in 1899 he repeated what he had written in his essay 'Den moderne norske Literatur' [Modern Norwegian Literature, 1896] printed in both the German magazine *Die Zukunft*, the American *Forum* and in a Dutch translation by Margaretha Meyboom (Leiden, 1896).[24] His criticism is directed at peasants, rural society, New Norwegian literature and the entire New Norwegian cultural movement. The essay and the speech constituted a formidable attack on the movement, which had become increasingly visible through the quantity of literature and other writings and the literary quality of works by a truly great man of letters such as Garborg. Bjørnson's attack, using words such as 'Bondebegrænsningen' [the peasant limitation] and 'Indskrænkning' [narrow-mindedness], led others from the dominant Bokmål field to make even stronger contrasts and more explicit objections, and for a while to regard New Norwegian literature as more of a threat than offering a contribution to national unity.

Meanwhile, this debate sharpened the minds of the New Norwegian activists. The inspiration gained from the legalisation of New Norwegian in schools and churches led to a great many creative activities. Once the municipalities, mostly in the west and in parts of the inland, decided to use New Norwegian in schools, another important step was to choose the new

23 Linneberg, A., 'Romantikk for borgar – realisme for bonde? Arne Garborgs *Haugtussa* og litteraturkritikken, I-II', *Syn og Segn* 2-3 (1979), p. 92-107, 150-163.

24 Bjørnson, B., 'Den moderne norske literatur', in: B. Bjørnson, *Artikler og Taler II* (Kristiania 1913), pp. 305-331. See for more information on the Dutch translation by M. Meyboom: Broomans, P., 'Hur skapas en litteraturhistorisk bild? Den nordiska litteraturens "fräschhet" i Nederländerna och Flandern', in: Dahl, P. and Steinfeld, T., eds., *Videnskab og national opdragelse. Studier i nordisk litteraturhistorieskrivning*, vol. 2 (Copenhagen, 2001), pp. 515-541.

language for official purposes within the communities. Local newspapers changed the language in which they were edited and very often also altered their names.

New Norwegian Theatre: making way for New Norwegian drama

Arne Garborg's wife, Hulda Garborg, also became an author and wrote a series of novels, mostly in Bokmål. However, she also became as important a figure as her husband in pioneering the use of New Norwegian.[25] Both Garborgs were interested in presenting theatre in New Norwegian, sharing the primary and most ambitious aim of those concerned with New Norwegian literature to make drama in the language possible. However, there was no institutional theatre that would stage a play in the language. Hulda Garborg had published *Mødre* in New Norwegian in 1895 with the play being performed that year with little success at the Kristiania Theatre, the year before Arne Garborg's *Læraren* [The Teacher, 1896] became the best non-amateur play written in the language at the time. The main problem for *Mødre* at the time was that the actors had not yet mastered the language – when Spellaget staged the play a few years later in 1899 it did quite well.[26] Being more of an activist, Hulda started a theatre group, Det Norske Spellaget [The Norwegian Play Association], in 1898, which travelled around the country for several years performing comedies and lighter dramas. In 1913 the group managed to establish their own alternative theatre in Kristiania, Det Norske Teatret [The Norwegian Theatre], with the two main aims of facilitating the writing of original dramas in New Norwegian and establishing a professional stage in the capital whose use of the language might function as a model and ideal for people who wanted to speak it regardless of their different dialects. These were very idealistic aims which were never really achieved.

The development New Norwegian theatre begun by Hulda Garborg and her colleagues led to the increased production of plays by her and a number of other writers in the years to come. In 1928, when The Norwegian Theatre

25 See also: Van Elswijk, R., 'Spread the Word. Arne og Hulda Garborg as Cultural Transmitters of Nynorsk', in: Broomans, P. and Ronne, M., eds., In *the Vanguard of Cultural Transfer. Cultural Transmitters and Authors in Peripheral Literary Fields* (Groningen, 2010), pp. 13-31.

26 Dale, J.A., *Nynorsk dramatikk i hundre år* (Oslo, 1964), p. 54.

celebrated its fifteenth anniversary, one of the leading critics in Bokmål, the playwright Helge Krog, spoke highly of its work as 'an excellent example of how a theatre may stimulate the writing of drama'.[27] However, Krog also mentioned that few plays of high quality had been produced in this period. To improve the quality, translations from foreign languages were needed, and in the late 1920s, the theatre performed plays by Shakespeare, the Irish writer Sean O'Casey, the Czech Karel Čapek and the German Gerhart Hauptmann, amongst others. The translation of plays increased during the 1930s and after the Second World War. From the 1950s onwards, The Norwegian Theatre took the lead in staging absurdist drama, especially Beckett, as well as plays in the political tradition of Bertolt Brecht, and the great names of Western drama such as Pinter, Ionesco, O'Neill and Arthur Miller. The Norwegian Theatre also quite rightfully took pride in its leading position in bringing classical Greek drama to the stage.

From the beginning, The Norwegian Theatre received a lot of negative criticism for its stage language from the public as well as professional critics; however, this was also the case for intellectuals and playwrights writing in Bokmål. The theatre staged quite a number of plays which had been written in Bokmål and translated into New Norwegian. After the Second World War even Ibsen was translated and staged in New Norwegian, as were other Scandinavians such as Strindberg, Kaj Munk and Lars Norén to name just a few. However, performing Ibsen in New Norwegian heightened the conflict in relation to both language and culture. The first occasion was 1948, and was a double provocation: the director Hans Jakob Nilsen claimed that *Peer Gynt* was an anti-romantic play and controversially rejected Edvard Grieg's music and engaged Harald Sæverud to compose a new score. The Norwegian Theatre was also important for productions of music drama, in particular after the Second World War, with several American musicals and a couple of New Norwegian musical plays being performed.

Although The Norwegian Theatre was in many ways of huge importance to the entire New Norwegian movement, it cannot be said to have quite succeeded in bringing about new drama of the highest quality. The expressionist and poetic drama of Tore Ørjasæter (1886-1968), Aslaug Vaa (1889-1965) and Tarjei Vesaas (1897-1970) does not seem to

27 *Ibidem*, p. 74. 'et ypperlig eksempel på hvordan et teater kan anspore den dramatiske diktning'.

have encouraged the theatre leaders to promote new experiments in the writing and production of plays, although in the 1960s and 1970s they provided a stage for experimentation and renewal called 'Scene 2'. Some experiments were undertaken by a younger generation of writers at the time, with some significant results. Edvard Hoem, for example, wrote plays of his own as well as translating Shakespeare and other playwrights for The Norwegian Theatre. Jon Fosse is considered to be the summit of this unique development within the New Norwegian movement, but we must not forget that Fosse's starting point was at Den Nationale Scene [The National Stage] in Bergen. Fosse also finally broke through the barrier of the Nationaltheatret [The National Theatre] itself, which with two or three exceptions had not staged anything else in New Norwegian. No doubt the existence of The Norwegian Theatre also made the use of New Norwegian and different dialects possible at a number of regional theatres.

'Folkeskrifter' for popular education

An equally important organisation was of course Noregs Mållag [The New Norwegian Language Association] along with local and regional groups. Among these was Studentmållaget [The New Norwegian Student Association], which was comprised of young academics and writers, who, in cooperation with the Youth Association, organised the *Norske Folkeskrifter* [Norwegian People's Educational Booklets] series. This was launched in 1902 but slowly faded after the Second World War. They published booklets of many kinds, some about literature, authors and other cultural topics, but also a great many didactic books and educational writings about housekeeping, agriculture, forestry, electricity and so on, mostly very useful books for people doing manual work of various kinds. These 'folkeskrifter' had few parallels in Bokmål.

A dispersed literary field

In spite of undertakings such as those mentioned above, the building of a New Norwegian literary field was not consistently pursued in the twentieth century. New publishing houses did not completely reject New Norwegian, especially not the novels and short stories, and the Olaf Norlis Forlag publishing house for some decades even became the most important publisher of books in New Norwegian. However, there were problems, a major one being that the growth of New Norwegian literature was hindered by a subtle and more or less unconscious ignorance of the language by those in publishing companies, as well as critics, writers of literary history and others. Leading – often conservative – newspapers in Oslo, whose opinions often influenced literary historians, might ignore experimental and innovative New Norwegian authors. For example, Kristofer Uppdal's original expressionist poetry from around the First World War was barely noticed, nor were his working-class novels, the ten volume series *Dansen gjenom skuggeheimen* [The Dance through the World of Shadows, 1911-1924]. In addition, while Olaf Bull (1883-1933) and Olav Nygard (1884-1924) were both skilful poets, Bull writing in Bokmål and Nygard in New Norwegian, in his literary history from the early 1930s, Kristian Elster wrote ten pages on Bull and ten lines on Nygard.

From the dissolution of the union with Sweden and throughout the interwar period Norwegian literature in both languages was dominated by novels. These were often long series, including trilogies, tetralogies, or more – up to six or even ten volumes – becoming more thematically oriented towards Freudian psychology by the 1930s. In addition to Uppdal, there were a number of great novelists in Bokmål, including Sigrid Undset (1882-1949) and Knut Hamsun (1859-1952). The great New Norwegian novelist Olav Duun (1876-1939) was also at a similar level. This period was also one of great poetry, and along with outstanding poets in Bokmål, especially Olaf Bull, at least three New Norwegian poets, Kristofer Uppdal (1878-1961), Olav Aukrust (1883-1929) and Olav Nygard, wrote highly valued poetry, each in their own style.

Impulses from German expressionism reached Norwegian poetry through Uppdal, especially after his visit to Germany in 1913-1914. This can also partly be said of his series of novels, making it the most imposing working-class literary work in a Norwegian language. Nygard's poetry was of another kind, highly stylised classical verses with wonderful rhymes with an inventive use of New Norwegian, often in the ottava rima or octave form. We might say that Nygard celebrated the richness of the New Norwegian language, something which might also be said of Olav Aukrust, whose poetry celebrated and impressed upon us the nostalgic attitude of modern Norwegians as heirs to a great medieval spiritual culture.

The great New Norwegian poets up to the 1920s were men. Really original modern poetry by women only emerged with the debuts of Halldis Moren (1907-1995) in 1929 and Aslaug Vaa in 1934. Together with Inger Hagerup (1905-1985), writing in Bokmål, all three can be called pioneers of *modern* Norwegian poetry by women. Similarly, few women wrote prose in New Norwegian until the interwar period, especially compared to the rich tradition of women writing in Bokmål dating from the days of Camilla Collett (1813-1895).

Translations and the New Norwegian literary field

Translation was not only important for the theatre. From the very beginning Aasen and Vinje tested their new language by translating texts from other languages. Aasen in particular did so to determine whether New Norwegian was sufficiently rich to provide an adequate rendering of different texts from the European tradition. Thus, he translated fragments from Shakespeare and Cervantes, poems by Luther, Schiller, Byron, George Eliot and others, as well as modern academic prose from English and German. No doubt he also did this to prove to his critics that his language really was capable of such transformation, poetically as well as semantically.

As time went on and the number of academics using New Norwegian increased, many felt obliged to provide their less well-educated compatriots with worthy and important texts from great literature. Arne Garborg was the first to translate Homer's *Odyssey* (1918) and in 1921 the New Norwegian Student Association started the series *Klassiske bokverk* [Classic Books]. After twenty-six books in the series, it was discontinued during the Second World War, with the last publication being Augustine's *Confessions.* Among the books in the series were Greek tragedies, dialogues by Plato and other classical philosophical works from Greek and Latin. Another series was *Bokverk frå millomalderen* [Medieval Books], and of course a series of Icelandic sagas and other medieval books from Old Norse and Old Icelandic – Norrøne bokverk.

The translation activity also continued after the war, however, the conscious organisation of established series no longer played such an important role. At the same time, the New Norwegian series from before the 1940s were followed by those in Bokmål. The two sides inspired each other and in several areas New Norwegian was definitely able to compete. In this regard I consider that New Norwegian had an important advantage because those supporting Bokmål had long been satisfied with Danish translations of classics.

From about the time that New Norwegian was introduced into schools, the translation of children's and youth books began with *Robin Hood, Robinson Crusoe* and other English classics, as well as books from German, and occasionally from other languages. Translations remain an important part of New Norwegian children's literature today.

Children's literature

The increasing number of authors and books around 1900 also provided a stock of children's literature originally written in New Norwegian in a time which has sometimes been called a golden age for Norwegian children's literature. New Norwegian played its part, with Rasmus Løland writing stories about ordinary boys in a traditional rural society and their often complicated relationships with adults. Løland is regarded as one of the best Norwegian authors of children's books and due to him New Norwegian children's literature became more realistic and poetic and less moralistic and religious than it probably would have been otherwise. A number of authors followed Løland, but they did not always have his understanding of the young characters or defend them as well. Very often the stories were about poor children in the countryside, sometimes orphans, and with titles such as *Vi må greie oss selv* [We have to manage on our own] (Ingeborg Refling Hagen, 1935), prompted readers to consider their own lives. Popular serial books for boys or girls were, with few exceptions, written in Bokmål, while the 'manage-on-our-own books', with didactic aims and less emphasis on aesthetic considerations, dominated New Norwegian children's literature for a couple of decades. Not until the 1970s were the dominant didactic demands overtaken by a depiction of freer young subjects acting independently of the adult environment. This renewal was initiated by Guri Vesaas, the children's literature editor of the New Norwegian publishing company Det Norske Samlaget [The Norwegian Book Association]. She contacted already establish authors and asked them to write children's books. Gradually, this approach was successful and other editors from Bokmål companies followed.

Current New Norwegian literature and some concluding remarks

The revival of modern New Norwegian children's literature was part of a general literary renewal occurring in the 1960s, led by New Norwegian and Bokmål authors and poets alike, often published together in literary magazines such as *Profil*, *Vinduet* [The Window], and *Basar*. This followed an earlier, remarkable modernist renewal of fictional prose by the imposing author Tarjei Vesaas (1897-1970) around the end of the Second World War.

Vesaas wrote lyrical prose and was also a poet, as was his wife Halldis Moren Vesaas. Among other things, they introduced the great expressionist modernist Edith Södergran from Finland to the Norwegian public. For the great poet, Olav H. Hauge (1908-1994), the presence of artists such as the Vesaas couple was no doubt of considerable importance, just as all three were for the new generation of the 1960s, which included Einar Økland, Tor Obrestad, Eldrid Lunden and Paal-Helge Haugen.

The modernisation of Det Norske Samlaget into a truly modern publishing house was also important for the New Norwegian authors of the 1960s generation, and not only for their children's books, as to some extent it also led to a revival of New Norwegian literature. The new publisher between 1958 and 1972, Johannes Aanderaa (1927-1991), strongly promoted young, new authors and the publishing house became a meeting place where authors felt welcome and well treated. Aanderaa's new deal was fruitful, and necessary, as those running the bigger companies did not appreciate the New Norwegian manuscripts any more than before. For example, Einar Økland delivered a poetry manuscript to the publishing house Gyldendal in 1966 and was told that his book would be published; however, after a few weeks he was told that the director did not want another New Norwegian poet because Tor Obrestad had already been accepted.[28]

Some poets of the generation from the 1960s were influenced by contemporary American poetry and prose from the Beat Generation and others. There were also impulses from Latin American prose and poetry, introduced not least by the great novelist and essayist Kjartan Fløgstad. Since 2000, we have also been observing promising young authors writing in New Norwegian. Among these are some outstanding young women, including the burlesque and now well-known Olaug Nilssen and her friend Gunhild Øyehaug, whose last novel *Vente, blinke* [To wait, to flash, 2008] is highly regarded among critics and other readers. Nilssen has been the leader of Skrivekunstakademiet [The Writing Academy] in the Bergen area, in the County of Hordaland, while Øyehaug teaches poetry at the same institution. The two also edited the literary periodical *Kraftsentrum* (2005-2009). Through skilful activities and resolute and courageous actions these two young women in their 30s are currently solid and worthy

28 Tusvik, S., 'Plantefelt, flatehogst eller tynning i underskogen', in: Fjeldstad, A., Danielsen, Ø. and Tusvik, S., eds., *Litteraturen mellom staten og marknaden. Rappårt frå konferanse på Ustaoset 16.-18.09.1922* (Oslo, 1992), p. 102.

representatives of contemporary New Norwegian literature, maintaining its strength and quality and of course acting as role models for younger people wanting to become New Norwegian writers.

In conclusion, with reference to Stephen J. Walton's book on Ivar Aasen, I have presented Aasen's and Vinje's efforts as part of a counter-hegemonic movement.[29] The literary and cultural growth from these efforts was successful to such an extent that responsible intellectuals and politicians came to accept the New Norwegian movement as an important and fruitful cultural fact. Under the first parliamentary government of the leftist liberal party in the 1880s it was decided that New Norwegian and Bokmål should develop equal status as official languages, thus legally ensuring that both would be part of national unity. Most importantly, the legislation made it possible for people to vote for the introduction of New Norwegian as the official language in schools, churches and local and regional administration. As the minor competitor, however, the New Norwegian movement in some ways continued to be counter-hegemonic. In addition to the institutional acceptance of New Norwegian in schools, the growth of New Norwegian literature, and above all the highly recognised quality of several novelists and poets writing in this language along with institutions such as Det Norske Teatret and Det Norske Samlaget, have secured a place for New Norwegian culture within the Norwegian public sphere.

In a recent essay, 'Eit sant mirakel' (A true miracle), the author Kjartan Fløgstad maintains that "from a very strong position the New Norwegian belles-lettres becomes even stronger" from around the year 2000.[30]

29 Walton, *Farewell the Spirit Craven.*

30 Fløgstad, K., 'Eit sant mirakel', *Aftenposten* (Oslo, July 1, 2012).

Towards a Monolingual Canon

Faroese and Danish on the Faroe Islands

« Malan Marnersdóttir »

The focus of this article is links between literature written in Faroese and in Danish. These languages have coexisted on the Faroe Islands since the Lutheran Reformation in the fifteenth century.

As the title of this article indicates, the relationship between the two languages has changed: whereas Danish was the official language and the only written language on the Faroes, it is now considered the first other language. Faroese took over the role of main language with the institution of Home Rule in 1948 which also stipulates that Danish has to be taught well. At that time, a Faroese literary canon had been under construction for about a century and a half, beginning with the collection of traditional oral poetry. The crossing of language boundaries has been vital in the construction of a Faroese literature in terms of both new forms and new ideas.

Background

The Faroes are a group of 18 islands covering an area of 1,399 km^2 in the North Atlantic. Today the population is almost 50,000, which is three times as large as it was in 1901.

Norwegian farmers settled on the Faroes in the ninth century, and in the fourteenth century the country came under Danish rule, together with Norway. The Lutheran Reformation of 1537 meant that Danish became both the language of faith and the official language on the Faroes. The most influential literary transfer has been the Danish Bible and the new hymns of the Reformation. The official Faroese Bible was first published in 1961 and the official hymn book in 1960. Despite the fact that for centuries all reading on the Faroes was in Danish, the spoken language has always been Faroese.

The colonial hegemony also included economic regulations. The Danish crown commissioned Faroese trade to different commercial companies.[1] From 1709 to 1856 the Royal Danish Monopoly was responsible for all imports to and exports from the Faroes, which meant that the Faroese were not allowed to trade with anybody else. In the last decade of the eighteenth century these restrictions provoked the first literary opposition towards the colonial hegemony when Poul Poulsen Nólsoy (1766-1808) composed his satirical dance ballad *Fuglakvæðið* [The Bird Ballad]. In the century that followed there was rising opposition, inspired by the ideas of Romanticism, to the linguistic hegemony. Providing Faroese with an orthography was an important step towards being able to answer back to the centre of the empire, which is an important goal in most postcolonial literatures, as Bill Ashcroft, Gareth Griffiths and Helen Tiffins have described in the book *The Empire Writes Back.*[2] The struggle to install Faroese as the language of the country was successful, and this was due in no small part to literature. In the nineteenth and twentieth centuries the idea arose that the language was the main defining characteristic of a nation and this formed the basis for the struggle for independence. Literature has played an important part in preparing for the nation-building which has taken place since the late nineteenth century, and literature in Faroese was a particularly efficient means in this struggle for an independent position within the Danish kingdom. The Faroese language has survived and Faroese literature is a fact. How it will develop in the future will depend on its ability to adjust to new situations in the global culture and the media of communication.

Most influences from abroad on the Faroes came and still come from Denmark, and are principally related to the administrative, social and cultural organization of society. Global philosophical, artistic and literary trends and movements arrive somewhat late on the Faroes, often after a process of Danish filtration through television, radio, film distribution, books, magazines and library systems. On the other hand, with modern media direct global influences have increased and made it a more simultaneous process.

Faroese literature shows a number of postcolonial characteristics. First, there is an effort to replace Danish as a medium with Faroese. However, Faroese literature has found inspiration and taken on forms from Danish and

1 Cf. Joensen, J.K., Mortensen, A. and Petersen, P., *Føroyar undir fríum handli í 100 ár* (Tórshavn, 1955); West, J.F., *Faroe. The Emergence of a Nation* (London, 1974), chapters 2-4.

2 Ashcroft, B., Griffiths, G. and Tiffin, H., *The Empire Writes Back: Theory and Practice in Post-colonial Literatures* (London, 1989).

other Scandinavian literatures. The national songs of the late nineteenth century, for instance, were based on similar songs in Scandinavian literature.[3] The term 'mimicry' in postcolonial studies applies to the ambivalence in the relationship between colonizer and colony.[4] In the transfer of literary forms between Denmark and the Faroes there are imitations that veer towards mocking exaggeration in terms of national pride.

Most transfer from Faroese literature occurs via Danish, either through works by Faroese authors who write in Danish, such as William Heinesen (1900-1991), or via translations of Faroese works into Danish. The translations into Danish prepare the way for translations into other languages. However, some works by Faroese writers have recently been translated directly from the Faroese, such as the German volume of short stories *Von Inseln weiss ich* (2006) and the Dutch collection of poetry *Windvlinders* (2008).[5]

The history of the development from a culture of an exclusively Danish literature to one of a mixed Faroese-Danish oral and written literature, and then to one of an almost monolingual Faroese literature is complicated and this article will only give a short version of it.[6]

On the Faroes there has been no attempt to create an official list of the most valuable literary works as has been the case in Denmark, where not only literature but also architecture, music, art, design and theatre each have an official canon mainly intended for the school curriculum. Instead, an implied or tacit canon of Faroese literary works exists. It consists of the works read and discussed at schools and universities. The literary histories of Christian Matras (1935) and Árni Dahl (1980-83) list authors and works, as do readers in Faroese, but the evaluation of these works is mainly indirect – that is, the more valuable a work is considered to be, the more is said about it. It is characteristic of these Faroese canons – except for Dahl's – that they do not include works in Danish by Faroese authors but only the Faroese translations of their works. This is the case for the

3 Sigurðardóttir, T., *At rejse ud for at komme hjem: den færøske sangdigtning 1876-1892 som del af og udtryk for færøsk nationalidentitet i støbeskeen* (Copenhagen, 1987).

4 Ashcroft, B., Griffiths, G. and Tiffin, H., *Post-Colonial Studies. The Key Concepts* (London/New York, 2000).

5 Stössinger, V. and Dömling, A.K., eds., *"Von Inseln weiss ich..." Geschichten von den Färöer-Inseln (transl. by Borchert, R. et al.) (Zürich, 2006);* Van Elswijk, R., ed., *Windvlinders. Poëzie van de Faerøer* (Groningen, 2008).

6 Cf. Marnersdóttir, M., 'Grænser i færøsk litteratur', in: Zilliacus, C. et al., eds., *Gränser i nordisk litteratur* (Åbo, 2008), pp. 65-80.

works of William Heinesen and Jørgen-Frantz Jacobsen (1900-1938), which appeared on the school curriculum after 1975 once Faroese translations were available[7].

Colonial poetry – oral poetry turned into writing

The earliest evidence of the transfer of European poetry to the Faroes is in the medieval ballads of the Faroes. This old oral poetry has motifs in common with important European poetry. The ballad cycle of Sjúrður (Sigurd) and the dragon Frænir (Fafnir) was composed by anonymous authors, probably in the fourteenth century. It has common roots with poems about Sigurd in the 'Older' *Edda*, which was written down in the thirteenth and fourteenth centuries, as well as with the Icelandic *Völsunga saga* [Volsunga Saga] from the late thirteenth century. The German *Nibelungenlied* is another interesting intertext of the Faroese ballad.

In the oral tradition, the union of singing the ballad text with dancing in a chain constitutes a unique form which still is practised in the Faroes.[8] These oral ballads are the oldest Faroese poetry and they form the basis both for the restoration of Faroese writing and for literature in Faroese.

The language of faith, for example reading from the Bible and singing hymns, was already Danish, and sometime after the 1590s the ballad and dance tradition, which had been solely Faroese, became bilingual. This happened when Danish-language ballads were introduced by Anders Sørensen Vedel's (1542-1616) book of Danish folk songs *Hundredevisebogen* [The Book of a Hundred Ballads] from 1591 and the philologist Peder Syv's (1631-1702) extended version, republished in 1695. The Danish folk ballads became very popular on the Faroes as dance ballads to the extent that the politician, farmer and poet Jóannes Patursson (1866-46) wrote in his memoirs that in his childhood in the village of Kirkjubø, Danish-language ballads predominated.[9] It is only recently that the Danish ballads on the Faroes have attracted the interest of researchers: the Danish musicologist

7 Ellefsen, A., 'William Heinesen i undervisningsøjemed', in: Í Ólavsstovu, V. and Kløvstad, J.N., eds., *Tårnet midt i verden – en bog om William Heinesen* (Tórshavn, 1994), pp. 153-163.

8 Nolsøe, M., 'Folkevisa og folkevisemiljøet på Færøyane', in: Andreassen, E., ed., *Kvæðagreinir* (Tórshavn, 1988), pp. 3-21.

9 Patursson, J., *Tættir úr Kirkjubøar søgu* (Tórshavn, 1966), pp. 45.

Marianne Clausen has been studying the melodies of the Danish ballads collected in the Faroes.[10]

Transfer from the Faroes

The collection of Faroese oral poetry began in 1639 when Ole Worm (1588-1654) received some ballads written down on the Faroes. Unfortunately, this collection was lost in the big fire at the library of the University of Copenhagen, but a copy of some of the stanzas had been preserved thanks to Peder Syv.

In the eighteenth century, ballad collection was taken up by the Faroese scholar of economics Jens Christian Svabo (1746-1824), who invented his own spelling based on the dialect of his home village of Sandavágur. His aim in writing down ballads was to preserve examples of the old Faroese language because he believed it was about to become extinct.[11] Therefore, he also wrote a big dictionary manuscript, which he dedicated to the King.[12] While Svabo was studying at the University of Copenhagen in the 1770s, he sold his collection of ballads which was stored at the Royal Library.[13]

The Faroese ballads caught the interest of Danish scholars at the beginning of the nineteenth century and the collection of ballads became more organized due to the work of Hans Christian Lyngbye (1782-1837). He published the first book of Faroese texts, *Færøiske Qvæder* [Faroese Ballads], in 1822. The book was based on the work of collectors on the Faroes who had used Svabo's spelling, two of whom were the vicar of Suðuroy, Johan Hendrik Schrøter (1771-1851), and the shepherd Johannes Clemensen (1794-1869), who came from Sandur.[14] Until Lyngbye's book was published, the Faroese had never seen these ballads, or for that matter anything else, in print in Faroese, whereas they did know the Danish folk ballads from books. It is very likely that it was Herder's ideas about folk and language, which became so powerful with Romanticism that caused

10 She has published works about Faroese hymn singing and the melodies of the oral poetry. Her work on the Danish ballad melodies was published in 2010.

11 Svabo, J.C., *Dictionarium Færoense. Færøsk-dansk-latinsk ordbog*, Matras, C., ed., vol. II, *Indledning og register* (Copenhagen, 1970), p. XI.

12 *Ibidem*, p. IX.

13 *Ibidem.*

14 Króki', *Fróðskaparrit* 42 (1994), pp. 29-35.

Faroese oral poetry to attract the interest of scholars in Denmark and collectors on the Faroe Isles. The Danish interest in Faroese folklore and these first attempts to collect it in writing were the first step towards the colony being able to answer back to the central colonial power.

At the same time as this transfer of Faroese poetry to Denmark, poets on the Faroes began to compose new ballads with contemporary plots as well as historical ones from the Icelandic sagas and from Norwegian and Danish history. These poets, Jens Christian Djurhuus (1773-1853) and his son Jens Hendrik Djurhuus (1799-1892), also wrote some of them down – the other ballads by father and son Djurhuus lived on as oral poetry, and were collected in the same way as the old ballads. In addition, the colonial bailiff and governor from 1830 until 1848, Christian Pløyen (1803-67), wrote a new ballad in Danish entitled *Grindavísan* [The Whale Hunt Ballad], which to this day is a much-appreciated dance ballad.

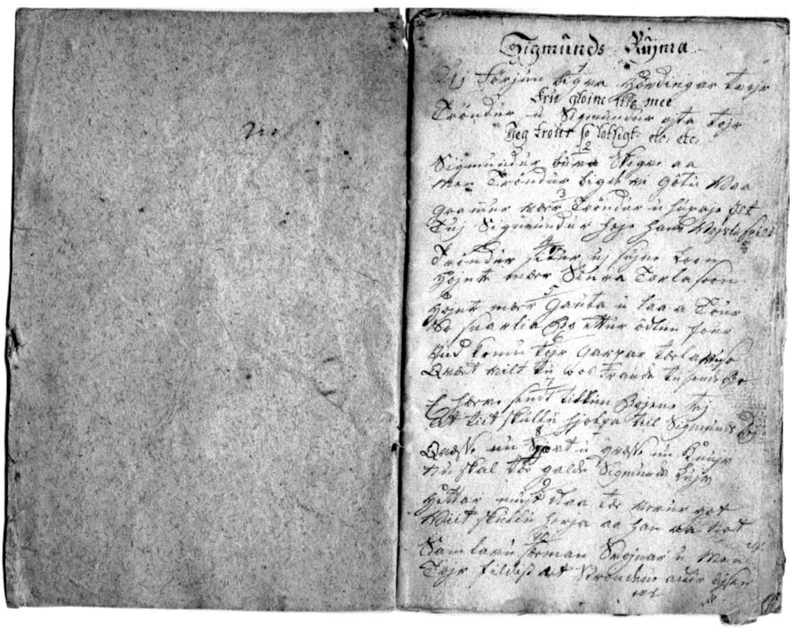

Jens Christian Djurhuus' Sigmunds Ríma, one of three texts in the oldest literary manuscript in Faeroese literature written in the beginning of the 19th century.

Source: Manuscript. National Library. Faroese National Heritage. Date: Beginning of the 19th century.

Vencelaus Ulricus Hammershaimb.

Source: http://www.myheritageimages.com/F/storage/site115859131/files/00/00/66/000066_548468os356331e0841v37.jpg.

Until the end of the nineteenth century, almost all writing on the Faroes and about the Faroes was in Danish. Svabo's first attempt to construct a Faroese orthography did not form a linguistic museum but became the basis for the development of the orthography from which modern Faroese would rise. Contemporary Faroese orthography was developed in 1846 by a Faroese student of theology, Vencelaus Ulricus Hammershaimb (1816-1909). This orthography is historical and is based on Old Norse. It was created in order to prove that Faroese was a language in its own right and that there was a literature at hand to write down.[15] It also provided Hammershaimb with an appropriate tool for writing down the old dance ballads that he collected on the Faroes in 1847-48 and published in the 1840s and 1850s. In 1891 Hammershaimb published *Færøsk Anthologi* [Faroese Anthology], which proposed a literary canon consisting of oral poetry texts, riddles, legends and pieces of contemporary prose he had written himself. The work also comprises a grammar explaining in Danish the structure of Faroese and a second volume containing a dictionary by Jakob Jakobsen (1864-1918), a student of Nordic philology.

The first major volume of modern poems, *Føriskar vysur* [Faroese Songs], was published in 1892 using another spelling. This spelling was based on phonetics and was developed by Jakob Jakobsen. Disagreement about these two spelling methods – the historical and the phonetic – resulted in a struggle that caused the break-up of Føringafelag [The Faroese Association], which was established in 1889 with the aim of promoting the Faroese language and culture. The outcome of the struggle was that the historical orthography won.

The existence of two orthographies at the end of the nineteenth century did not mean that everybody on the Faroes began to write Faroese. Faroese was not taught at school at all and for a period at the beginning of the twentieth

15 Matras, C., 'Det færøske skriftsprog af 1846', in: Næs, M. and Poulsen, J.H.W., eds., *Greinaval – málfrøðigreinir* (1951), pp. 97-115 (Tórshavn, 2000), explains the process very well.

century the teachers were not allowed to speak Faroese to the older pupils. In 1938 this stipulation was abolished and Faroese became a compulsory subject at primary school.[16] From then on Faroese children learned Faroese and Danish to the same level. However, a long way into the twentieth century many Faroese still did all their writing in Danish. In the beginning of the twentieth century, however, some people did learn to write Faroese themselves or went to the *Fólkaháskúli* [folk high school], which was established in 1899 and was the only institution at the time that taught Faroese.

A society in need of a new ideology

From the 1870s to the 1890s, National Romanticism answered the need for a new ideology. The ideological changes in the nineteenth century followed economic and demographic changes. Until 1856 the country was closed and was a Lutheran agricultural society where all trade was concentrated in the Royal Monopoly.[17] In the following decades both Faroese and foreign business people who had settled on the Faroes, established a wide range of trades and enterprises, and in the 1870s the first fishing vessels were purchased from Scotland, which made it possible to sail to the rich fishing grounds around Iceland. This started a great era of cod fishing and salt fish production for the markets in southern Europe.

The promotion of the Faroese language and culture served the development of the new society.[18] Despite the fact that Føringafelag ended its activities because of internal disagreements on the orthography, the idea of Faroese as the national language of the Faroes became the mainstream of Faroese political and cultural thought of the twentieth century. The most important literary outcome of the national movement was the songs about the Faroese language and landscape published in books such as *Føriskar vysur.* These songs have become icons of Faroese-ness, and people still sing them at parties, meetings and festivals.

At the same time there were poets writing and publishing in Danish. A hymn poet, Ole Hansen (1834-1916) from the village of Eiði, had his hymns

16 Thomasen, A., *Færøsk i den færøske skole: fra århundredskiftet til 1938* (Odense, 1985).

17 The Danish King was responsible for all imports from and exports to the Faroes until 1856, when all trade became free. After this people were free to set up companies. Fishing and the manufacture of fish products could begin to answer the need of a fast-growing population, which from 1805 to 1901 tripled from 5,265 to 15,230.

18 Sigurðardóttir, *At rejse ud*; Debes, H.J., *Færingernes land: historien om den færøske nutids oprindelse*, Cold, S.A. and Hvidt, K., eds. (Copenhagen, 2001).

published in Norway, and the farmer Gregorius Johannesen (1823-90) from Gøta published in 1884 what was probably the very first volume of poems printed on the Faroes: *Udvalgte Digte* [Selected Poems]. His poems praise the King and have historical themes.

The idea of Faroese as a language that also comprised a literature was a true child of Romanticism. The orthography struggle shows that internal disagreements about how to answer back to the colonial power concerned the form of the writing rather than the content, as in the national ideas and feelings. In the late eighteenth century Faroese poetry had already become known in Denmark. Claus Lund (1739-1815) was the first Faroese to call himself an intellectual. He published poems and ballads with Faroese subject matters in Danish literary magazines such as *Minerva* and *Den danske Tilskuer* [The Danish Spectator] in the 1790s.[19]

As the collection of Faroese oral poetry became known in Denmark, the Danish poet Carl Ploug (1813-94) based the refrain of one of his poems on a Faroese ballad refrain. It is the poem *Slaget ved Slesvig* [The Slesvig Battle] from 1848[20]:

Slutter kreds og staar fast
Alle danske Mænd!
Gud han raader
Naar vi fange Sejr igen.[21]

The Faroese ballad refrain goes:

Stígum fast á várt gólv
sparum ei vár skó.
Gud man ráða,
hvar vær drekkum onnur jól.[22]

....

19 Marnersdóttir, M., 'Claus Lund – en "Litteratus" in Tórshavn i 1790'erne', in: Uecker, H., ed., *Opplysning i Norden* (Frankfurt a.M., 1998), pp. 357-364.

20 Weyhe, E., 'Eitt samtíðarligt kvæði – og ein ókend uppskrift' [uppskrift', in: Marnersdóttir, M., Joensen, L. and Kristjánsdóttir, D., eds., *Bókmentaljós* (Tórshavn, 2006), pp. 145-160.

21 'Let us form a circle, all Danish men! God decides when we triumph again'. Translation by Malan Marnersdóttir.

22 'Let us stamp on our floor, let us not spare our shoes. God decides where we celebrate next Christmas.' Translation by Malan Marnersdóttir.

This is one of very few examples of direct literary transfer from the Faroese colony to the literature of the Danish colonial power. Ploug's poem celebrates the Danish soldiers in one of the major fights in the Danish-German war of 1848, which took place close to the town Slesvig in Southern Jylland. After a series of wars between Denmark and Germany in 1848-1864, Slesvig finally became German.

Some Danish novels of the early twentieth century are set in a Faroese environment and describe Faroese themes, for example the works by Jørgen Falk Rønne (1865-1939), who was a vicar on the Faroes from 1888 to 1894. He published a volume of stories called *En modig pige: og andre fortællinger fra Færøerne* [A Courageous Girl, and Other Stories from the Faroe Islands] and a novel entitled *Lykkens Land. Roman fra Færøerne* [The Land of Happiness. A Novel from the Faroe Islands] in 1919.

Transfer of classic forms

Lyngbye's *Færøiske Qvæder* was the first of three books in Faroese to be published in the decade from 1822 to 1832. The other two books were transfers to Faroese. The second book of the three was a translation of *The Gospel by S. Matthew* by the Reverend and ballad collector J.H. Schrøter. Schrøter's translation was the first time a book from the Bible had become available in Faroese. The audience was not used to reading Faroese and was certainly not used to using Faroese for matters of faith, which may have been one of the reasons that the translation was condemned.[23]

The third book to be published in Faroese between 1822 and 1832 was the Icelandic saga *Færeyinga saga* [Saga about the Faroese], which the Danish scholar Carl Christian Rafn (1795-1864) edited to create a trilingual book with both the Old Norse, Faroese and Danish texts. This Faroese story is from the thirteenth century and it is the only story about the Faroes in the first centuries after Norwegian farmers settled on the islands.

These three books form the foundation of Faroese literature and it is notable that all of them transferred ancient forms – the medieval ballad, biblical prose and Old Norse prose – into Faroese in a period in which almost nothing else existed for the general public in written Faroese.

In the twentieth century Jens Hendrik Oliver Djurhuus (1881-1948) was the first modern poet to introduce literary forms from Greek antiquity to Faroese. He published his first volume of poems in 1914. The poem *Atlantis*

23 Matras, C., *Evangelium sankta Matteusar II. Um týðingina av bókini* (Tórshavn, 1973).

(1917) refers to the Greek myth of the sunken civilization of Atlantis and the first line 'Hana sveipti havsins lætta og hjómhvíta froða' [The light and white foam of the waves wrapped her] alludes to the *Iliad*, which Djurhuus translated into Faroese as well – it was published posthumously in 1967. Djurhuus was a child of the national movement and his aim was to prove that it was possible to express abstract thoughts and feelings in Faroese.

Transfer of Danish literature – two geographical poems

One of the most striking examples of cultural transfer from Danish to the Faroese nation-building literature is a geographical poem from 1921, *Føroyar* [The Faroe Islands].[24] This 29-stanza poem was written by Hans Andrias Djurhuus (1883-1951) and its opening line reads 'Lítið yvir Føroya land' [Take a look over the Faroes]. The poem both imitates and mocks its model, the *Vort Land* [Our Country, 1889] by the Danish national poet Christian Richardt (1831-1892).

The introduction in Djurhuus's poem depicts the country in general terms and the poem then goes into more detail. It ends by repeating the call to look very carefully at the country. The body of the poem divides the islands into groups with the Northern, Middle and Southern Islands, a strategy which makes the country seem bigger. Each island is named and described in terms of its mountains, history or wealth. *Færeyinga saga*, the Icelandic saga about the Faroese mentioned above, has an important role in the poem as it gives the descriptions of the country historical legitimacy. Some important scenes from the saga endow certain places with historical significance – for instance, Svínoy (st. 7), Norðagøta (st. 15), Skúvoy (st. 23) and Sandvík (st. 23). The poem also alludes to a myth about a giant and his wife who came to take the Faroes over to Iceland. They did not succeed because as they were about to begin towing the islands away, the sun rose and they were turned into two cliffs at the northernmost tip of the island Eysturoy.

The poem describes the islands, names many details and points out different qualities of the landscape and society. By naming the places, the poem gives a lesson in geography, and the pedagogical intention is obvious from the imperative forms used throughout the poem. The poet was a teacher and many of his poems were produced directly on the blackboard. As a lesson in geography, the poem can also be understood as a comment on the geographical maps of the time. The only map with Faroese place

24 'Føroyar' was published in the first volume of the journal *Varðin* in 1921, pp. 49-56.

names which the poem's audience would have known was the map in Rafn's edition of *Færeyinga saga*. In 1921, all maps of the Faroe Islands were in Danish; that is, the place names were rendered in a Danish form.[25] From this perspective, H.A. Djurhuus's poem conquers the country and makes it Faroese.

A selection of ten stanzas from Djurhuus's poem is included in *Songbók Føroya fólks* [Songbook of the Faroese people], which was first published in 1913 and functions as a national songbook.[26] This selection from Djurhuus's poem is accorded a high status by the editors as it comes right after the two national hymns. The stanzas form a song that mentions all the islands but no further details such as villages, mountains, historical places or explicit evaluations. This keeps the poem universal.

The interesting issue in our context is that Djurhuus's song is a response to the aforementioned *Vort Land*, a very long poem by Christian Richardt that was published in 1889. It has 72 stanzas of which five are about the Danish colonies: two stanzas are about Iceland, one is about the Faroe Islands and one is about Greenland. However, the West Indies, which were a colony of Denmark from the seventeenth century until 1917, are only described indirectly in two lines as, 'Sukker-Colonier, Palmestrand med Kolibrier' [sugar colonies, palm beaches with hummingbirds]. Djurhuus's 29 stanzas are an overwhelming counterpart to Richardt's single stanza about the Faroes and his adaptation of the rhyme and rhythm of Richardt's poem underlines the exaggeration. By replacing the centre of the hegemony with one of the overseas possessions and allowing this to fill out the whole text, Djurhuus's song becomes a postcolonial answer to the hegemonic power. The use of Richardt's poem shows the ambiguity of mimicry. It mirrors the relationship between the colonizer and the colonized. The colonizer makes rules and restrictions and offers models to the colony, which suffers under some of the restrictions and copies others. The colony imitates the colonizer's cultural and literary forms in order to promote its own, which is given an edge by the mockery that underlies the exaggeration in Djurhuus's poem.

---

25 Weyhe, E., 'Tey nýggju føroyakortini', *Ársfrágreiðing* 1998 (Tórshavn, 1999), pp. 6-7; Nørlund, N.E., Færøernes kortlægning – en historisk fremstilling (Copenhagen, 1944).

26 *Songbók Føroya fólks* [Songbook of the Faroese People] 3rd edition 1931 to the hitherto 10th edition 2008.

However, the national ideology of the two songs is the same: one has to know the country and remember every inch of it. In order to create a Faroese national identity, Djurhuus mimics the poem of the colonizer with great success.[27]

Heinesen and Jacobsen

The work of William Heinesen and that of his contemporary Jørgen-Frantz Jacobsen comprises interesting mixed linguistic characteristics. As this article has shown, Faroese literature was bilingual and this continued to be the case until about the middle of the twentieth century. Some authors published works in Faroese and some in Danish. The latter prevailed in the novel genre in the beginning of the century, mainly thanks to William Heinesen and Jørgen-Frantz Jacobsen. They embody the most important transfer from Faroese to Danish literature and into the world in the middle of the twentieth century. It was not only because of personal, biographical reasons that William Heinesen and Jørgen-Frantz Jacobsen became Danish-writing authors. Their family background in the Danish-speaking circles of the capital Tórshavn and the fact that Faroese was not on the school curriculum to the same extent as Danish when they grew up meant that their abilities in Faroese were not developed. Nevertheless, both authors spoke Faroese, wrote articles in Faroese and supported the independence movement, but their primary writing language was Danish.[28]

Leyvoy Joensen has persuasively argued that these two Danish-writing Faroese authors took care of the external part of the literary building of the nation.[29] The plots and motifs of their works are Faroese, and their Danish is a hybrid of Danish and Faroese. The insertion of Faroese expressions such as place names creates metonymic gaps or black holes of meaning that can be seen in other post-colonial literary works such as Naipaul's

27 Marnersdóttir, M., 'Genskrivning, efterligning og modstand i færøsk historie og litteratur', *TijdSchrift voor Skandinavistiek*, vol. 30, no. 2 (2009), pp. 137-164.

28 Sørensen, H. Flohr, 'Mit forhold til det danske sprog er fatalt bestemt. William Heinesens dansksprogede forfatterskab. Baggrund og konsekvenser', *Fróðskaparrit* 47 (1999), pp. 5-31. Jones, W. Glyn, *Færø og kosmos* (Copenhagen, 1974).

29 Joensen, L., 'Barbara and the Dano-Faroese Moment', *Úthavsdagar – Oceaniske dage. Annales societatis scientiarum færoensis*, supplementum XXIX (Tórshavn, 2000), pp. 64-87.

novel *The Mystic Masseur*.[30] In the Danish texts of Heinesen and Jacobsen words and lines from or directly in Faroese create passages into the Faroese language and culture as a whole.[31]

Heinesen and Jacobsen wrote in Danish and were excluded from the Faroese literary canon and the first literary history, *Føroysk bókmentasøga* [History of Faroese literature], published in 1935 by the poet and scholar Christian Matras. Works by Heinesen and Jacobsen were rarely taught in Faroese schools, except occasionally in Danish classes, until they were translated into Faroese in the 1970s.[32] Árni Dahl's literary history from the beginning of the 1980s includes Faroese authors who wrote in Danish in a separate chapter, 'Danish-writing Faroese'.[33] A comprehensive Faroese literary history should take into account that Danish was the written language of the country for many centuries and that Danish-writing Faroese authors have contributed to a great extent to Faroese literature.

Heinesen and Jacobsen are the only Faroese authors to have been included in Danish literary histories from the 1950s and onwards.[34] The Danish scholar Hans Hauge has criticized contemporary Danish literary historians for not including all Faroese and Greenlandic literature, as well as for not including Icelandic literature until 1944 (the year of Icelandic independence). By analogy with Edward Saïd's concept of 'orientalism', Hauge has coined the term 'Norientalism' for the Nordic phenomena.[35] The term applies to the newest Danish literary history *Dansk litteraturs historie* [The History of Danish Literature], 2006, in which Heinesen and Jacobsen are the only representatives of Faroese literature.

30 Naipaul, V.S. *The Mystic Masseur* (London, 1957). See also Ashcroft, W.D., 'Is that the Congo? Language as Metonymy in the Post-Colonial Text', *World Literature Written in English*, 29:2 (1989), pp. 3-10.

31 Marnersdóttir, M. 'William Heinesens *Det gode håb* i lyset af post-kolonial teori', *TijdSchrift voor Skandinavistiek*, vol. 25, no. 2 (2004), pp. 181-198.

32 Ellefsen, 'William Heinesen'.

33 Dahl, Á., *Bókmentasøga* (Tórshavn, 1981-1983), I (1981): p. 130 and II (1983): pp. 31, 57.

34 Marnersdóttir, M., 'Vit eiga William', *Brá* 20 (1993), pp. 32-42.

35 Hauge, H., 'Norientalisme eller nordisk postkolonialisme', *Nordisk litteratur* (Copenhagen etc, 2003), pp. 8-11.

Guðrið Helmsdal.

Source: http://www.ms.fo/wp-content/uploads/2011/03/Gu%C3%B0ri%C3%B0-Helmsdal-e1305555186223.jpg.

Other writers also contributed in Danish to the Faroese literary history. During the Second World War, Faroese authors such as Richard B. Thomsen (1888-1970) wrote novels about the sudden wealth among the population due to the war economy. The titles of some of his novels are in Faroese whereas the text is in Danish, for example, *Blámannavík* [The Creek of the Blue/Black Men, 1944]. Eilif Mortansson (1916-1989), who lived in Denmark, also wrote novels in Danish with Faroese motifs. Several of these novels were translated into Faroese, for instance, *Blámannavík* by Thomsen was published in Faroese translation in 1988 and *Snæbjørn* [Polar Bear, 1954] by Mortansson in 2000. Thus, they became an element in the struggle for a monolingual literature.

A shift took place in the literary transfer from Faroese to Danish when Regin Dahl (1918-2007) began to translate his poems and published them with the original Faroese texts and the translations juxtaposed. This shift would have advanced further if poets had begun to publish in both languages as did the modernist poet Guðrið Helmsdal (1941) in the volume *Morgun í mars* [Morning in March]. Here some poems are in Faroese and some in Danish, and they are not translations of each other. This shift would have been a sign that the development of the Faroese language and its literature had reached a stage of self-assurance and of acceptance of the ability to use both Faroese and Danish in poetry. This has not been the case.

Faroese writers born in the 1930s and later

Since 1938, people have learned Faroese from their first day at school. This means that writers whose first book was published from the 1950s onwards write Faroese. These authors also began to move away from the pre-war nation-building literature. Instead of describing the transformation from a peasant culture to the fishery culture of the early twentieth century, the post-war novels describe a society with a modern fishing industry that has easier access to entertainment and travel, not only by car around the islands but also abroad. Parallel to this development, the national issues change, and authors such as Jens Pauli Heinesen (1932-2011) tend to criticize the lack of self-determination. His novels from the 1960s and 1970s describe the inability of the Faroese to decide and rule in a democratic way. With his generation of authors, Faroese literature became monolingual. All authors who are born and live on the Faroe Islands now publish their books in Faroese.

A brief comparison of the number of novels published functions as an indicator of the development towards a monolingual literature on the Faroes: from 1909, when the first novel in Faroese was published, until 1969 the number of novels by Faroese authors published was 47. Out of these, 32 were in Danish and fifteen in Faroese. Between 1970 and 2005, the total number of novels published was 69 and only six were in Danish.[36] This is emblematic of the development of Faroese and of the common consciousness of the Faroese: from being bilingual the literature has now become monolingual. The creation of a modern literature in Faroese has excluded Danish from the canon. From a national and a linguistic point of view, this monolingual high literature has proved the success of the language struggle. Now writers can concentrate on aesthetics and the development of literary genres.

New linguistic hybrids

Faroese literature has tended to contain a very clean – purist – vocabulary. Danish expressions and wordings which are common in spoken Faroese have been more or less explicitly banned from written Faroese and have been a point of evaluation. However, in contemporary works of literature there is a tendency to include more and more English vocabulary. This

36 Marnersdóttir, M., *Hvør av øðrum. Samanseting, frásøgn og millumtekstleiki í føroyskari skaldsøgu eftir 1970* (Tórshavn, 2000), pp. 389ff.

tendency has an aesthetic aim and results in the same kind of hybrid as when Faroese expressions are inserted into a Danish text, or Danish expressions into a Faroese text. However, it is not interpreted in the same way but is taken more as a sign of globalization, and therefore functions as a literary device. The last volume of poems by Carl Jóhan Jensen (1957) is *September í bjørkum, sum kanska eru bláar* [September in Birches that Might be Blue, 2006] and the subtitle of the volume is in English, *The afflictions of the reverend J.H.Ö. Dünn*, referring to J.H.O. Djurhuus, who did not write poetry in English. In addition, all of the poem titles are in English with open references to English-writing poets such as Wordsworth and Yeats. The poems also allude to Faroese and Norwegian poetry. The explicit English intertextuality can be taken as a sign of openness towards cultures other than the Danish one. It pays tribute to Anglo-American language and literature and thus is a sign of opposition to Danish hegemony on the Faroes, but it is also a less critical sign of the worldwide dominance of the Anglo-American influence – or cultural imperialism of the twenty-first century.

Lisbeth Nebelong (Photo: Linda Hansen).

The issue of new multilingual approaches also relates to the question of whether works of Danish and Norwegian authors should be included in the Faroese canon.[37] The events in Danish novels such as Arthur Krasilnikov's

37 Simonsen, K., 'Ein modernað skaldsøga um Føroyar', *Outsider magazine* (2005), pp. 168-170.

excellent *Hvalens øje* [The Eye of the Whale], Lisbeth Nebelong's *Når engle spiller Mozart* [When Angels Play Mozart] and *Færøblues* [Faroe Blues], and the Norwegian novel *Buzz Aldrin, hvor ble det av deg i alt mylderet?* [Buzz Aldrin, what has become of you in the swarm?] by John Harstad take place on the Faroes and thus contribute to Faroese culture with their important views of the Faroes from the outside. A question would therefore be: should these works of literature be included in a Faroese literary history as examples of answers back from representatives of both the original settlers of the Faroes, such as Harstad, and of the contemporary colonial power that has given away a good deal of its power but still has the final word in matters of foreign policy, military defence and currency, such as Nebelong?

The different stories about the struggle of the Provençal, Breton and Basque peoples for the recognition of their language and literature show that they have encountered greater difficulties than the Faroese and Greenlandic people. This could be linked to the tradition in these countries of a much stronger central power than in Scandinavia. Iceland is the great role model for many Faroese people and in terms of literature the ideals of both countries are pretty much the same. In Greenland a similar but also very different development has taken place.

Although Danish is excluded from Faroese poetry and fiction and the transfer from other literatures tends to be directly from the foreign language to Faroese, the triumph of making Faroese literature monolingual may lose its importance if we take into consideration that in the twenty-first century the impact of cultural transfer through literature tends to be overshadowed by the impact of other media such as TV, cinema and the internet. It could be added that as long as there is something to fight for there is hope, as the struggle itself keeps the death of Faroese-language literature at bay.

It is a fact that over the last two hundred years the Faroese literature and language have known great success and triumphed over extinction. This short outline of the development of Faroese literature in terms of literary transfer between the Faroe Islands and Denmark has shown the lines along which this success has been achieved and has indicated a number of contemporary challenges.[38]

38 A new Faroese literary history published in 2011 acknowledges the bilingualism in Faroese letters and analyses works in Danish as well as in Faroese.

Part IV

Literary History/Within Borders/Without Borders

Anticolonial and Postcolonial De-/Constructions of the Nation

Ethnonational Mobilisation in Meänmaa

« Anne Heith »

This article will examine discursive constructions of the nation through an analysis of Bengt Pohjanen and Kirsti Johansson's survey of Tornedalian Finnish literature, *Den tornedalsfinska litteraturen. Från Kexi till Liksom* [Tornedalian Finnish Literature: From Kexi to Liksom], published in 2007.[1] One theoretical point of departure is constituted by the claim that there are a number of discourses of 'nation' which are attuned to specific historical, ideological and geographical contexts: 'there is not a single discourse of "race, ethnicity and nation" but a series of such discourses attuned to the historical demands of specific countries, regions and internal social and political dynamics'.[2] The article wishes to highlight connections between this theoretical vantage point, on the one hand, and deconstructions and critical reformulations of a national optic which has shaped images of the Nordic nation-states as 'small, peaceful nations with relatively homogeneous populations contained within "natural borders"', on the other.[3] These images were the result of redefinitions which suppressed the turbulent histories of the kingdoms of Denmark-Norway and Sweden-Finland, which were 'organized as aggressive maritime miniempires with a great appetite for military conquest'.[4] One result of this turbulent history was that borders were redrawn. This is exemplified by the 1809 border between Sweden and Finland which was drawn along the Torne River. For

1 The term 'Tornedalian Finnish' is used in this article as the term that is used by Pohjanen and Johansson in the history of Tornedalian Finnish literature that will be discussed. However, the term generally used today is 'Tornedalian'.

2 Fenton, S., *Ethnicity* (Cambridge/Malden, MA, 2005), p. 48.

3 Löfgren, O., 'Regionauts: The Transformation of Cross-Border Regions in Scandinavia', *European Urban and Regional Studies*, vol. 15, no. 3 (2008), p. 197.

4 *Ibidem.*

the people living in the Torne Valley the consequences were far-reaching as the border cut through a region of highly integrated villages lying on both sides of the river. Consequently, the Finnish-speaking population on both sides was divided by the new state border and the Tornedalian Finns in Sweden became an ethnic and linguistic minority. This minority status constitutes a major incentive behind the present-day cultural mobilisation of the Tornedalian Finns, in particular when viewed against the backdrop of the homogenising effects of assimilation politics.[5]

The concept of 'nation' is important to the argument of this article, but may be defined in different ways. *The American Heritage Dictionary of the English Language*, for example, provides four definitions: 1) A relatively large group of people organised under a single, usually independent government; a country. The territory occupied by such a group of people; 2) The government of a sovereign state; 3) A people who share common customs, origins, history, and frequently language; a nationality; 4) A federation or tribe, especially one composed of Native Americans. The territory occupied by such a federation or tribe.[6]

The modern European nation-states are generally defined in accordance with the first definition. The history of this particular kind of organisation into states started with the Peace of Westphalia in 1648, which resulted in the spread of an international system for the formation of independent sovereign states.[7] The development of the new system within various European countries reveals significant similarities related to connections between modernity, industrialisation, democratisation and 'the nationalisation of the masses', or 'the making of peasants into citizens'.[8] To a large extent the

5 Löfgren particularly highlights 'the strong homogenizing effects of the period of strong "welfare state nationalism" in Denmark and Sweden after the Second World War' when discussing development in the Öresund Region after the bridge connecting Sweden and Denmark was opened; Löfgren, 'Regionauts: The Transformation of Cross-Border Regions in Scandinavia', p. 202.

6 *The American Heritage Dictionary of the English Language*, updated 2005, online publication.

7 Hettne, B., Sörlin, S., and Østergård, U., *Den globala nationalismen* (Stockholm, 2006), pp.17-39.

8 Mosse, G.L., *The Nationalization of the Masses: Political Symbolism and Mass Movements in Germany from the Napoleonic Wars Through the Third Reich* (New York, 1975); Weber, E., *Peasants into Frenchmen: The Modernization of Rural France 1870-1914* (London, 1976). Mosse discusses the role of art and aesthetics in the 'nationalization of the masses in Germany', while Weber analyses the relationship between the 'making of peasants into Frenchmen' and the 'modernization of rural France'.

success of a nationalisation process was related to the existence of institutions supervised by the state, such as the educational system, conscription armies, mass media, health care, and various social and cultural institutions. Furthermore, the spread of a common language, history and literature supported by state institutions played a significant role in the process of making citizens. According to the sociologist Liah Greenfeld, there is a strong connection between national identity and modernity. Greenfeld even claims that national identity constitutes the founding principle of modernity. One effect is that collective identities have increasingly been seen as connected with independent nation-states. In the Swedish context, the modernisation of society after the Second World War is strongly connected to the vision of a 'People's Home', first formulated by the Social Democrat Per Albin Hansson in a speech delivered in 1928. This vision provided a powerful model for a brand of nationalism which has been termed 'welfare state nationalism'.[9] From the perspective of present-day cultural mobilisation among ethnic and linguistic historical minorities in Sweden, this discourse of nationalism is problematic, both because of its culturally homogenising effects and because of the exclusion of ethnic minorities from the notion of the Swedish nation: 'The Swedish People's Home in Per Albin Hansson's classical version was no doubt planned for ethnic Swedes'.[10]

The intention of the title of this article, 'Anticolonial and Postcolonial De-/Constructions of the Nation', is to draw attention to negotiations about how to define 'nation'. Clearly, definitions of the concept involve ideological and political aspects. In his famous article, 'DissemiNation: Time, Narrative and the Margins of the Modern Nation', Homi K. Bhabha discusses this theme from a postcolonial perspective.[11] His main point is that homogenising nationalist pedagogies have contributed to constructing the notion of the nation as a homogeneous entity, but that this construction is challenged by anticolonial and postcolonial alternative narratives which deconstruct homogenising narratives of modernity. He particularly emphasises the need to question 'that progressive metaphor of modern social cohesion – *the many*

9 See Löfgren's discussion of development in Denmark and Sweden after the Second World War; Löfgren, 'Regionauts: The Transformation of Cross-Border Regions in Scandinavia', p. 202.

10 Hettne, Sörlin and Østergård, *Den globala nationalismen*, p. 400 (my translation). This observation is important with respect to this article's discussion of the response from ethnic minorities to notions of an ethnically pure nation-state.

11 Bhabha, H.K., 'DissemiNation: Time, Narrative and the Margins of the Modern Nation', in: Bhabha H.K., *The Location of Culture* (London/New York, 2008), pp. 199-244.

as one – shared by organic theories of the holism of culture and community, and theorists who treat gender, class or race as social totalities that are expressive of unitary collective experiences'.[12] In this context he highlights the potential of minority discourse to subvert homogenising narratives of the modern nation and its nationalising pedagogies through bottom-up performances of alternative narratives.[13] One characteristic of Bhabha's analysis of the struggle to define the nation and how to narrate it, which is relevant to the argument of this article, is that he distinguishes between the pedagogical knowledges of state institutions disseminated from the top, down to the people, and performative, popular subversions expressed through minority and 'marginal' discourses which confront, contradict or negate the logic of the idea of '*the many as one*'.[14]

With Bhabha's analysis as a theoretical point of departure, the present article argues that Pohjanen and Kirsti Johansson's survey of Tornedalian Finnish literature, *Den tornedalsfinska litteraturen. Från Kexi till Liksom*, offers a performative deconstruction of a Swedish homogenising discourse of the modern nation-state. The ideological vantage point is that of anticolonial and postcolonial criticism of internal colonialism and assimilation politics which have contributed to the marginalisation of the Tornedalian Finnish ethnic and linguistic minority in Sweden. While deconstructing a top-down national pedagogy connected with modernity and its dissemination through state institutions, *Den tornedalsfinska litteraturen* also presents an alternative interpretation of the nation, namely the idea of the nation as constituted by an ethnic and linguistic group whose traditional homeland overlaps the borders of present-day nation-states. In this case the group is the Tornedalians, who share common customs, origins, history and language. This coincides with the third definition presented in *The American Heritage Dictionary of the English Language*. Beliefs in shared ancestry and ideas of a common culture are intimately linked to assertions of both ethnic identity and national identity. However, it is important to keep in mind that both ethnicity and nation are constructed in discourse: 'the claims about ancestry and culture may in both cases be as much a matter of fiction and myth as a matter of fact'.[15]

12 *Ibidem*, p. 204

13 See the section 'Of Margins and Minorities', Bhabha, 'DissemiNation', pp. 217-226.

14 *Ibidem*, p. 223

15 Fenton, S. and May, S., 'Ethnicity, Nation and "Race": Connections and Disjunctures', in: Fenton S. and May, S., eds., *Ethnonational Identitites* (Houndsmill/New York, 2002), p. 2.

One important aspect of challenges to culturally homogenising narratives of the nation-state, which tend to conflate the nation with the state, is that the state may be represented as multiethnic, multicultural, multilingual and multinational. This does not imply that there has to be a consensus within an ethnic group with regard to the supposition of a historically shared 'common culture': '[t]he supposition of a historically shared "common culture" in an ethnic group is open to question just as it is in the case of a nation'.[16]

As mentioned above, this article aims to analyse Pohjanen and Johansson's contribution to a discursive construction of a Tornedalian Finnish nation in *Den tornedalsfinska litteraturen.* This construction implies the use of symbols which are traditionally employed to represent a nation, namely maps and flags. Both these symbols are found on the cover of *Den tornedalsfinska litteraturen.*

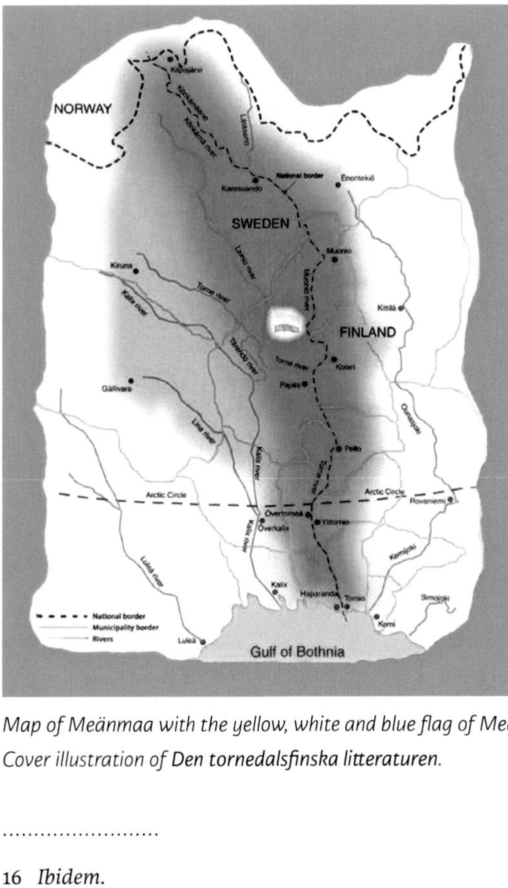

Map of Meänmaa with the yellow, white and blue flag of Meänmaa in the centre.
Cover illustration of **Den tornedalsfinska litteraturen**.

16 *Ibidem.*

While Fenton and May emphasise the closeness in meaning of 'nation' and 'ethnie' (or ethnic group) they also highlight that the status of *nation* is often connected with claims of a greater degree of formal civic recognition, self-determination or self-governance. This is one reason why the term is controversial and often avoided in political forums which hesitate to grant or deny rights to minorities and indigenous peoples.[17] During the 1980s, anticolonial perspectives influenced Sámi challenges to colonialism from the vantage point of the academic disciplines of historiography and the social sciences, and from that of artistic representations.[18] Since then the status of ethnic and linguistic minorities has changed in Nordic countries. Today the Sámi are recognised as a national minority in Norway, Sweden and Finland, and there is a consensus among political decision-makers that Sámi culture and the major Sámi language, North Sámi, should be preserved.[19] The emergence of Sámi ethnonationalism is based on the construction of a transnational nation, Sápmi, which overlaps northern Norway, Sweden and Finland, as well as the Kola peninsula in Russia.[20] This is one example of a nation without a state, constituted by an ethnic group. One element of the comparatively new construction of a Sámi nation is that it reflects the fact that the identity formations of groups of people that have been culturally and politically marginalised through history tend to evolve in opposition to the majority culture which is conceived of as oppressive: 'ethnic [minority] groups define themselves in a situation where others are defining them, often with some expressions of hostility, suspicion and rejection. Thus ideas of nation and ideas of who properly belongs to the nation are essential to the self-awareness of ethnic groups'.[21] The issue of identity formation in the cultural mobilisation of ethnic minorities and indigenous peoples is closely related to power asymmetries and tensions between majority and minority cultures,

17 Fenton and May, 'Ethnicity, Nation and "Race"', pp. 4-5.

18 Magga, O.L., 'Are We Finally to Get Our Rights?', in: Brøsted, J. et al. eds., *Native Power: The Quest for Autonomy and Nationhood of Indigeous Peoples* (Bergen/Oslo/Stavanger/Tromsø, 1985); Gaup. N., *Kautokeino-opprøret*, English title: *The Kautokeino Rebellion* (Rubicon, 2008); Valkeapää, N.A., *Beaivi áhcážan*, English translation, *The Sun, My Father* (Kautokeino, 1997).

19 For a survey of language legislation in Sweden concerning the Sami languages, see Kulonen, U-M., Seurajärvi-Kari, I. and Pulkkinen, R., eds., *The Saami. A Cultural Encyclopaedia* (Vammala, 2005), p. 180. For a brief survey, see Solbakk, J.T., ed./author, *The Sámi People: A Handbook* (Karasjok, 2006), which presents facts about Sámi culture and surveys of the language situation in all the states overlapped by Sápmi.

20 Kulonen, Seurajärvi-Kari and Pulkkinen, eds., *The Saami*, pp. 294-295.

21 Fenton, *Ethnicity*, p. 165.

which provides a rationale for the use of anticolonial and postcolonial critical perspectives on cultural mobilisation among the Sámi and Tornedalian Finns.

The fairly recent change in the status of the Sámi people provides an example of a break with the history of nation-building and nationalisation of the populations of Norway, Sweden and Finland during the nineteenth and first part of the twentieth century. This development is paralleled by Tornedalian Finnish cultural mobilisation. Today the status of the Swedish Tornedalian Finns may be described as that of an ethnic and linguistic minority in the Swedish-Finnish borderland. In the discourse of present-day Tornedalian Finnish ethnonational mobilisation, this borderland is referred to as 'Meänmaa', which is Tornedalian Finnish for 'Our land'. The name has had a breakthrough in mainstream media – being used recurrently in the Finnish news programme, *Uutiset*, broadcast on Swedish national television.

Both Sámi and Tornedalian Finnish ethnonational mobilisation are closely related to challenges to and negotiations concerning the content of national culture in the Scandinavian nation-states. These challenges to and negotiations of state-centred 'narrations of the nation' have been successful in several respects. One example from a Swedish context is that both Sámi and Meänkieli (Tornedalian Finnish literally meaning 'Our language') were granted the status of official national minority languages in Sweden in 2000.[22] This development is related to transformations in 'the narration of the nation'[23] and critical examinations of processes of nation-building and state-centred culturally homogenising nationalism. These are incentives, both of Sámi and Tornedalian Finnish cultural mobilisation, which, under the influence of anticolonial and postcolonial perspectives, aim at decolonising the minds of the Sámi and Tornedalian Finns.[24]

22 Gröndahl, S., 'Inledning. Från "mångkulturell" till "mångspråkig" litteratur?', in: Gröndahl, S., ed., *Litteraturens gränsland. Invandrar- och minoritetslitteratur i nordiskt perspektiv* (Uppsala, 2002), pp. 11-34; Heith, A., *Texter – medier – kontexter* (Lund, 2006), pp. 50-52.

23 See Bhabha, 'DissemiNation', pp. 199-244.

24 The decolonisation of the minds of the Sámi is a theme explored by Vuokko Hirvonen, who wrote the first academic thesis entirely in a Sámi language (North Sámi), published in 1998. The theme of decolonising the minds of colonised peoples is central both to Ngugi Wa Thiong'o's *Decolonizing the Mind*, which has also been a source of inspiration in the analysis of minorities in the North, and Smith's *Decolonizing Methodologies*. Hirvonen's thesis was published in English in 2008: Hirvonen, V., *Voices from Sápmi: Sámi Womens' Path to Authorship* (Kautokeino 2008).

One important source of inspiration for the Maori researcher Linda Tuhiwai Smith's proposal of a decolonising methodology involving the decolonisation of minds is Foucault's notion of the cultural archive and his analysis of strategies for disciplining individuals.[25] It is relevant to the analysis of this article that Foucault's emphasis on the role of systems of classification and representation for establishing cultural hierarchies may be used when analysing mechanisms of inclusion and exclusion at play in nationalisation processes which have aimed at cultural and linguistic homogenisation. The creation of national cultural archives complied with the nationalisation of the inhabitants of modern nation-states. One important discourse in this context is that of historiography, which has always played a major role in the 'nationalisation of the masses', both by providing a narrative of a common past and by legitimising the nation. This constitutes one incentive for present-day critical examinations of national historiography which has marginalised and disempowered ethnic and linguistic minorities. Assimilation politics, which has resulted in the loss of language and status, is one target of this kind of research and cultural production. Although the historian Lars Elenius – who has written extensively on the history of Fenno-Ugric minorities in Northern Sweden – has pointed out that there is no uniform history of a politics of exclusion and disempowerment of the Tornedalian Finnish minority in Sweden, it is obvious that the emotional response to Swedish assimilation politics, as well as ethnic and linguistic discrimination, expressed in literary writing by authors such as Bengt Pohjanen (1944) and Mikael Niemi (1959) provides a more complicated picture than Elenius's survey of the legislation and politics which have affected the Fenno-Ugric minorities.[26] According to Elenius, the Swedish Tornedalian Finns were not subject to political discrimination, but they were subjected to assimilatory language politics from the latter part of the nineteenth century onwards.[27]

25 Smith, L.T., *Decolonizing Methodologies: Research and Indigenous Peoples* (London/New York, 2006), p. 51, pp. 68-69.

26 Elenius, L., *Nationalstat och minoritetspolitik. Samer och finskspråkiga minoriteter i ett jämförande nordiskt perspektiv* (Lund, 2006); Heith, A., 'Contemporary Tornedalian Fictions by Ester Cullblom and Annika Korpi', *Nora: Nordic Journal of Feminist and Gender Research* 2 (2009a), note 8, p. 86.

27 Elenius, *Nationalstat och minoritetspolitik*, p. 255.

One poem significant to the early Tornedalian Finnish cultural mobilisation in Sweden, Bengt Pohjanen's 'I was born without language', presents a sombre picture of identity loss connected with the loss of language.[28] The poem, which was published for the first time in the 1970s,[29] depicts an emotional response to assimilation politics, resulting in loss of self-esteem. It forcefully foregrounds the theme of discipline and punishment in a state-regulated mandatory school: 'I was whipped at school/ into language, clarity/ nationality/ I was whipped to contempt/ for that which was mine/ the want of a language/ and the border'.[30] The mode of experiencing depicted by Pohjanen is connected to a practice which involves socialisation into a culture of poverty and failure. Although decades have passed since the poem was first printed, the theme of socialisation into failure still prevails today, for example in Mikael Niemi's breakthrough as a writer of fiction, which came with *Populärmusik från Vittula* (*Popular Music from Vittula*) in 2000. In the novel's fourth chapter the narrator enumerates what the Swedish Tornedalian Finnish children were taught at school: 'We spoke broken Finnish without being Finns, we spoke broken Swedish without being Swedes. We were nothing'.[31]

In his book on internal colonialism, Michael Hechter claims that the practice of socialisation into cultures of poverty was systematically carried out in a British context with respect to the establishment of power asymmetries between the centre of the British nation and its Celtic fringes, as well as in an American context with respect to the treatment of Black

28 For an English translation of the poem, see Heith, A., 'Fluid Identities and the Use of History: The Northern Lights Route and the Writings of Bengt Pohjanen', in: Fornäs, J. and Fredriksson, M., eds., *Inter. A European Cultural Studies Conference in Sweden* (Linköping, 2007), p. 235. This translation is reprinted on Pohjanen's homepage: www.sirillus.se.

29 It was published for the first time in 1973 in a suite of poems with the title 'Jag är född utan språk' [I was born without language] in the ecumenical journal *Vår Lösen*. It was also reprinted at the very beginning of Bengt Pohjanen and Eeva Muli's Meänkieli grammar, *Meänkieli rätt och lätt. Grammatik i Meänkieli* (Överkalix, 2005), p. 5.

30 Heith, 'Fluid Identities and the Use of History', p. 235.

31 Niemi, M., *Populärmusik från Vittula* (Stockholm, 2000), p. 50 (my translation).

Americans.[32] Socialisation into cultures of poverty and failure, identity loss and loss of self-esteem certainly are recurring themes in Swedish Tornedalian Finnish literary writing, as well as in present-day research on indigenous peoples and ethnic and linguistic minorities that have suffered from the effects of colonialism and nationalisation which conflate nation and state. The process of being socialised into a 'culture of poverty', or the effacement and denial of the cultural roots of a linguistic minority through assimilation, may furthermore be interpreted as versions of disciplining as analysed by Foucault in *Discipline and Punish*.[33] One of Foucault's points is that discipline (he is particularly concerned with the eighteenth and nineteenth centuries) has functioned in terms of 'formulas of domination', at work in schools, hospitals and military organisations.[34] Considering the role of state-regulated education as a 'formula of domination' designed around the language and cultural capital of the imagined nation promoted by the political elite in power, Pohjanen's alternative view of this process from the vantage point of somebody being disciplined and disempowered due to ethnicity and language, and Niemi's elaboration of the same theme more than three decades later, make it evident that the paradigm of culturally homogenising nationalism has come under attack through the cultural mobilisation performed by Swedish Tornedalian Finnish authors.

A Critical View on the Discourse of National Historiography

Cultural homogenisation in compliance with a nationalism based on the ethnic majority as a model for minorities to imitate[35] is being challenged

32 Hechter, M., *Internal Colonialism. The Celtic Fringe in British National Development, 1536-1966* (London, 1975). Although Hechter's proposal of a connection between internal colonialism and socialisation into cultures of poverty and failure is useful for the analysis of the situation of the Tornedalian Finnish minority in Sweden, other elements of his analysis which tend to present the relationship between 'colonisers' and 'colonised' as too static and homogeneous are less useful.

33 Foucault, M., *Discipline and Punish: The Birth of the Prison* (London, 1977).

34 *Ibidem*, p. 137.

35 Hettne, Sörlin and Østergård elaborate upon this model with examples from various states, for example India; Hettne, Sörlin and Østergård, *Den globala nationalismen*, p. 375. They make the point that this model is also applicable to critical examinations of Swedish assimilation politics.

by present-day Sámi, Swedish Tornedalian Finnish and Norwegian Kven[36] cultural mobilisation. The current struggle to define the meaning of 'nation' is related to a number of transformations in demographics and the view of ethnic and linguistic minorities. As a result, the notion of a culturally and ethnically homogeneous nation-state has become increasingly obsolete. In a state which acknowledges the rights of linguistic minorities to preserve and cultivate their languages, nationalism cannot be understood as a conflation of nation and state. Nor can Herderian (or other) notions of nationalism which emphasise a common culture, nature and consciousness (subsumed under the idea of a 'National Spirit' or 'Geist') provide viable descriptions of nationalism in states which officially, through legislation, have declared themselves culturally heterogeneous, multilingual and multiethnic. This implies that the meaning of 'nationalism' has to be complemented with the notion of polynational states and with that of nations overlapping state borders. It also involves national archives of knowledge, based on the paradigm of homogenising nationalism, being complemented by the alternative histories and knowledges of ethnic and linguistic minorities.

Bengt Pohjanen and Kirsti Johansson's survey of Tornedalian Finnish literature provides one example of a critical view on the discourse of state-centred national historiography. Against the backdrop of the role of a belief in a shared ancestry, necessary for the assertion of both ethnic and national identities, it is of particular interest to consider what elements Pohjanen and Johansson propose as part of a Tornedalian Finnish ancestry and origin in the context of present-day Sweden. One such element is found in the subtitle: 'From Kexi to Liksom'. On this basis, the history begins with the farmer-poet Antti Keksi's poem about the breaking of ice in the Torne River in 1677.[37]

36 The Kvens in northernmost Norway are a Fenno-Ugric ethnic and linguistic minority. In 1995 they became a national minority in Norway in accordance with the Council of Europe's Convention on National Minorities; Niemi, E., 'Kvenene – fra innvandrere til utvandrere', in: Mellem, R., ed., *Innsyn i kvensk historie, språk og kultur.* Seminarrapport, Tromsø, mars 2002 (Tromsø, 2003), pp. 43-57. The intensification of Kven ethnonational mobilisation in recent years is reflected in a collection of articles published after a seminar on Kven history, language and culture held at Tromsø University in 2002; Mellem, R., ed., *Innsyn i kvensk historie, språk og kultur.* Seminarrapport, Tromsø, mars 2002 (Tromsø, 2003).

37 The name 'Keksi' is alternatively spelt 'Kexi' and 'Keksi' in *Den tornedalsfinska litteraturen.* I will use the spelling 'Keksi' except when quoting passages where the other spelling is used.

Keksi's poem has been published in Finnish, Meänkieli and Swedish, which reflects current linguistic pluralism rather than the language situation in the seventeenth century when the Torne Valley was regarded as a peripheral region within the Swedish kingdom where Finnish was spoken.[38] Elenius actually states that before 1809, the year a new border divided the Tornedalians, the Torne Valley *was* a peripheral valley in the Swedish kingdom. This is of course a problematic statement when considered from a critical decolonising perspective which rejects the spatial vocabulary of colonialism due to its marginalisation of groups of people on the basis of their assumed distance from the colonial centre.[39]

One element of the Swedish cultural archive produced in compliance with homogenising nationalism which is challenged by Pohjanen and his co-author Johansson is related to the system of classification of Tornedalian culture from an outsider's perspective. This type of classification is a recurring ingredient, for example, in travellers' tales and museum exhibitions which have contributed to producing knowledge about people and places constructed as 'strange' or 'foreign'. One instance of this which Pohjanen particularly highlights is Selma Lagerlöf's contribution to the education of Swedish schoolchildren with *The Wonderful Adventures of Nils* (*Nils Holgerssons underbara resa genom Sverige*), a geography book

38 Elenius, *Nationalstat och minoritetspolitik*, p. 255.

39 In her discussion of a decolonising methodology from the vantage point of indigenous studies, Smith emphasises the role played by conceptions of space in the marginalisation of indigenous peoples and various ethnic groups. She particularly highlights the function of notions of 'The Centre' and 'The Outside' for establishing borders between the centre and outside/margin/periphery; Smith, *Decolonizing Methodologies*, pp. 50-53. The strategy of decentring centres which have marginalised various groups of people is of major importance to a number of research fields, most notably indigenous studies, postcolonial studies and feminist and gender studies. See also Narayan, U. and Harding, S., eds., *Decentering the Center: Philosophy for a Multicultural, Postcolonial, and Feminist World* (Bloomington/Indianapolis 2000). Another instance of the role of a centre and margin dichotomy, this time in a Finnish national context, is provided by Juha Ridanpää's analysis of Rosa Liksom's literary writings. Ridanpää particularly emphasises the impact of 'postcolonialistic [sic] ideas' for his own discussion of the relationship between the North and the South in a Finnish context; Ridanpää, J., 'Rosa Liksom's Literary North: Traditional Confrontations or New Discursive Practices?', in: Möller, F. and Pehkonen, S., eds., *Encountering the North. Cultural Geography, International Relations and Northern Landscapes* (Aldershot/Burlington, 2003), p. 107.

commissioned by the Swedish Elementary Schoolteachers' Association's textbook committee.[40] The book was published in two volumes in 1906-1907 and became a great success both in Sweden and abroad. Although the socialising role of *Nils Holgerssons underbara resa genom Sverige* in mandatory state-regulated schools has evaporated – it has long since lost its role as educational material for Swedish schoolchildren learning national geography and history – the book remains a symbol of homogenising nationalism in the context of Pohjanen's contribution to present-day Swedish Tornedalian Finnish cultural mobilisation. This is emphasised by Pohjanen when elaborating upon the theme of visitors' and travellers' marginalisation of Tornedalian culture: 'Selma painted a picture of Sweden as it really was NOT. Nils Holgersson never saw us'.[41]

Myth-making and fictionalisation are two strategies used by Pohjanen and Johansson in their deconstruction of Swedish national literary history. One important element of their proposal for an alternative history is the appropriation and circulation of the Finnish Kalevala tradition. This strategy, which proposes that Tornedalian Finns on both sides of the present-day Swedish-Finnish border share a mythic past with the Finnish nation, has a performative function. From the vantage point of cultural studies, Stuart Hall has emphasised the active use of history and myth-making in constructions of cultural identity. When discussing this theme he makes the point that constructions of common origins involve the proposition that there are shared characteristics which provide a connecting glue in the form of solidarity and allegiance: '[i]dentification is constructed on the back of a recognition of some common origin or shared characteristics with another group, or with an ideal, and with the natural closure of solidarity and allegiance established on this foundation'.[42]

One major characteristic of Swedish Tornedalian Finnish cultural mobilisation is that identity is multiplied when nation and state are not conflated, due to a distinction made between citizenship and nationality.[43]

40 Heith, A., '"Nils Holgersson Never Saw Us": A Tornedalian Finnish Literary History', in: Hansson, H. and Norberg, C., eds., *Cold Matters, Northern Studies Monographs*, no. 1 (Umeå, 2009b), pp. 42-43.

41 *Ibidem*, p. 47 (my translation).

42 Hall, S., 'Introduction. Who needs "identity"?', in: Hall, S. and Du Gay, P., eds., *Questions of Cultural Identity* (London/Thousand Oaks/New Delhi, 2005), p. 2.

43 For a short survey of theories of citizenship, see Bellamy, R., *Citizenship: A Very Short Introduction* (Oxford, 2008).

In the case of Tornedalian Finnish cultural mobilisation performed in *Den tornedalsfinska litteraturen*, this is reflected in the deployment of elements from the Kalevala tradition. Given that *The Kalevala* is Finland's national epic and that it was part of the patriotic movement in the nineteenth century which had a great impact on the shaping of a Finnish national identity and ideas of a shared past and origin, it is a deconstructive move on the part of Pohjanen and Johansson when they use this material in their present-day proposal of a common Tornedalian Finnish identity.[44]

Pohjanen and Johansson's proposition of a Tornedalian Finnish literary history in fact involves the construction of a number of beginnings which differentiate Tornedalian Finnish literary production from Swedish and Finnish national historiography. As we saw above, the subtitle, 'From Kexi to Liksom', indicates one of the beginnings proposed – the dissemination of Antti Keksi's poem of 1677. However, this poem, which is part of an oral tradition, was not printed until 1829. In the Swedish national encyclopaedia (*Nationalencyklopedin*), Keksi is said to be the first author from the Swedish province of Norrbotten. From the vantage point of the administrative centre, before 1809 the Torne Valley, in the northeastern part of Norrbotten, was seen as a peripheral region where Finnish was spoken.[45] This linguistic backdrop implies that Keksi's poem did not exist in the linguistic shape in which it was later reproduced in *Den tornedalsfinska litteraturen* (that is Swedish, Finnish and Meänkieli). As a matter of fact the notion of a specific Tornedalian Finnish language did not exist in the seventeenth century. The term 'Meänkieli' is of fairly recent origin, connected to the emerging cultural mobilisation among the Tornedalian Finns in the 1970s and 1980s.

According to one account, the term 'Meänkieli' was introduced in a brochure distributed to Tornedalian homes in the 1970s. The brochure informed schoolchildren and their parents about the possibility of studying Meänkieli at school if the language was used at home ('hemspråk').[46] Another account claims that the term was used in print for the first time in an article published in the regional newspaper *Haparandabladet* in the early 1980s.[47] Whatever the case may be, the first appearance of the term 'Meänkieli' in print, the launching of the notion of Meänkieli as a specific language on parity with other national languages (such as Swedish and Finnish), reflects

44 Heith, 'Nils Holgersson Never Saw Us', p. 50.

45 Elenius, *Nationalstat och minoritetspolitik*, p. 255.

46 *Ibidem*, pp. 295-298.

47 Edlund, L. and Frängsmyr, T., eds., *Norrländsk uppslagsbok*, vol. 3 (Umeå, 1995), p. 147.

the importance of the role of language in ethnonational mobilisation. In other words, according to Elenius, the language question was decisive for the emergence of Tornedalian Finnish ethnopolitical mobilisation.[48] When the role of language is considered, the publication of Keksi's seventeenth-century poem in Swedish, Finnish and Meänkieli in *Den tornedalsfinska litteraturen* may be related to performative aspects of ethnonational mobilisation. As already mentioned, this may involve a deconstruction of established national cultural archives. It certainly implies a focus on the future just as much as a preoccupation with origins and ancestry. Ethnonational identities, as well as other brands of identification, are very much about becoming: 'identities are about questions of using the resources of history, language and culture in the process of becoming rather than being'.[49]

The other author highlighted in the subtitle of *Den tornedalsfinska litteraturen*, Rosa Liksom (1958, pseudonym for Anni Ylävaara), also draws attention to the importance of not conflating nation and state. According to the knowledge produced from the vantage point of the Swedish and Finnish state-centred national cultural cores, Liksom is a Finnish author of fiction who writes about both urban settings and sparsely populated regions. In an analysis which employs perspectives from cultural geography and postcolonial theory, Juha Ridanpää discusses the role of the themes of the centre and margin and their relationship to power in collections of short stories by Rosa Liksom.[50] Although Ridanpää discerns some ambiguities when it comes to the interpretation of Liksom's representations of the North and South in a Finnish context, he has no doubts about the ideological implications of the division: [t]his relationship between centre and margin is about using power, about domination in relation to bureaucratic, economic, political and cultural activities, which form all kinds of inequalities and subordinate relationships'.[51]

48 Elenius, *Nationalstat och minoritetspolitik*, p. 255.

49 Hall, 'Introduction. Who needs "identity"?', p. 4.

50 The collections Ridanpää mentions are: *Yhden yön pysäkki* (1985), *Unohdettu vartti* (1986) and *Tyhjän tien paratiisit* (1989); Ridanpää, 'Rosa Liksom's Literary North', pp. 103-125. A collection of short stories, Liksom, *One Night Stands*, was published in English in 1993.

51 Ridanpää, 'Rosa Liksom's Literary North', p. 107. In connection with this statement Ridanpää makes an explicit reference to Ashcroft, B., Griffiths, G. and Tiffin, H., *The Empire Writes Back: Theory and Practice in Post-colonial Literatures* (London, 1989), thus proposing that a North-South division in a Finnish national context indeed represents a version of colonialism.

Ridanpää's analysis is not the only one to highlight power asymmetries between North and South in a Finnish national context through the use of critical perspectives from postcolonial theory.

The impact of notions of a centre and its margins for literary production is also emphasised in Matti Savolainen's explorations of literary production in the margins of the Finnish nation-state, as well as in Veli-Pekka Lehtola's examinations of Sámi identity-formation on the fringes of the national centre.[52] According to Ridanpää, Savolainen and Lehtola there is a tradition of marginalising authors from the North in the Finnish nation-state, context. With this in mind, Rosa Liksom's conscious deployment of elements which represent and distinguish between 'northernness' and 'southernness' may be interpreted as a preoccupation with the theme of internal colonialism. This backdrop also adds a specific significance to the fact that she is identified as the 'contemporary', modern author in the subtitle of *Den tornedalsfinska litteraturen.*

In the context of Tornedalian Finnish cultural mobilisation, the 'established' fact that Liksom is a Finnish author does not prevent Pohjanen and Johansson from classifying her as a Tornedalian Finnish one. One obvious reason for this is the fact that she was born in Meänmaa (on the Finnish side of the border). More importantly, there is a strategic dimension to the inclusion of Liksom among the authors presented in *Den tornedalsfinska litteraturen.* As mentioned above, her representations of a national centre, which may be interpreted as a marginalisation of the North, concords with Pohjanen and Johansson's critical view of discourses of nationalisation which have negatively affected the Tornedalian Finns. Liksom is also the only woman author presented in *Den tornedalsfinska litteraturen.* Furthermore, she is relatively young and contemporary when compared to the other authors presented. The fact that she is not exclusively associated with Meänmaa, but just as much (perhaps even more) with urban Helsinki, makes it possible for her to transgress the prevailing geographical dichotomy between province and centre. When it comes to aesthetics, Liksom represents innovation. She is considered a somewhat unconventional prose writer with a personal literary style. Thus, with the notion of ethnonational identity formation as a process which

52 Savolainen, M., 'Keskusta, marginalia, kirjallisuus', in: Savolainen, M., ed., *Marginalia ja Kirjallisus. Ääniä suomalaisen kirjallisuuden reunoilta* (Helsinki, 1995), pp. 7-35; Lehtola, V.P., *Rajamaan identiteetti. Lappilaisuuden rakentuminen 1920- ja 1930-luvun kirjallisuudessa* (Helsinki, 1997), p. 26.

involves 'becoming rather than being', Liksom fills an important function by providing a complement to the male authors of previous generations who are discussed. Liksom's work may also be related to the themes of migration, lack of belonging and urban life. It is a strategic move on the part of Pohjanen and Johansson to characterise Liksom as 'new and different', and perhaps even a vital move, if Tornedalian Finnish literary production is to play any role in a process of ethnonational becoming.[53] This proposition relies on the hypothesis that newness and diversity are important ingredients of present-day identity formation inspired by postcolonial perspectives, and on the acknowledgement of the impact of gender, migration and age.

There has been considerable critique from feminist points of view of traditional Tornedalian village life.[54] Conflicting narratives, some of which view traditional life with nostalgia and others which are openly critical, make it evident that the relationship between gendering and tradition may be a controversial theme.[55] To sum up Liksom's role in *Den tornedalsfinska litteraturen*, it can be related to issues of gender and migration as well as ideological aspects connected to notions of internal colonialism. In colonial cultural geography, which has defined the North as marginal, there has been a tendency to view authors from northern Scandinavia as marginal by definition. When approaching this theme within a Finnish national context, Ridanpää comments upon the minor part which northern literature has in the history of Finnish literature. He concludes that '[t]his (...) means (...) culture and literature and everything associated [sic] were defined from the South. The northern manner of perceiving what art really is just did not fit

53 Pohjanen, B. and Johansson, K., 'Rosa Liksom – ny och annorlunda', in: *Den tornedalsfinska litteraturen.* Från Kexi till Liksom (Överkalix, 2007), pp. 96-106.

54 Cullblom, E., *Män styr och kvinnor flyr Tornedalen. Kvinnliga strategier i en värld av manlig maktdominans* (Luleå, 1997); Juntti-Henriksson, A.K., *Women Narratives from Tornedalen – Northernmost Sweden. Gender and Culture in Perspective* (Luleå, 2008); Heith, 'Contemporary Tornedalian Fictions by Ester Cullblom and Annika Korpi', pp. 76-80.

55 Cullblom, E., *Första tvättmaskinen i Ohtanajärvi – och andra berättelser från Tornedalen* (Luleå, 2006); Cullblom, E., *Berta och byn. En kvinnas liv i Tornedalen* (Luleå, 2007); Korpi, A., *Hevonen Häst* (Stockholm, 2005); Heith, 'Contemporary Tornedalian Fictions by Ester Cullblom and Annika Korpi', pp. 72-88.

into southern literary categories'.[56] In this colonial geography Liksom both enforces notions of North and South as significantly different, as well as invokes other binaries, such as rural versus urban. When it comes to the construction of cultural liminalities, Liksom avoids crude dichotomies which present static and homogeneous images of North and South, rural and urban. Her representations, being both ambiguous and complex, add a dose of experimentation and flux to *Den tornedalsfinska litteraturen*, which, as mentioned, is a prerequisite if Pohjanen and Johansson's proposal of a Tornedalian Finnish literary tradition is to encompass aesthetic renewal and progress.[57] Considering the role of aesthetic experimentation in traditional literary histories, the emphasis on Liksom's 'newness' and 'difference' should not be underestimated.

The Role of Publishers

The role of national education, as well as a common language, in the idea of a people which forms a nation, was emphasised by Johann Gottfried von Herder as early as the eighteenth century: 'Denn jedes Volk ist Volk: es hat seine National-Bildung wie seine Sprache'.[58] As Benedict Anderson points out, this conception of 'nation-ness' had a wide influence in nineteenth-century Europe and on subsequent theorising about the nature of nationalism.[59] Anderson also foregrounds the development of 'national print-languages' as contributing to the notion of 'nation': '[t]he "nation" thus became something capable of being consciously aspired to from early on (...), the "nation" proved an invention on which it was impossible

56 Ridanpää, 'Rosa Liksom's Literary North', p. 112. The issue of gender and geography with respect to inclusion in and exclusion from a nation's cultural archive is specifically addressed by Sinikka Tuohimaa who has studied northern Finnish women authors. Tuohimaa claims that they have been forgotten, which of course is one way of saying that they have been marginalised; Tuohimaa, S., 'Pohjois-Suomen unohdetut naiskirjailijat', in: Majasaari K. and Rytkönen M. eds., *Silmukoita verkossa. Sukupuoli, kirjallisuus ja identiteetti* (Oulu, 1997), pp. 46-47.

57 Of course there are also other Tornedalian Finnish authors who experiment, Pohjanen himself for example. My point is that Liksom is foregrounded as a representative of renewal and 'difference' ('ny och annorlunda') in *Den tornedalsfinska litteraturen*.

58 Quoted from Kemiläinen, A., *Nationalism: Problems Concerning the Word, the Concept and Classification* (Jyväskylä, 1964), note 128, pp. 40-41.

59 Anderson, B., *Imagined Communities: Reflections on the Origin and Spread of Nationalism* (London/New York, 2006), p. 68.

to secure a patent'.[60] Anderson goes on to elaborate on the role of print-language for the construction of nations.

One aspect of *Den tornedalfinska litteraturen* related to the construction of an imagined community of Tornedalian Finns is its conscious aspiration to present Meänkieli as a language which has evolved from the era of oral transmission of Keksi to a contemporary print-language. This is evident in Johansson's presentation of her co-author, Pohjanen, as one of the great Fenno-Ugric linguistic innovators on par with Mikael Agricola (1510-1557) and Elias Lönnrot (1802-1884), which involves Pohjanen being attributed the role of the 'father of Meänkieli as a print-language'.[61] Agricola, who translated *The New Testament* into Finnish in 1548, is considered the father of Finnish literature and the creator of a Finnish written language. Lönnrot, who collected, arranged and published the volume of *The Kalevala* which has become the standard edition in Finland, had a tremendous impact on the creation of Finnish national identity.[62] It is obvious that Fenno-Ugric ethnicity and the Tornedalian Finnish language play major roles in Pohjanen and Johansson's contribution to Tornedalian Finnish cultural mobilisation. This of course challenges homogenising Swedish nationalism, exemplified in *Den tornedalsfinska litteraturen* by Lagerlöf's *Nils Holgerssons underbara resa genom Sverige*, as well as other texts where Tornedalian Finnish culture is viewed from the outside. It is a commonplace in historiography to use denominations such as 'state-regulated colonisation politics', when referring to the colonisation of the North.[63] As the discussion above shows, anticolonial and postcolonial theory may be applied when analysing constructions of a centre and its margins in the establishment of national cultural archives which have excluded or diminished the value of authors from the North. Ridanpää describes the situation as follows from the vantage point of the construction of a Finnish cultural archive:

> With a few exceptions, Lapland, northern Finland and northern authors have been systematically left out when listing what Finnish

60 *Ibidem*, p. 67.

61 Pohjanen and Johansson, *Den tornedalsfinska litteraturen*, pp. 85-86; Heith, 'Nils Holgersson Never Saw Us', p. 45.

62 Heith, 'Nils Holgersson Never Saw Us', p. 45.

63 Elenius, 'Statlig kolonisationspolitik i Sverige', *Nationalstat och minoritetspolitik*, pp. 57-74.

> literature is all about and reaching the list of nationally known authors from the North has been very exceptional, even today. Rosa Liksom has been one of those exceptions.[64]

Rosa Liksom (Photo: Pekka Mustonen).

From the theoretical vantage point of a decolonising methodology, Pohjanen and Johansson's *Den tornedalsfinska litteraturen* presents a challenge to 'state-regulated colonisation politics', which complies with an assimilation politics that has marginalised Tornedalian Finnish culture. In opposition to the spatial vocabulary of colonialism, notions of 'The Centre' are re-semanticised in both Sámi and Tornedalian Finnish ethnonational mobilisation, which involves the claim that there is a traditional Sámi homeland, Sápmi, as well as a Tornedalian Finnish nation, Meänmaa. Placing the emphasis on Meänmaa as a centre of Tornedalian Finnish culture with a specific history, culture and language in *Den tornedalsfinska litteraturen* entails a strategy of deconstructing and re-semanticising the content of 'The Centre' and its margin, or periphery, promoting the notion of a Tornedalian Finnish nation with a cultural centre of its own. This strategy is based on a critique of traditional binaries which by definition have attributed the role of the Other to ethnic and linguistic minorities – to those who are considered to be outside the centre. This critical perspective

64 Ridanpää, 'Rosa Liksom's Literary North', p. 112.

on traditional centres has led to the founding of new publishing houses which explicitly challenge old publishers in capitals or other national centres who have complied with culturally homogenising nationalism. Davvi Girji and DAT are two examples of Sámi publishers located in Sápmi and publishing in Sámi.[65] Kamos and Barents Publisher, both founded by Bengt Pohjanen, are two Swedish Tornedalian Finnish examples. The importance of publishers located *in* the North, is implicit also in Ridanpää's discussion of the situation in Finland. He concludes that when viewed from the outside 'a strong horizon of exoticism [sic] and strangeness has been laid over the image of Lapland. Trying to exceed or break this horizon has been basically an impossibility for northern authors'.[66] No doubt Ridanpää is right when emphasising the element of exotification in travellers', visitors' and other non-locals' representations of the North, but there are also other strategies, such as exclusion and devaluation, both critically examined in *Den tornedalsfinska litteraturen.*

Den tornedalsfinska litteraturen was published by Barents Publisher. Considering the importance of the existence of a print-language for the formation of a nation, suggested by Anderson, the publishing houses which publish in Sámi and Meänkieli and which concentrate on material related to Sápmi and Meänmaa respectively, play a major role in ethnonational linguistic mobilisation which challenges traditions of internal colonialism. This implies that classifications which reinforce notions of the North as a periphery and ideas of ethnic and linguistic minorities as marginal, are viewed as problematic. This is the case, for example, in Lars Wendelius's analysis of differences in status between various Swedish publishers. Wendelius proposes that the publishing business constitutes a hierarchical system with four levels. The most prestigious publishers, according to Wendelius, are Bonniers and Norstedts, both 'old', quality publishers located in Stockholm. On the bottom level of the hierarchy, 'provincial publishers' and 'pronounced ethnic publishers' can be found with other publishers categorised as marginal.[67] From the vantage point of a decolonising analytical framework, this kind of categorisation, which recirculates and reinforces the spatial vocabulary of colonialism, is extremely problematic. One of the major points of Sámi and Tornedalian

65 Solbakk, *The Sámi People*, p. 295.

66 Ridanpää, 'Rosa Liksom's Literary North', p. 112.

67 Wendelius, L., *Den dubbla identiteten. Immigrant- och minoritetslitteratur på svenska 1970-2000* (Uppsala, 2002), p. 25.

Finnish ethnonationalism is that the traditional centres of the Norwegian, Swedish and Finnish states are challenged and complemented with new centres, representing Sápmi and Meänmaa. Publishers play an important role in this process, establishing and consolidating Sámi and Tornedalian Finnish print-languages.

Concluding Remarks

This article has argued that present-day cultural mobilisation in the northern parts of Norway, Sweden and Finland is also transforming the cultural geography of the Nordic nation-states. After the Cold War ended, the issue of limits and boundaries in the North changed. In this context, borders became less static and more permeable than previously as the notion of 'The Northern Dimension' replaced older more stringent, state-centred conceptions of bordering.[68] This article proposed that bordering regimes, at play in the ideological landscape of the building of the modern welfare state after the Second World War, played a major role in the nationalisation of the populations of Norway, Sweden and Finland and that this has changed today as ethnic allegiances and linguistic minority status are employed in deconstructions of state-centred national cultural archives. Notions of internal colonialism provide one important theoretical vantage point for the cultural mobilisation of ethnic and linguistic minorities, particularly in contestations of a spatial vocabulary which has systematically marginalised the North. One example of the employment of decolonising methodologies and the performance of postcolonial critique is Pohjanen and Johansson's contribution to Tornedalian Finnish cultural mobilisation, *Den tornedalsfinska litteraturen*. In promoting the notion of a Tornedalian Finnish nation – the region of Meänmaa, with a language of its own, Meänkieli – Pohjanen and Johansson contribute to a deconstruction of both Swedish and Finnish state-centred constructions of a culturally homogeneous nation.

68 Joenniemi, P., 'Changing Politics along Finland's Borders: From Norden to the Northern Dimension', in: Ahonen, P. and Jukarainen P., eds., *Tearing Down the Curtain, Opening the Gates: Northern Boundaries in Change* (Jyväskylä, 2000), pp. 114-132.

Cultural Transmission

Diaspora Writing from the Balkans

« Elka Agoston-Nikolova »

When discussing major and minor language interaction and transmission processes from one national literature to another, one should also include those individuals (in this case writers and poets) who for various reasons transcend national borders. Do they offer other insights such as a particular perception of individual (and national) identity or a particular treatment of the notions of *time* and *place*, *home* and *abroad*?

The Balkans is a specific geopolitical area with multicultural, multilingual communities. Before the formation of nation states in the region in the nineteenth century, almost all Balkan inhabitants used, if not every day but quite often, at least three languages: their own regional language (Slavic, Albanian etc.), Greek for the Slavic orthodox believers and Turkish for the administration and authorities.

In his 1976 novel *The Three-Arched Bridge*, the Albanian writer Ismail Kadare tells the story of the building of a bridge in fourteenth-century Albania to connect Europe with its eastern parts. A monk, who is acting as translator to the Albanian count and leading the negotiations with the Ottoman party, comments on the 'horrible' language of the foreigners:

> The new arrivals did indeed speak the most horrible tongue. My ears have never heard such babble. Slowly I began to untangle the sounds. I noticed that their numbers were Latin and their verbs generally Greek or Slav, while they used Albanian for the names of things and now and then a word of German.[1]

In *Die gerettete Zunge* [The Tongue Set Free, 1979] from 1977 Elias Canetti gives a good portrayal of the multiethnic nature of a Bulgarian town at the beginning of the twentieth century:

1 Quoted after Apter, E., *The Translation Zone. A New Comparative Literature* (Princeton/Oxford, 2006), p. 131.

> Roustchuk, on the Danube, where I was born, was a wonderful city for a child, and when I say that it was in Bulgaria I am giving an imperfect picture, for there lived many different peoples and on a day one could hear seven or eight languages spoken. Next to the Bulgarians who came from the surrounding villages, there lived many Turks who had their own city quarter next to that of the Spanioles, the Spanish Jews, and our own city part. There were also Albanians, Armenians and Gypsies. From the other side of the Danube Romanians crossed over and sporadically Russians.[2]

With the establishment of nation states and the development of national languages and national consciousness this multiethnic picture changed and seemed to have been banished forever. The question of emigrant literature or simply literature written outside the nation state became connected with the national question. To which national literature should such literary work belong: the one corresponding with the nationhood of the author or the one corresponding with the language in which it is written?

As an example, the Balkan writer Grigor Parlichev (1830-1893), who was born into a Slavic-speaking family in Macedonia, wrote his major literary works, the two long epic poems *The Armatole* and *Skenderbey*, in Greek, while his heroes were Albanians. To which national literature should his work belong? Having lived in different Balkan countries he spoke nearly all of the Balkan languages.

The wars of the 1990s in former Yugoslavia together with recent globalization processes and migration demand a reconsideration of the old question of roots, multiculturalism and bilingualism. Increasing migration from the former Yugoslav republics to Western Europe and the USA during and after the disembodiment of Yugoslavia has resulted in an exile literature that is sometimes written in the language of the host country. Should such writing, and each artistic creation for that matter, necessarily reflect an ethnic or national identity?

It is with these questions in mind that I propose to look now at South Slavic diaspora literature with the aim of considering which kind of cultural transmission we are speaking of here, both in the host and in the home countries. The period under consideration will be from the Second World War down to the present day. In this period we can distinguish three waves of emigration. The first wave came about after or at the time of the establishment of the Communist regimes and concerned voluntary or,

2 Canetti, E., *The Tongue Set Free* (New York, 1979), pp. 4-5.

mainly forced political exile. Writers from this wave of emigration were acclaimed in Western Europe and the United States and could soon enjoy a protected economic position. They were published and translated. Most well-known in Western Europe are writers from Central Europe and Russia such as Vladimir Nabokov (1899-1977), Josef Brodsky (1940-1996), Česlav Miloš (1911-2004) and Milan Kundera (1929). Let me add here the names of Danilo Kiš (1935-1989) and Georgi Markov (1929-1978) from a list of South Slavic exiles. Although banned at home as 'traitors', they were eagerly read clandestinely. The Bulgarian Georgi Markov's work is a strong indictment of the communist system in Bulgaria, portraying the stupidity of its leaders and the cruelty of its secret service. Markov was a broadcaster on the BBC World Service and his works were read on Radio Free Europe, Deutsche Welle and the Voice of America. He was silenced in the notorious 'umbrella poisoning' in September 1978, when a poisoned dart was supposedly fired at him from the tip of an umbrella.

Besides being politically engaged, exile writers from the first wave wrestled with the problems of the identity as an outsider and the loss of home. Having lost, maybe forever, the possibility of returning home, they wrote about what Kiš called 'the plight of the man without a fatherland'.[3] Julia Kristeva (1941), another exile from that period, examines this process in *Strangers to Ourselves*.[4] The writer has a shattered sense of belonging, a shuttling back and forth between two different cultures and two different languages. Such writing challenges the notions of home and abroad: one is an outsider in both worlds. For Kristeva the modern writer is by definition an outsider and even more so in the era of globalization.

In *L'Homme dépaysée* (1996), Tzvetan Todorov coins the term transculturation to describe the hierarchical relationship between the languages one speaks. This hierarchy changes all the time so one no longer knows where home is. 'Je vis désormais dans un espace singulier, à la fois dehors et dedans: étranger "chez moi" (à Sofia), chez moi "l'étranger" (à Paris)'.[5]

In his *Lauta i ožiljci*, a collection of stories from 1994, translated into Dutch as *De luit en de littekens*, Danilo Kiš presents the reader with two confusing and contradictory images of his birthplace. One is that of 'a magical place' (p. 112), the other 'the worst rat hole I visited' (p. 114). Such are the treacherous workings of the memory. For Brodsky memory is never

3 Kiš, D., *De luit en de littekens* (Amsterdam, 1996), pp. 112, 114.

4 Kristeva, J., *Strangers to Ourselves* (New York, 1991).

5 Todorov, T., *L'Homme dépaysée* (Paris, 1996), p. 23.

linear, 'It stumbles, coils, recoils, and digresses to all sides'. It resembles 'a library in alphabetical disorder and with no collected works by anyone'.[6]

Nabokov never used the word 'real' without quotation marks. His work underlines the notion that what is remembered is at best fragmentary and fictional. For him 'the supreme form of reality resides in the imagination'. His novel *The Real Life of Sebastian Knight* (1941) stresses the fragmentariness and inconclusiveness of both the remembered and the 'illusion of real life'. The reader eventually realizes that Sebastian's real life lies elsewhere but that it remains a mystery.[7] The propaganda at home was meant to demonize and silence such writers. But it had the reverse effect and such writers became the heroes of the underground.

The second wave of emigration can be timed with the fall of Communism and the 1990s wars in former Yugoslavia. A number of writer dissidents from former Yugoslavia in particular lived in exile in Western Europe and the US, but their integration was much more difficult and the possibilities for publication much more restricted than for the writers from the first wave of exile. Dubravka Ugrešić (1949), David Albahari (1948), Aleksandar Hemon (1964) and others chose to live and write abroad. Primarily read as Serbian, Croatian and Bosnian writers after the dissemination of the Yugoslav Federation, they represented a non-existent country (the lost home) in every respect.

Dubravka Ugrešić, who was born in Zagreb, was before the war a scholar, literary critic and well-known writer of novels, children's books, and film and television scripts. Ugrešić refused to submit to the limiting scope of obsessive Croatian nationalism under president Tudjman, and therefore chose to live in exile. She was stigmatized by the national media as a yugo-nostalgic, a national mass murderer, a traitor to the fatherland and a witch.[8] She became a so-called enemy of the people, was threatened and consequently forced to live abroad. She currently resides in Amsterdam. In exile she has written books, all of which challenge traditional ideas of genre by combining autobiography and diary with critical essays on the political and cultural situation in former Yugoslavia and (Western) Europe. In her 2005 collection of essays *Nikog Nema Doma* [Nobody's Home], she describes the plight of such non-mainstream individuals:

6 Brodsky, J., *Less Than One* (Middlesex, 1987).

7 Nabokov, V., *The Real Life of Sebastian Knight* (London, 1960).

8 Ugrešić, D., *The Culture of Lies* (London, 1994).

> I live in Amsterdam, yet I do not write in Dutch. What are the Croats to do with me? I write in Croatian, but I have a 'bad reputation' and I come home only for the Christmas holidays. What are the Serbs and the Bosnians to do with me? They can read me in the language in which I write: BCS (Bosnian-Croatian-Serbian) which does not exist anymore.[9]

David Albahari lives in Canada and writes in Serbian, whereas Aleksandar Hemon, who lives in the US, writes in English. The Bulgarian writers Iliya Troyanov (1965) and Dimitré Dinev (1968) both write in German and live in Germany and Austria respectively. With the exception of Iliya Troyanov, literary criticism of and media attention for their work sticks to nationality labels or a general 'Made in the Balkans'. Ugrešić complains of such reductionism:

> Why? Because the reception of literary texts has shown that the luggage of identification bogs them down. It has further been shown that labels actually alter the substance of a literary text and its meaning. Also the identifying label is, in fact, an abbreviated textual interpretation, almost always skewed. Moreover, the label opens up room for reading something into a text that is not there. And, finally, because the identifying label discriminates against the text.[10]

At 'home' the works of these writers are ignored either because of their lack of 'patriotism' or 'love of the country' or simply because of a lack of media information. Dimitré Dinev and Iliya Troyanov were both 'discovered' by Bulgarian readers after they had won important literary awards abroad.

The third wave of exile introduces the 'intellectual nomad' of Edward Said (1935-2003), who published *inter alia* the essay collection *The World, the Text and the Critic* (1983). An increasing number of intellectuals from outside Western Europe have left their native countries and settled abroad, sometimes moving from one country to another, speaking different languages and often writing in a language other than their native one. Goran Stefanovski (1952), a well-known playwright from Macedonia, settled in England in the 1990s, and writes essays and plays in English. Iliya Troyanov (1965), having left Bulgaria at the age of five when his parents

9 Ugrešić, D., *Nobody's Home* (London, 2007), p. 166.

10 *Ibidem*, p. 168.

fled from Communism, has lived in Africa and Western Europe and written novels in German. Tzveta Sofronieva, who was born in Bulgaria in 1963, currently lives in Berlin and writes poetry and prose in Bulgarian, German and English and sometimes in all three at once.

Tzveta Sofronieva (Photo: Yves Noir).

How can this writing of the third wave be read and analyzed? Until now Eastern European exile writing has often been read and analyzed as a political statement, but literature of the third wave is neither part of the national canon nor a 'literature of exile'. It is creative, experimental, self-reflexive individual writing which transcends national borders. Seyhan Azade's study of 'writing outside the nation' introduces a new genre of literary studies: transnational literature.[11] This is about narratives of cultural movement and translation, multiple identities, travel and cross-cultural events. It is difficult to label such writers as belonging to a particular national literature. How can one define Moses Isegawa (1963), who comes from Uganda, lives in the Netherlands but writes in English, or the Indian-born Joydeep Roy-Bhattacharaya, who moved from Calcutta to New York, where he studies philosophy, and has written a novel on Hungarian intellectual circles of the 1960s? Iliya Troyanov's novel, *Der Weltensammler* [The Collector of Worlds] from 2006, is written in German

11 Seyhan, A., *Writing outside the Nation* (Princeton, 2001).

and is about the eccentric Richard Burton, who as an officer in the British army in the nineteenth century travelled and lived in India, Arabia and Africa taking on different identities.[12]

Tzveta Sofronieva's vision is of a world that is neither integral nor multiple but proliferating, 'My language was once a home, now it is a feather in Europe's wings'.[13] Having discarded old labels, writers find it difficult to find new ones. After all, each writer belonging to this second or third wave of immigrants is either already a legitimate part of the national literature of the host country or chooses to be in 'exile' and thus chooses endless motion and border crossing in every possible sense.

To conclude, I would like to present Tzveta Sofronieva's 2008 poem *Ein unbekanntes Wort.* It can be read from two different points of view – that of the poet and that of the reader. Let us consider the poet's point of view. One could ask why does she need to mix three different languages – German, Bulgarian and English – in one poem? Considered from the point of view of national literature and one (major) language, such writing could be regarded as proof of the poet's lack of words in the host language, in this case German. The poet herself would answer that she is fluent in German and has written poems in German but wanted here to stress the sounds and patterns of 'unknown words', which represent a considerable part of any emigrant's existence. This phenomenon has finally been assigned a literary term in post-colonial literary theory: the metonymic gap.[14] The Bulgarian words create such a gap, which reminds the poet of the other language existing in her and at the same time influences the listener (German, English or Bulgarian) by introducing unknown words. This deliberately chosen device transcends the notions of home and home language, which in traditional literary approaches are connected within the boundaries of the nation state. Having thus arrived at the point of view of the reader or listener here, for this poem should be recited, it must be mentioned that the main character in the poem is the poet's twelve-year-old daughter, who is multilingual and for whom there is nothing strange about a mixture of different languages within the same utterance. She represents the global youth nowadays, who easily switch from one language to another, communicate in different SMS languages and chat with friends all over

12 Troyanov, I., *Der Weltensammler* (München, 2006).

13 Spasova, K., 'Her Cities and Languages', *Altera Journal for Gender, Language and Culture* (Sofia, 2007), pp. 42-44.

14 See Ashcroft, B., *Post-Colonial Transformation* (London/New York, 2001).

the world. The present-day literary reality requires new paradigms and new theoretical approaches to express cultural transmission and cultural translation as increasingly practised all over the world.

Ein unbekanntes Wort
Tzveta Sofronieva

Носталгия ist ein Fremdwort:
Homesickness, Heimweh, Nostalgie.
Auf Bulgarisch existiert das Wort nicht
und meine Tochter sagte gestern:
Мамо, имам heimweh за теб.
Der Ort des Bewohnens kann Berlin sein,
Beverly Hills, Bitterfeld, Konska, Paris.
Hauptsache es riecht nach Mama,
nach ihren immer schneller alternden Händen,
die mit Uhus reden können
und stark umarmen.

Wer kommt in meine Arme?
Den hab ich lieb!

Я кажи ми, гълъбче ле бяло,
отгде идеш, що си ми видяло.
Wer kommt, erwartet und geliebt,
in meine Flügel, die eines Kolibris?
Kommt ein Vogel geflogen...
Гугутка гука в усои, леле,
гукни ми гукни, гугутке,
гукни ми гукни пай пукни, леле,
и аз така съм гукала, хееей,
и аз така съм гукала, леле,
кога съм била при мама.
Home, home, sweet home.
Ein Täubchen singt in der Hecke,
ich habe auch so gesungen
als ich bei Mama aufwuchs.

Oh, when my mom combed me
my hair grew long.
Ach, als Mutter mich wusch,
strahlte mein Gesicht.
Du, Vögelein, singe wie damals,
Sing, sing, blow up and die.
Sick, sick, weh, weh, heim, heim.

Ein Wort des Vermissens.

Abwesenheit und Sehnsucht – gefährlich.
Schmerz für Daheim, Zuhause – Krankheit.
Sitzt man da unbeweglich?
Aber es gibt auch Aufbruch, Asyl, Fremdwohnen,
Ein- und Auswandern, изгнание, гурбет,
хъшове, странстване, Wege.
Der Mensch geht und kommt, um wieder zu gehen.
Und auf dem Weg
erreicht das Zurückkehren
auf der anderen Seite das Abbrechen.
Das ist es.
Ein sich drehender Kreis.
Ich habe nie daran gedacht,
Worte der Zugehörigkeit oder Anerkennung
zu gebrauchen.[15]

15 Sofronieva, T., *Eine Hand voll Wasser* (Aschersleben, 2008), English title: *A hand full of water* (transl. by Wright, C.), pp. 42-46.

About the Authors

Elka Agoston, PhD in Slavonic Literature, was lecturer in South Slavonic Languages and Literature, Balkan Studies (folklore and ethnic identity), Studies on Central and South Eastern Europe, as well as gender topics (representations of women in literary texts) at the University of Groningen. Her research and publications focuses mainly on the oral literature of the Balkan Slavs and the question of ethnic and national identity in the literature of the South Slavs. Most recent publication - *South East European Writing in Diaspora* (ed. Elka Agoston-Nikolova), Rodopi, Amsterdam, 2010.

Nikolaj Bijleveld read Religious Studies and Scandinavian Studies at the universities of Groningen and Copenhagen. He gained his PhD in 2007 with a dissertation on the role of the Dutch clergy in the nationalization of Dutch culture in the first half of the 19th century. He has published on Dutch and Danish nationalism, religion, culture and elites in the modern period. Nikolaj Bijleveld is copy-editor and secretary of Virtus, a peer-reviewed yearbook on the history of the nobility. He is a study advisor at the University of Groningen.

Petra Broomans is Associate Professor of European Literatures and Cultures (Swedish) at the University of Groningen and visiting professor at Ghent University. She was the coordinator of the project 'Scandinavian Literature in Europe around 1900: the Influence of Language Politics, Gender and Aesthetics' (2004-2010) and the initiator of *Studies on Cultural Transfer and Transmission* (see www.soctat.org). She has published numerous articles on the reception and image of Scandinavian literature in Europe. One of the related projects is the 'Bibliography of Swedish and Swedish-Finnish literature in Dutch translation (1491-2007)' (2013). She is also editor-in-chief of the series *Studies on Cultural Transfer and Transmission* (CTaT) and president of the board of the International Association for Scandinavian Studies (IASS). Together with Jeanette den Toonder she coordinates the theme group Beyond Horizons in Cultural Transfer (Research Centre Arts in Society, UG). For further information please visit her website: www.petrabroomans.net.

Roald van Elswijk read Scandinavian Studies and Early Germanic at the University of Groningen. His main research interests include literary criticism, sociolinguistics and Nynorsk. Roald van Elswijk has published articles, essays and reviews in a number of anthologies and periodicals. Alongside his research projects, he takes a keen interest in translating and has published poetry translations, children's literature and biographies from Danish, Icelandic and Norwegian into Dutch.

Andrea Graw-Teebken read History at the University of Southern Denmark, Odense / Denmark and Dutch History and Language at the University of Groningen / the Netherlands. She gained her PhD in 2008 on the interdisciplinary doctoral programme SPIRIT, Aalborg University / Denmark with the dissertation 'Nationalisierte Grenzräume. Eine Untersuchung nationaler Diskurse in Ostfriesland und Schleswig, 1815 bis 1867'. She also gained a European Doctorate from the Universitá ca` Foscari Venezia / Italy in 2009. From 2007 to 2008 she worked at the Department of Border Region Studies, University of Southern Denmark, Sønderborg / Denmark. Since 2008, she has worked as an academic co-worker at the Region Sønderjylland-Schleswig, member of the Association of European Border Regions, working on cross-border cooperation, and in 2011-12 she headed the regional people-to-people programme. Andrea Graw-Teebken has published in several German and Danish journals.

Anne Heith is Associate Professor of Comparative Literature at the Department of Culture and Media Studies, Umeå University, Sweden. Between 2008 and 2011 she was a researcher in Border Poetics, Tromsø University, Norway. She was a guest researcher at the Hugo Valentin Centre, Uppsala University, Sweden, in 2010 and 2012. She participates in a number of networks and projects researching bordering practices and identities. Her research interests include national and postnational identities, ethnic literary studies, postcolonialism, indigenous studies, migration and literature, and critical race and whiteness studies.

Adriaan van der Hoeven lectures on Finnish literature and culture at the University of Groningen, The Netherlands. His special fields of interests include the reception of Finnish literature and culture in the Netherlands, and the relationship between text and image, notably the visual arts based on the epic *The Kalevala*. He has produced several translations of Finnish literature (in particular poetry, e.g. Caj Westerberg, Jouni Inkala, Tomi Kontio, Sirkka Turkka, Risto Oikarinen, and Anni Sumari, but also prose, e.g. Annika Idström, and plays, e.g. Laura Ruohonen, and Juho Lehtola).

Roger Holmström is Professor emeritus [akademilektor] of Comparative Literature at Åbo Akademi University. His extensive writings on 20th-century Finland-Swedish literature include his 1988 thesis *Karakteristik och värdering. Sudier i finlandssvensk litteraturkritik 1916-1929*, a two-volume biography of Hagar Olsson (1993,1995) and a study of Bo Carpelan's novel *Urwind* (1998). In 2005 he published a study of manners and customs of the Finland-Swedish people called *Att ge röst. Omvärld och identitet i några nyländska folklivsberättelser*. He also edited the volumes *Från kulturväktare till nightdrivers* (1996) and *Det förgrenade ljuset. En bok om Bo Carpelan och hans diktning* (2006). His current research focuses on classics and canonization in Finland-Swedish 20th-century literature.

Goffe Jensma is head of the Department of Frisian Language and Culture at the University of Groningen. He specialises in the field of Minority Studies and Multilingualism.

Ester Jiresch read History and Scandinavian Studies in Vienna and Stockholm. She recently finished her PhD research at the Groningen Research School for the Study of the Humanities (GRSSH) at the University of Groningen, on the role of networks in the work of female cultural transmitters of Scandinavian literature and culture in Europe around 1900 – comparing the Dutch/Flemish and Austrian/German-speaking regions. She has published several articles and books, including *Im Netzwerk der Kulturvermittlung. Sechs Autorinnen und ihre Bedeutung für die Verbreitung skandinavischer Literatur und Kultur in West- und Mitteleuropa um 1900.* (Groningen 2013: Barkhuis).

Janke Klok is Henrik-Steffens-professor at the Humboldt-Universität zu Berlin. In 2011 she published her PhD dissertation *Det norske litterære Feminapolis 1880-1980. Skram, Undset, Sandel og Haslunds byromaner – mot en ny modernistisk genre*. She has published several articles on Scandinavian literature in the field of literary transfer and gender studies in, inter alia, *From Darwin to Weil. Women as Transmitters of Ideas* (2009), *Feminist Review. Urban Spaces* (2010), *The invasion of Books in Peripheral Literary Fields* (2011), *Gymnadenia* (2011) and *Nordlit* (2015). She has translated novels and poetry by classic and contemporary Norwegian authors, is co-author of the biography *'Mijn vak werd mijn leven'. Amy van Marken (1912-1995)* (2010), editor of the series Wilde aardbeien (2003-) and *TijdSchrift voor Skandinavistiek* (2012-), and co-editor of the bibliography *Noorse auteurs in Nederlandse vertaling 1741- 2012/Norske forfattere oversatt til nederlandsk 1741-2012* (2013).

Malan Marnersdóttir is Professor of Literature and Dean of humanities, social sciences and education at Fróðskaparsetur Føroya, the University of the Faroe Islands. She has published widely on Faroese literature, novels, intertextuality, post-colonial studies and gender studies. She is one of the two authors of the Faroese Literary History vol.1. Her current research focuses on 20th-century writers like William Heinesen, Karsten Hoydal and others for vol. 2.

Idar Stegane, PhD, is professor emeritus of Scandinavian literature at the University of Bergen. Among other things, Stegane edited *Olav H. Hauges dikting* (1974), *Det nynorske skriftlivet* (1987), *Artiklar om litteratur* (2010). He was a co-writer of B. Fidjestøl et al.: *Norsk litteratur gjennom tusen år* (1994, new ed. 2001) and co-editor of the anthology *Norske tekster. Lyrikk* (1998, new ed. 2007). He has written articles on Nordic poetry in the series *Nordisk poetisk modernisme* 1 – 7 (2005–2013), and was co-editor of no. 1. and no. 6.

Bibliography

Aasen, I., 'Om vort Skriftsprog', in: Aasen, I., *Skrifter II* (Oslo, 1926), pp. 47-50.

Acerbi, G., *Reizen door Zweeden en Finland, tot aan de uiterste grenzen van Lapland. In de jaren 1798 en 1799*, vol. I-II (Haarlem, 1804-1806).

Acerbi, G., *Travels through Sweden, Finland, and Lapland, to the North Cape, in the years 1798 and 1799*, vol. I (London, 1802).

Adriansen, I., *Nationale symboler i Det Danske Rige 1830-2000*, vol. I-II (Copenhagen, 2003).

Allen, C.F., 'Ueber die Sprache und Volksthümlichkeit im Herzogthum Schleswig oder Süderjütland', *Anti-Schleswig-Holsteinische Fragmente*, 6 (Copenhagen, 1848).

Anderson, B., *Imagined Communities. Reflections on the Origin and Spread of Nationalism* (London/New York, 1983, 2006).

Anderson, B., 'Old Languages, New Models', in: Anderson B., *Imagined Communities: Reflections on the Origin and Spread of Nationalism* (London/New York, 2006), pp. 67-82.

Apter, E., *The Translation Zone. A New Comparative Literature* (Princeton/Oxford, 2006).

Ashcroft, B., *Post-Colonial Transformation* (London/New York, 2001).

Ashcroft, B., Griffiths, G. and Tiffin, H., *Post-Colonial Studies. The Key Concepts* (London/New York, 2000).

Ashcroft, B., Griffiths, G. and Tiffin, H., *The Empire Writes Back: Theory and Practice in Post-Colonial Literatures* (London, 1989).

Ashcroft. W.D., 'Is that the Congo? Language as Metonymy in the Post-Colonial Text', *World Literature Written in English*, 29:2 (1989), pp. 3-10.

Bang, H., *Tine* (Copenhagen, 1989, 1909)

Baumann, G. and Gingrich, A., eds., *Grammars of Identity/Alterity: A Structural Approach* (New York, 2004).

Bellamy, R., *Citizenship: A Very Short Introduction* (Oxford, 2008).

Beller, M. and Leerssen, J., eds., *Imagology. The Cultural Construction and Literary Representation of National Characters – A Critical Survey*, series: *Studia Imagologica*, vol. 13 (Amsterdam/New York, 2007).

Bhabha, H.K., *The Location of Culture* (London/New York, 1994, 2004), p. XX.

Bhabha, H.K., ‘DissemiNation: Time, Narrative and the Margins of the Modern Nation’, in: Bhabha H.K., *The Location of Culture* (London/New York, 2008), pp. 199-244.

Bijleveld, N., ‘Language, National Culture and the Clergy in Nineteenth-Century Denmark’, in: Broomans, P., Jensma, G., Vandevoorde, H. and Van Ginderachter, M., eds., *The Beloved Mothertongue. Ethnolinguistic Nationalism in Small Nations: Inventories and Reflections* (Louvain, Paris, Dudley, MA, 2008), pp. 93-107.

Bjerrum, A., ‘De danske sprogprøver hos C.F. Allen’, *Festskrift til Peter Skautrup 21. januar 1956* (Aarhus, 1956), pp. 297-309.

Bjørn, C., *1848: Borgerkrig og revolution* (Copenhagen, 1998).

Bjørnson, B., ‘Den moderne norske literatur’, in: Bjørnson, B., *Artikler og taler II* (Kristiania, 1913), pp. 305-331.

Blaunfeldt, M.F., *Das Schleswigsche Sprachrescript vertheidigt wider die Angriffe des Herrn Conferenzraths Raaslöff von M.F. Blaunfeldt, Hardesvogt in der Hüttener Harde im Herzogthum Schleswig* (Copenhagen, 1863).

Bollmann, C., *Eine Verschwörung: Von Carl Bollmann, ehemaligem Kabinetssecretair Sr. Hoheit des regierenden Herzogs von Koburg* (Flensburg, 1862).

Bondestam, A., ed., *Sallys saga: En bok om Sally Salminen till 50-årsminnet av ‘Katrina’* (Helsingfors, 1986).

Bourdieu, P., *The Rules of Art. Genesis and Structure of the Literary Field* (Stanford California, 1996), French title: *Les Règles d’art* (Paris, 1992).

Bracker, J., ‘Die dänische Sprachpolitik 1850-1864 und die Bevölkerung Mittelschleswigs’, *Zeitschrift der Gesellschaft für Schleswig-Holsteinische Geschichte* (1972), pp. 127-225 and (1973), pp. 87-213.

Brodsky, J., *Less Than One* (Middlesex, 1987).

Broomans, P., ed., *From Darwin to Weil. Women as Transmitters of Ideas* (Groningen, 2009).

Broomans, P., Jensma, G., Vandevoorde, H. and Van Ginderachter, M., eds., *The Beloved Mothertongue. Ethnolinguistic Nationalism in Small Nations: Inventories and Reflections* (Louvain, Paris, Dudley, MA, 2008).

Broomans, P., ‘Hur skapas en litteraturhistorisk bild? Den nordiska litteraturens “fräschhet” i Nederländerna och Flandern’, in: Dahl, P. and Steinfeld, T., eds., *Videnskab og national opdragelse. Studier i nordisk litteraturhistorieskrivning*, vol. 2 (Copenhagen, 2001), pp. 515-541.

Broomans, P., 'I fadershuset. Om kön och nationell identitet i nordisk litteraturhistorieskrivning', in: Marnersdóttir, M. and Cramer, J., 'Nordisk litteratur og mentalitet. Foredrag fra den 22. Studiekongres i International Association for Scandinavian Studies (IASS) arrangeret af Føroyamálsdeid, Fróskaparsetur Føroya, Færøernes Universitet 3.-9. august 1998', *Annales Societatis Scientiarum Færoensis,* Supplementum XXV (Tórshavn, 2000), pp. 41 - 55.

Busch, M., *Der Schmerzensschrei von der Eider. Ein Nachtrag zu den 'Schleswig-Holsteinischen Briefen' von Moritz Busch* (Leipzig, 1860).

Deleuze, G. and Guattari, F., *Kafka. Towards a Minor Literature* (Minneapolis/London, 1986)

Deleuze, G. and Guattari, F., 'What is a Minor Literature?', in: Deleuze, G. and Guattari, F., *Kafka. Towards a Minor Literature* (Minneapolis/ London, 1986), pp. 16-27.

De Wever, B., 'From Language to Nationality. The Case of the Dutch-speaking Belgians in the Nineteenth Century', in: Broomans, P., Jensma, G., Vandevoorde, H. and Van Ginderachter, M., eds., *The Beloved Mothertongue. Ethnolinguistic Nationalism in Small Nations: Inventories and Reflections* (Louvain, Paris, Dudley, MA, 2008), pp. 49-61.

Canetti, E., *The Tongue Set Free* (New York, 1979).

Clausen, M., ed., *Andalig visuløg í Føroyum upptikin 1902-2002. Spiritural Songs in the Faroe* (Hoyvík, 2006).

Clausen, M., *The Melodies – Løgini. Føroya kvæði. Corpus Carminum Færoensium*, vol. 8 (Copenhagen, 2003).

Glissant, É., *Poetics of Relation* (Ann Arbor, 1997).

Clement, K.J., *Das wahre Verhältnis der süderjütischen Nationalität und Sprache zur deutschen und frisischen im Herzogthum Schleswig: Eine historische und ethnographische Beleuchtung des 6ten Hefts der anti-schleswig-holsteinischen Fragmente von Dr. K.J. Clement* (Hamburg, 1849).

Conrad, F., 'Den nationale litteraturhistorieskrivning 1800-1861', in: Feldbæk, O., *Dansk identitetshistorie*, vol. II (Copenhagen, 1991), pp. 391-468.

Consett, M., *Een togtje door Zweden, Zweeds-Lapland, Finland en Denemarken* (uit het Engelsch, naar de 2de uitg.) (Dordrecht, 1818).

Cullblom, E., *Berta och byn. En kvinnas liv i Tornedalen* (Luleå, 2007).

Cullblom, E., *Första tvättmaskinen i Ohtanajärvi – och andra berättelser från Tornedalen* (Luleå, 2006).

Cullblom, E., *Män styr och kvinnor flyr Tornedalen. Kvinnliga strategier i en värld av manlig maktdominans* (Luleå, 1997).

Dahl, Á., *Bókmentasøga*, vol. II-III (Tórshavn, 1981-1983).

Dale, J.A., *Nynorsk dramatikk i hundre år* (Oslo, 1964).

Damsholt, T., *Fædrelandskærlighed og Borgerdyd. Patriotisk diskurs og militære reformer i Danmark i sidste del af 1700-tallet* (Copenhagen, 2000).

Debes, H.J., *Færingernes land: historien om den færøske nutids oprindelse*, Cold, S.A. and Hvidt, K., eds. (Copenhagen, 2001).

Dietrichson, L., *Omrids af den norske poesis historie. Literærhistoriske forelæsninger. II: Den norske literatur efter 1814* (Copenhagen, 1869).

Djurhuus, H.A., 'Føroyar', *Varðin* 1 (1921), pp. 49-56.

Djurhuus, J.H.O., *Yrkingar 1898-1948*, Matras, C., ed. (Tórshavn, 1988).

Djurhuus, J.H.O., 'Atlantis', *Yrkingar* (Copenhagen, 1923).

Edlund, L. and Frängsmyr, T., eds., *Norrländsk uppslagsbok*, vol. 3 (Umeå, 1995).

Elenius, L., *Nationalstat och minoritetspolitik. Samer och finskspråkiga minoriteter i ett jämförande nordiskt perspektiv* (Lund, 2006).

Ellefsen, A., 'William Heinesen i undervisningsøjemed', in: Í Ólavsstovu, V. and Kløvstad, J.N., eds., *Tårnet midt i verden – en bog om William Heinesen* (Tórshavn, 1994), pp. 153-163.

Enquist, P.O., *The Royal Physician's Visit* (New York, 2001).

Feldbæk, O., *Danmarks historien*, vol. IX (Copenhagen, 2003, 1990).

Feldbæk, O. and Winge, V., 'Tyskerfejden 1789-1790. Den første nationale konfrontation', in: Feldbæk, O., ed., *Dansk identitetshistorie*, vol. II (Copenhagen, 1991), pp. 9-109.

Feldbæk, O., ed., *Dansk identitetshistorie*, vol. I-IV (Copenhagen, 1991-1992).

Feldbæk, O., 'Skole og identitet 1789-1848. Lovgivning og lærebøger', in: Feldbæk, O., ed., *Dansk identitetshistorie*, vol. II (Copenhagen, 1991), pp. 268-269.

Fenton, S., *Ethnicity* (Cambridge/Malden, MA, 2005).

Fenton, S. and May, S., 'Ethnicity, Nation and "Race": Connections and Disjunctures', in: Fenton S. and May, S., eds., *Ethnonational Identitites* (Houndsmill/New York, 2002), pp. 1-20.

Fischer Hansen, I. et al., eds., *Litteraturhåndbogen* (Copenhagen, 1994).

Flo, R., 'Norske bøker', *Syn og Segn* (1896), pp. 372-388.

Fløgstad, K., 'Eit sant mirakel', *Aftenposten* (Oslo, July 1, 2012).

Foucault, M., *Discipline and Punish: The Birth of the Prison* (London, 1977).

Foucault, M., *The Archeology of Knowledge* (New York, 1972).

Frandsen, S.B., *Holsten i Helstaten. Hertugdømmer inden for og uden for det danske monarki i første halvdel af 1800-tallet* (Copenhagen, 2008).

Frandsen, S.B., 'Det nya Norden efter Napoleon. Den dansk-tyske helstat 1814-1864', in: Engman, M. and Sandstrøm, Å., eds., *Det nya Norden efter Napoleon. 25de Nordiska Historikermøtet* (Stockholm, 2004), pp. 19-54.

Færeyinga saga, Rafn, C.C., ed., *Old Norse with Faroese and Danish translations* (Copenhagen, 1832).

Garborg, A., 'Forleggjarvanskar', *Festskrift til William Nygaard* (Kristiania, 1913), pp. 204-206.

Garborg, A., *Henrik Ibsen's "Keiser og Galilæer". En kritisk studie* (Kristiania, 1873).

Gaup. N., *Kautokeino-opprøret*, English title: *The Kautokeino Rebellion* (Rubicon, 2008).

Gellner, E., *Nations and nationalism* (Oxford, 1983).

Greenfeldt, L., *Nationalism: Five Roads to Modernity* (Cambridge Mass., 1992).

Grundtvig, N.F.S., 'Sommeandres og mit Tyskerhad', in: Christensen, G. and Koch, H., eds., *N.F.S. Grundtvig. Værker i Udvalg*, vol. V (Copenhagen, 1943).

Grundtvig, N.F.S., *Om Danemarks kvide der lød en sang* (1839), quoted in: *Folkehøjskolens sangbog*, no. 183.

Gröndahl, S., ed., *Litteraturens gränsland. Invandrar- och minoritetslitteratur i nordiskt perspektiv* (Uppsala, 2002).

Gröndahl, S., 'Inledning. Från "mångkulturell" till "mångspråkig" litteratur?', in: Gröndahl, S., ed., *Litteraturens gränsland. Invandrar- och minoritetslitteratur i nordiskt perspektiv* (Uppsala, 2002), pp. 11-34.

Gustafsson, H., 'The Conglomerate State: A Perspective on State Formation in Early Modern Europe', *Scandinavian Journal of History*, vol. 23, no. 3-4 (1998), pp. 189-213.

Habermas, J., *Strukturwandel der Öffentlichkeit. Untersuchungen zu einer Kategorie der bürgerlichen Gesellschaft* (Neuwied, 1962), English translation: Burger, T. and Lawrence, F., *The Structural Transformation of the Public Sphere. An Inquiry into a Category of Bourgeois Society* (Cambridge, 1989).

Hall, S., 'Introduction. Who needs "identity"?', in: Hall, S. and Du Gay, P., eds., *Questions of Cultural Identity* (London/Thousand Oaks/New Delhi, 2005), pp. 1-17.

Hammershaimb, V.U., *Færøsk Anthologi*, vol. I-II (Copenhagen, 1891) (repr. Tórshavn, 1969).

Hammershaimb, V.U., *Færöiske Kvæder* (Copenhagen, 1851-1855) (repr. Tórshavn, 1969).

Hammershaimb, V.U., *Savn úr Annaler for nordisk Oldkyndighed og historie og Antiquarisk tidsskrift*, 1846-1854 (repr. Tórshavn, 1969).
Hansson, P.A., 'Folkhemmet, medborgarhemmet', in: Berkling, A.L., ed., *Från Fram till folkhemmet. Per Albin Hansson som tidningsman och talare* (Stockholm, 1982), pp. 227-234.
Harstad, J., *Buzz Aldrin, hvor ble det av deg i alt mylderet?* (Oslo, 2005).
Hastings, D. and Wilson, T.M., *Borders: Frontiers of Identity, Nation and State* (Oxford/New York, 1999).
Hauge, H., 'Norientalisme eller nordisk postkolonialisme', *Nordisk litteratur* (Copenhagen etc, 2003), pp. 8-11.
Hechter, M., *Internal Colonialism. The Celtic Fringe in British National Development, 1536-1966* (London, 1975).
Heiberg, S., 'Herskab gennem tiderne', in: Heiberg, S. and Venborg Pedersen, M., eds., *Herregården*, vol. I (Copenhagen, 2004), pp. 37-118.
Heith, A., 'Contemporary Tornedalian Fictions by Ester Cullblom and Annika Korpi', *Nora: Nordic Journal of Feminist and Gender Research* 2 (2009a), pp. 72-88.
Heith, A., '"Nils Holgersson Never Saw Us": A Tornedalian Finnish Literary History', in: Hansson, H. and Norberg, C., eds., *Cold Matters, Northern Studies Monographs*, no. 1 (Umeå, 2009b), pp. 41-53.
Heith, A., 'Litteraturhistorieskrivning och det nationellas förändringar', *Tidskrift för litteraturvetenskap* 2 (2008a), pp. 17-19.
Heith, A., 'Förhandlingar och förvandlingar av det nationella i den tornedalsfinska litteraturen', *Horisont* 3 (2008b), pp. 17-19.
Heith, A., 'Fluid Identities and the Use of History: The Northern Lights Route and the Writings of Bengt Pohjanen', in: Fornäs, J. and Fredriksson, M., eds., *Inter. A European Cultural Studies Conference in Sweden* (Linköping, 2007), pp. 227-241.
Heith, A., *Texter – medier – kontexter* (Lund, 2006).
Henningsen, B., Klein, J., Müssener, H. and Söderlind, S., eds., *Skandinavien och Tyskland 1800-1914. Möten och vänskabsband* (Berlin, 1997).
Henriksen, S.H., 'Det blandede sprogdistrikt mellem krigene', *Sønderjysk Månedsskrift*, vol. 28 (Aabenraa, 1952), pp. 136-143.
Herder, J.G., *Sämtliche Werke*, Suphan, B., ed., vol. XIII (Berlin, 1877-1913).
Hettne, B., Sörlin, S., and Østergård, U., *Den globala nationalismen* (Stockholm, 2006).
Hirvonen, V., *Voices from Sápmi. Sámi Women's Path to Authorship* (Kautokeino, 1998, 2008).

Hobsbawm, E.J., *Nations and Nationalism since 1780. Programme, Myth, Reality* (Cambridge, 2000, 1992, 1990).

Holzapfel, O., 'Deutsch-dänische Grenz- und Anpassungsschwierigkeiten. Patriotismus und Nationalismus im Spiegel einiger schleswig-holsteinischer Liederbücher von 1802 bis 1864', *Jahrbuch für Volksliedforschung*, vol. 27/28, 1982/1983, pp. 225-234.

Hroch, M., *Das Europa der Nationen. Die moderne Nationsbildung im europäischen Vergleich* (Göttingen, 2005).

Hroch, M., 'From National Movement to the Fully-formed Nation: The Nation-building Process in Europe', in: Balakrishnan, G., ed., *Mapping the Nation.* (New York/London, 1996), pp. 78-97.

Hroch, M., *Social Preconditions of National Revival in Europe. A Comparative Analysis of the Social Composition of Patriotic Groups among the Smaller European Nations* (Cambridge, 1985), German title: *Die Vorkämpfer der nationalen Bewegung bei den kleinen Völkern Europas* (Prague, 1968).

Jensen, C.J., *September í bjørkum, sum kanska eru bláar* (Tórshavn, 2006).

Jensma, G., 'Minorities and Kinships. The Case of Ethnolinguistic Nationalism in Friesland', in: Broomans, P., Jensma, G., Vandevoorde, H. and Van Ginderachter, M., eds., *The Beloved Mothertongue. Ethnolinguistic Nationalism in Small Nations: Inventories and Reflections* (Louvain, Paris, Dudley, MA, 2008), pp. 63-78.

Joenniemi, P., 'Changing Politics along Finland's Borders: From Norden to the Northern Dimension', in: Ahonen, P. and Jukarainen P., eds., *Tearing Down the Curtain, Opening the Gates: Northern Boundaries in Change* (Jyväskylä, 2000), pp. 114-132.

Joensen, J.K., Mortensen, A. and Petersen, P., *Føroyar undir fríum handli í 100 ár* (Tórshavn, 1955).

Joensen, L., 'Barbara and the Dano-Faroese Moment', *Úthavsdagar – Oceaniske dage. Annales societatis scientiarum færoensis*, supplementum XXIX (Tórshavn, 2000), pp. 64-87.

Jones, W. Glyn, *Færø og kosmos* (Copenhagen, 1974).

Joseph, J.E., *Language and Identity: National, Ethnic, Religious* (London, 2004).

Juntti-Henriksson, A.K., *Women Narratives from Tornedalen – Northernmost Sweden. Gender and Culture in Perspective* (Luleå, 2008).

Jæger, H., 'Ivar Aasen', in: Jæger, H., *Illustrert norsk litteraturhistorie. Bind II* (Kristiania, 1896), pp. 478-486.

Kaufman, G., Ohrt, N. and Schulte-Wülwer, U., 'Vorwort', in: Schulte-Wülwer, U. and Hedinger, B., eds., *Louis Gurlitt 1812-1897. Porträts europäischer Landschaften in Gemälden und Zeichnungen* (München, 1997).

Kemiläinen, A., *Nationalism: Problems Concerning the Word, the Concept and Classification* (Jyväskylä, 1964).

Khemeri, J.H., *Ett öga rött* (Stockholm, 2003)

Kiš, D., *De luit en de littekens*

Koch, C.H., 'Forfatterportræt Henrich Steffens. Inledning', http://www.adl.dk/adl_pub/fportraet/cv/ShowFpItem.xsql?ff_id=64&p_fpkat_id=indl&nnoc=.

Koht, H., 'Ivar Aasen. Granskar og maalreisar', in: Garborg, A., Hovden, A. and Koht, H., *Ivar Aasen. Granskaren, maalreisaren, diktaren* (Kristiania, 1913), pp. 9-174.

Korpi, A., *Hevonen Häst* (Stockholm, 2005).

Krasilnikoff, A., *Hvalens øje* (Copenhagen, 2004).

Kriener, K., 'Sprache – Rasse – Volk: Aspekte des deutschen nationalen Diskurses', http://www.comlink.de/cl-hh/m.blumentritt/agr128s.htm.

Kristeva, J., *Strangers to Ourselves* (New York, 1991).

Krohn, J., *Suomalaisen kirjallisuuden vaiheet* (=SKS Toimituksia 86 Osa) (Helsinki, 1897).

Kulonen, U-M., Seurajärvi-Kari, I. and Pulkkinen, R., eds., *The Saami. A Cultural Encyclopaedia* (Vammala, 2005).

Küttner, K.G., *Reise durch Deutschland, Dänemark, Schweden, Norwegen und einen Theil von Italien in den Jahren 1797, 1798, 1799* (Leipzig, 1801), quoted in: Winge, V., *Dänische Deutsche – deutsche Dänen. Geschichte der deutschen Sprache in Dänemark 1300-1800 mit einem Ausblick auf das 19. Jahrhundert* (Heidelberg, 1992), p. 317.

Laestadius, A-H., *Hitta hem* (Stockholm, 2012)

Laestadius, A-H., *Ingen annan är som du* (Stockholm, 2011)

Laestadius, A-H., *Hej vacker* (Stockholm, 2010)

Laestadius, A-H., *Sms från Soppero* (Stockholm, 2007)

Lagerlöf, S., *Nils Holgerssons underbara resa genom Sverige* (Stockholm 1906-1907).

Lange, U., ed., *Geschichte Schleswig-Holsteins: Von den Anfängen bis zur Gegenwart* (Neumünster, 2003).

Langewiesche, D., 'Was heißt "Erfindung der Nation"? Nationalgeschichte als Artefakt – oder Geschichtsdeutung als Machtkampf', *Historische Zeitschrift*, vol. 277 (2003), pp. 593-617.

Langewiesche, D., *Nation, Nationalismus, Nationalstaat in Europa und Deutschland* (München, 2000).

Larsen, K., 'Kvæðauppskriftir Jóannesar í Króki', *Fróðskaparrit* 42 (1994), pp. 29-35.

Leerssen, J., 'Linguistic Geopolitics and the Problem of Cultural Nationalism', in: Broomans, P., Jensma, G., Vandevoorde, H. and Van Ginderachter, M., eds., *The Beloved Mothertongue. Ethnolinguistic Nationalism in Small Nations: Inventories and Reflections* (Louvain, Paris, Dudley, MA, 2008), pp. 15-36.

Leerssen, J., *National Thought in Europe. A Cultural History* (Amsterdam, 2008).

Lehmann, O., *Det tydske i Danmark: Et foredrag i arbejderforeningen af 1860 af Orla Lehmann* (Copenhagen, 1865).

Lehtola, V.P., *Rajamaan identiteetti. Lappilaisuuden rakentuminen 1920- ja 1930-luvun kirjallisuudessa* (Helsinki, 1997).

Leiva Wenger, A., *Författarna* (2013).

Leiva Wenger, A., *127* (2011).

Leiva Wenger, A., *Till vår ära* (Stockholm, 2001).

Leiva Wenger, A., 'Borta i tankar' in *Till vår ära* (Stockholm, 2001).

Liksom, R., *One Night Stands* (New York, 1993).

Liksom, R., *Tyhjän tien paratiisit* (Porvoo, 1989).

Liksom, R., *Unohdettu vartti* (Porvoo, 1986).

Liksom, R., *Yhden yön pysäkki* (Espoo, 1985).

Linneberg, A., 'Romantikk for borgar – realisme for bonde? Arne Garborgs *Haugtussa* og litteraturkritikken, I-II', *Syn og Segn* 2-3 (1979), pp. 92-107, 150-163.

Lundgreen-Nielsen, F., 'Danskhed - hvorfor og hvorledes?', in: Lundgreen-Nielsen, F., ed., *På sporet af dansk identitet. Syv humanistiske forskere fortæller historien om hvordan vi gennem tiderne er blevet os bevidste som dansk* (Copenhagen, 1992).

Löfgren, O., 'Regionauts: The Transformation of Cross-Border Regions in Scandinavia', *European Urban and Regional Studies*, vol. 15, no. 3 (2008), pp. 195-209.

Løland, R., 'Ei røda um bøker og andre ting', in: Løland, R., *Skrifter i samling IV* (Oslo, 1942), pp. 310-326.

Magga, O.L., 'Are We Finally to Get Our Rights?', in: Brøsted, J. et al., eds., *Native Power: The Quest for Autonomy and Nationhood of Indigeous Peoples* (Bergen/Oslo/Stavanger/Tromsø, 1985).

Malling, O., *Store og gode Handlinger af Danske, Norske og Holstenere, samlede ved Ove Malling*, Hansen, E., ed. (Copenhagen, 1992).

Marmier, X., *Brieven over het Noorden. Denemarken, Zweden, Noorwegen, Lapland en Spitsbergen* (uit het Fransch) (Deventer, 1841).

Marnersdóttir, M., 'Genskrivning, efterligning og modstand i færøsk historie og litteratur', *TijdSchrift voor Skandinavistiek*, vol. 30, no. 2 (2009), pp. 137-164.

Marnersdóttir, M., 'Grænser i færøsk litteratur', in: Zilliacus, C. et al., eds., *Gränser i nordisk litteratur* (Åbo, 2008), pp. 65-80.

Marnersdóttir, M., 'William Heinesens *Det gode håb* i lyset af post-kolonial teori', *TijdSchrift voor Skandinavistiek*, vol. 25, no. 2 (2004), pp. 181-198.

Marnersdóttir, M., *Hvør av øðrum. Samanseting, frásøgn og millumtekstleiki í føroyskari skaldsøgu eftir 1970* (Tórshavn, 2000).

Marnersdóttir, M., 'Claus Lund – en "Litteratus" in Tórshavn i 1790'erne', in: Uecker, H., ed., *Opplysning i Norden* (Frankfurt a.M., 1998), pp. 357-364.

Marnersdóttir, M., 'Vit eiga William', *Brá* 20 (1993), pp. 32-42.

Matras, C., 'Det færøske skriftsprog af 1846', in: Næs, M. and Poulsen, J.H.W., eds., *Greinaval – málfrøðigreinir* (1951), pp. 97-115 (Tórshavn, 2000).

Matras, C., *Evangelium sankta Matteusar II. Um týðingina av bókini* (Tórshavn, 1973).

Meerman, J., *Eenige berichten omtrent het Noorden en Noord-Oosten van Europa*, vol. 1 (The Hague, 1804).

Meijer, H., *Indische rekening. Indië, Nederland en de backpay-kwestie 1945-2005* (Amsterdam, 2005).

Mellem, R., ed., *Innsyn i kvensk historie, språk og kultur. Seminarrapport, Tromsø, mars 2002* (Tromsø, 2003).

Mohtadi, L., *Den dag jag blir fri. En bok om Katarina Taikon* (Stockholm, 2012).

Monrad, K., 'De Hollandse dimensie in de landschapschilderkunst van de Deense Gouden Eeuw', in: Bøgh Rønberg, L., Monrad, K. and Linnet, R., eds., *Twee Gouden eeuwen. Schilderkunst uit Nederland en Denemarken* (Zwolle, 2001), pp. 16-71.

Monrad, M.J., 'Ervingen. Sangspil i een Akt', *Norsk Tidsskrift for Videnskab og Literatur* (1854-1855), pp. 366-377.

Mortensen, K.P. and Schack, M., eds., *Dansk litteraturs historie* (Copenhagen, 2006).

Mosse, G.L., *The Nationalization of the Masses: Political Symbolism and Mass Movements in Germany from the Napoleonic Wars Through the Third Reich* (New York, 1975).

Myskja, K., 'The Norwegian', in: Myskja, K., *Ivar Aasens Poetry* (Fjærland, 2002), p. 5.

Nabokov, V., *The Real Life of Sebastian Knight* (London, 1960).

Naipaul, V.S. *The Mystic Masseur* (London, 1957).

Narayan, U. and Harding, S., eds., *Decentering the Center: Philosophy for a Multicultural, Postcolonial, and Feminist World* (Bloomington/ Indianapolis 2000).

Nebelong, L., *Færøblues* (Højbjerg, 2007).

Nebelong, L., *Når engle spiller Mozart* (Copenhagen, 2003).

Nielsen, N.Å., 'Sprogpolitik og dialektforskning i Slesvig 1851-64', *Sønderjysk Månedsskrift*, vol. 58, no. 10 (1982), pp. 283-290.

Niemi, E., 'Kvenene – fra innvandrere til utvandrere', in: Mellem, R., ed., *Innsyn i kvensk historie, språk og kultur. Seminarrapport, Tromsø, mars 2002* (Tromsø, 2003), pp. 43-57.

Niemi, M., *Populärmusik från Vittula* (Stockholm, 2000).

Nilsson, M., 'Literature in Multicultural and Multilingual Sweden: The Birth and Death of the Immigrant Writer', in: Behschnitt, W., De Mul, S., Minnaard, L., eds., *Literature, Language, and Multiculturalism in Scandinavia and the Low Countries* (Amsterdam, 2013), pp. 41-61.

N.N., *Actenstücke zur Geschichte des Hochdeutschen im Herzogtum Schleswig* (Copenhagen, 1856).

N.N., 'Zweden', *Algemeene konst- en letterbode*, LXVI, vol. 1, no. 19 (1854), p. 151.

Nolsøe, M., 'Folkevisa og folkevisemiljøet på Færøyane', in: Andreassen, E., ed., *Kvæðagreinir* (Tórshavn, 1988), pp. 3-21.

Nørlund, N.E., *Færøernes kortlægning – en historisk fremstilling* (Copenhagen, 1944).

O'Leary, B., ed., *Right-Sizing the State: The Politics of Moving Borders* (Oxford, 2000).

Olsen, S.T., *Die Dänenpolitik im deutschen Kaiserreich: Preußisch-deutsche Nationalitätenpolitik in der Region Nordschleswig/ Sønderjylland 1864-1914* (Hamburg, 1999).

Paasi, A., *Territories, Boundaries and Consciousness: The Changing Geographies of the Finnish-Russian Border* (Oulu, 1996).

Patursson, J., *Tættir úr Kirkjubøar søgu* (Tórshavn, 1966).

Pohjanen, B. and Johansson, K., *Den tornedalsfinska litteraturen I. Från Kexi till Liksom* (Överkalix, 2007)

Pohjanen, B. and Johansson, K., *Den tornedalsfinska litteraturen II. Från Kalkkimaa till Hilja Byström* (Överkalix, 2009).

Pohjanen, B., 'Vår identitet är i språket ', in: Pohjanen, B. and Johansson, K., eds., *Den tornedalsfinska litteraturen II. Från Kalkkimaa till Hilja Byström* (Överkalix, 2009), pp. 9-14.

Pohjanen, B. and Muli E., *Meänkieli rätt och lätt. Grammatik i Meänkieli* (Överkalix, 2005).

Pohjanen, B., 'Jag är född utan språk', *Vår Lösen* 3 (1973).

Poulsen, J.H.W., *Mál í mæti*, Johansen, A. and Joensen, H., eds. (Tórshavn, 2004).

Reintoft, H., *Nu er det længe siden* (Copenhagen, 2008).

Renan, E., 'Qu'est-ce qu'une nation?', conference in Sorbonne on March 11, 1882.

Ridanpää, J., 'Rosa Liksom's Literary North: Traditional Confrontations or New Discursive Practices?', in: Möller, F. and Pehkonen, S., eds., *Encountering the North. Cultural Geography, International Relations and Northern Landscapes* (Aldershot/Burlington, 2003), pp. 103-125.

Riecken, C., 'Zwischen Wissenschaft und politischem Erwachen: Nordfriesische Sprachforschung im 19. Jahrhundert', *Nordfriesland* (2001), pp. 24-27.

Rohweder, J., *Sprache und Nationalität: Nordschleswig und die Anfänge der dänischen Sprachpolitik in der ersten Hälfte des 19. Jahrhunderts* (Glückstadt, 1976).

Runblom, H., 'Introduction. Homeland As Imagination and Reality', in: Runblom, H., ed., *Migrants and the Homeland. Images, Symbols, and Realities* (Uppsala, 2000), pp. 9-30.

Rühs, F., *Finland en de Finnen*, vol. I-II (Leeuwarden, 1815).

Rühs, F., *Finland und seine Bewohner* (Leipzig, 1809).

Sahlins, P., 'Natural Frontiers Revisited: France's Boundaries in the 17th Century', *The American Historical Review*, vol. 95, no. 5 (1990), pp. 1423-1451.

Salminen, S., *Katrina* (Helsingfors/Esbo, 1936, 1994)

Salminen, S., *Min amerikanska saga* (Helsingfors, 1968).

Salminen, S., *Katrina*, transl. by Naomi Walford (New York, 1937).

Savolainen, M., 'Keskusta, marginalia, Kirjallisuus', in: Savolainen, M., ed., *Marginalia ja Kirjallisus. Ääniä suomalaisen kirjallisuuden reunoilta* (Helsinki, 1995), pp. 7-35.

Schulte-Wülwer, U., 'Louis Gurlitt – Leben und Werk', in: Schulte-Wülwer, U. and Hedinger, B., eds., *Louis Gurlitt 1812-1897. Porträts europäischer Landschaften in Gemälden und Zeichnungen* (München, 1997), pp. 27-144.

Schulte-Wülwer, U. and Hedinger, B., eds., *Louis Gurlitt 1812-1897. Porträts europäischer Landschaften in Gemälden und Zeichnungen* (München, 1997).

Schultz Hansen, H., Henningsen, L.N. and Porskrog Rasmussen, C., *Sønderjyllands historie*, vol. I (Aabenraa, 2008).
Schultz Hansen, H., *Danskheden i Sydslesvig, 1840-1918* (Flensburg, 1990).
Seyhan, A., *Writing outside the Nation* (Princeton, 2001).
Siemann, W., *Die deutsche Revolution von 1848/49* (Frankfurt a.M., 1985).
Sigurðardóttir, T., *At rejse ud for at komme hjem: den færøske sangdigtning 1876-1892 som del af og udtryk for færøsk nationalidentitet i støbeskeen* (Copenhagen, 1987).
Simonsen, K., 'Ein modernað skaldsøga um Føroyar', *Outsider magazine* (2005), pp. 168-170.
Smith, A.D., *The Cultural Foundations of Nations. Hierarchy, Covenant, and Republic* (Oxford, 2008).
Smith, A.D., *National Identity* (London, 1991).
Smith, L.T., *Decolonizing Methodologies: Research and Indigenous Peoples* (London/New York, 2006).
Sofronieva, T., *Eine Hand voll Wasser* (Aschersleben, 2008), English title: *A hand full of water* (transl. by Wright, C.).
Solbakk, J.T., ed./author, *The Sámi People: A Handbook* (Karasjok, 2006).
Songbók Føroya fólks (Tórshavn, 1913).
Spasova, K., 'Her Cities and Languages', *Altera. Journal for Gender, Language and Culture* (Sofia, 2007), pp. 42-44.
Steffens, H., *Indledning til philosophiske Forelæsninger* (Copenhagen, 1803).
Stegane, I., *Det nynorske skriftlivet. Nynorsk heimstaddikting og den litterære institusjon* (Oslo, 1987).
Steinby, A.-G., 'Katrina är fiktion, inte verklighet', *Hufvudstadsbladet*, July 30, 1997.
Stössinger, V. and Dömling, A.K., eds., *"Von Inseln weiss ich..." Geschichten von den Färöer-Inseln* (transl. by Borchert, R. et al.) (Zürich, 2006).
Suhm, P.F., *Danmarks, Norges og Holstens Historie udi tvende Udtog til brug for den studerende Ungdom* (Copenhagen, 1776), quoted in: Feldbæk, O., 'Fædreland og Indfødsret. 1700-tallets danske identitet', in: Feldbæk, O., ed., *Dansk identitetshistorie*, vol. I (Copenhagen, 1991), p. 196.
Svabo, J.C., *Dictionarium Færoense. Færøsk-dansk-latinsk ordbog*, Matras, C., ed., vol. II, *Indledning og register* (Copenhagen, 1970).
Sørensen, H. Flohr, 'Mit forhold til det danske sprog er fatalt bestemt. William Heinesens dansksprogede forfatterskab. Baggrund og konsekvenser', *Fróðskaparrit* 47 (1999), pp. 5-31.
Tarkiainen, V. and Kauppinen, E., *Suomalaisen kirjallisuuden historia* (Neljäs painos, Helsinki, 1967).

The American Heritage Dictionary of the English Language, fourth edition, updated 2005: http://dictionary.reference.com/browse/nationhood?__utma=1.563437068.1271323270.1271323270.12713.

Thiele, J.M., *Danske Folkesagn*, vol. III (Copenhagen, 1820).

Thiong'o, N.W., *Decolonizing the Mind: The Politics of Language in African Literature* (London, 1986).

Thomasen, A., *Færøsk i den færøske skole: fra århundredskiftet til 1938* (Odense, 1985).

Thráinsson, H., Petersen, H.P., Í Lon Jacobsen, J. and Svabo Hansen, Z., *Faroese. An Overview and Reference Grammar* (Tórshavn, 2004).

Todorov, T., *L'Homme dépaysée* (Paris, 1996).

Topelius, Z., *Maamme kirja. Lukukirja Suomen alimmille oppilaitoksille* (Kolmaskymmeneskolmas, korjattu painos, Porvoo, 1929).

Troyanov, I., *Der Weltensammler* (München, 2006).

Tuohimaa, S., 'Pohjois-Suomen unohdetut naiskirjailijat', in: Majasaari K. and Rytkönen M. eds., *Silmukoita verkossa. Sukupuoli, kirjallisuus ja identiteetti* (Oulu, 1997), pp. 46-47.

Tusvik, S., 'Plantefelt, flatehogst eller tynning i underskogen', in: Fjeldstad, A., Danielsen, Ø. and Tusvik, S., eds., *Litteraturen mellom staten og marknaden. Rappårt frå konferanse på Ustaoset 16.-18.09.1992* (Oslo, 1992), pp. 88-107.

Ugrešić, D., *Nobody's Home* (London, 2007).

Ugrešić, D., *The Culture of Lies* (London, 1994).

Valkeapää, N.A., *Beaivi áhcážan*, English translation, *The Sun, My Father* (Kautokeino, 1997).

Van der Hoeven, A.M., '"So Fresh, So New and So Perfectly Healthy": The Literature of Finland in the Netherlands 1875-1925', *Scandinavica*, vol. 45, no. 1 (2006), pp. 29-41.

Van der Hoeven, A.M., 'The Dutch translations of the Finnish epic *Kalevala*', in: Blokland, R. and Hasselblatt, C., eds., *Finno-Ugrians and Indo-Europeans: Linguistic and Literary Contacts. Proceedings of the Symposium at the University of Groningen, November 22-24, 2001* (Maastricht, 2002), pp. 112-147.

Van der Hoeven, A.M., 'Bibliografie van in het Nederlands verschenen literatuur op het gebied van de Finoegrische volken 1800-1900', in: Van der Hoeven, A.M. and Kylstra, A.D., eds., *Tien jaar Finoegristiek in Groningen 1966-1976* (Groningen, 1978), pp. 45-98.

Van Elswijk, R., 'Spread the Word. Arne and Hulda Garborg as Cultural Transmitters of Nynorsk', in: Broomans, P. and Ronne, M., eds., *In the Vanguard of Cultural Transfer. Cultural Transmitters and Authors in Peripheral Literary Fields* (Groningen, 2010), pp. 13-31.

Van Elswijk, R., ed., *Windvlinders. Poëzie van de Faerøer* (Groningen, 2008).

Van Ginderachter, M., 'How Useful is the Concept of Ethnolinguistic Nationalism? On imagined Communities, the Ethnic-Civic Dichotomy and Banal Nationalism', in: Broomans, P., Jensma, G., Vandevoorde, H. and Van Ginderachter, M., eds., *The Beloved Mothertongue. Ethnolinguistic Nationalism in Small Nations: Inventories and Reflections* (Louvain, Paris, Dudley, MA, 2008), pp. 1-13.

Venborg Pedersen, M., 'Gevormd tot het juiste karakter. Adellijke mentaliteit en de hertogen van Augustenborg aan het einde van de achttiende eeuw', *Virtus. Yearbook of the History of the Nobility* 15 (2008), pp. 121-141.

Viborg, K.F., *Folkeforsyndelsen og Folketugtelsen. Prædiken på Almindelig Bededag 1864* (Slagelse, 1864).

Viking, M. and Høvring, E., *Kulturkanon* (Copenhagen, 2006), pp. 168-169.

Vinje, A.O., 'Vaart Maalstrev', in: Vinje, A.O., *Norske Dikt* (Oslo, 1897), pp. 1-3.

Von Schubert, F.W., *Reis door Zweden, Noorwegen, Lappland, Finnland en Ingermannland in de jaren 1817, 1818 en 1820*, vol. I-III (uit het Hoogduitsch) (Deventer, 1826-1827).

Walton, S.J., *Farewell the Spirit Craven. Ivar Aasen and National Romanticism* (Oslo, 1987).

Warburton, T., 'Den välsignade damen', *Nya Argus* 2 (2006), pp. 29-30.

Weber, E., *Peasants into Frenchmen: The Modernization of Rural France 1870-1914* (London, 1976).

Welsch, W., 'Transculturality – the Puzzling Form of Cultures Today', in: Featherstone, M. and Lash, S., eds., *Spaces of Culture: City, Nation, World* (London, 1999), pp. 194-213.

Wendelius, L., *Den dubbla identiteten. Immigrant- och minoritetslitteratur på svenska 1970-2000* (Uppsala, 2002).

West, J.F., *Faroe. The Emergence of a Nation* (London, 1974), transl. *Færøerne. En nation og dens historie* (Copenhagen, 1974).

Westin, C., 'Migration, Time, and Space', in: Runblom, H., ed., *Migrants and the Homeland. Images, Symbols, and Realities* (Uppsala, 2000), pp. 33-42.

Weyhe, E., 'Eitt samtíðarligt kvæði – og ein ókend uppskrift', in: Marnersdóttir, M., Joensen, L. and Kristjánsdóttir, D., eds., *Bókmentaljós* (Tórshavn, 2006), pp. 145-160.

Weyhe, E., 'Tey nýggju føroyakortini', *Ársfrágreiðing* 1998 (Tórshavn, 1999), pp. 6-7.
Widén, G., 'En folkbok med sällsam lyskraft', *Hufvudstadsbladet*, April 21, 1994.
Wilster, C., 'Ludvig Holberg', quoted in: *Folkehøjskolens sangbog*, no. 187 (Odense, 1986).
Winge, V., 'Dansk og Tysk i Slesvig', in: Jørgensen, S.A., *Meddelelser fra Thorvaldsens Museum 2001* (Copenhagen, 2001), pp. 57-65.
Winge, V., *Dänische Deutsche – deutsche Dänen. Geschichte der deutschen Sprache in Dänemark 1300-1800 mit einem Ausblick auf das 19. Jahrhundert* (Heidelberg, 1992).
Winge, V., 'Dansk og tysk 1790-1848', in: Feldbæk, O., ed., *Dansk identitetshistorie*, vol. II (Copenhagen, 1991), pp. 110-149.
Zaldua, I., 'Eight Crucial Decisions (A Basque Writer is Obliged to Face)', in: Olaziregi, M.J. (ed.), *Writers in Between Languages: Minority Literatures in the Global Scene* (Reno, 2009), pp. 89-112.
Østergård, U., *Europa. Identitet og identitetspolitik* (Copenhagen, 2000, 1998).

Websites

http://adl.dk//adl_pub/fportraet/cv/ShowFpItem.xsql?ff_id=64&p_fpkat_id=indl&nnoc=
http://da.wikipedia.org/wiki/Heinrich_Steffens
http://dictionary.reference.com/browse/nationhood?__utma=1.563437068.1271323270.1271323270.12713
http://languagecharter.coe.int/docs/Translations/authentic_2c.pdf
http://languagecharter.coe.int/byLanguage.htm
http://no.wikipedia.org/wiki/Henrik_Steffens
http://www.bbkl.de/s/s4/steffens_h.shtml
http://www.comlink.de/cl-hh/m.blumentritt/agr128s.htm
www.sirillus.se
http://www.coe.int/t/dg4/education/minlang/aboutcharter/default_en.asp
http://www.eurominority.eu/version/eng/
http://www.eurominority.eu/version/eng/minority-type.asp
http://www.metisnation.ca/wp-content/uploads/2015/08/PST-LLP-Summary-Daniels-Case-July-2015-Update.pdf
http://www.unesco.org/culture/languages-atlas/
http://www.varromskahistoria.se/en/what-happened-sweden/activism

Index

About the Studies on Cultural Transfer and Transmission series

The Studies on Cultural Transfer and Transmission series (CTaT) deals with 'cultural transfer', defined as the one-way activity of translating a literary text, for example, and 'cultural transmission', considered as the reciprocal activity of sharing cultural and literary information. The research themes include gender, minorities, cultural transfer and transmission history.

Volumes in the series:

From Darwin to Weil
Women as Transmitters of Ideas
Petra Broomans (ed.)

In the Vanguard of Cultural Transfer
Cultural Transmitters and Authors in Peripheral Literary Fields
Petra Broomans and Marta Ronne (eds.)

The Invasion of Books in Peripheral Literary Fields
Transmitting Preferences and Images in Media, Networks and Translation
Petra Broomans and Ester Jiresch (eds.)

Rethinking Cultural Transfer and Transmission
Reflections and New Perspectives
Petra Broomans and Sandra van Voorst (eds.),
Karina Smits (assistant ed.)

Noorse auteurs in Nederlandse vertaling 1741-2012
Een bibliografie
Raf De Saeger
Onder redactie van / under redaksjon av Petra Broomans & Janke Klok

Zweedse en Zweedstalige Finse auteurs in Nederlandse vertaling 1491-2007
Een bibliografie
Samengesteld door / Sammanställd av
Petra Broomans (hoofdred./huvudred.) & Ingeborg Kroon

Battles and Borders
Perspectives on Cultural Transmission and Literature in Minor Language Areas
Edited by Petra Broomans (chief editor), Roald van Elswijk, Goffe Jensma, Ester Jiresch, Janke Klok

Forthcoming:

Travelling Ideas in the Long Nineteenth Century